ROGER DESCHNER

Choral Techniques

Choral Techniques

GORDON H. LAMB
University of Texas
at San Antonio

WM. C. BROWN COMPANY PUBLISHERS, Dubuque, Iowa

wcb

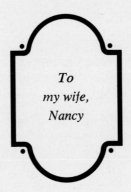

*To
my wife,
Nancy*

contents

This book is written for conductors of high school, college, church, and community choirs and for students preparing for such positions. It may also be of interest to music supervisors, principals, and others who desire information about the formation and operation of a choral department. It is especially designed to serve as a textbook for college and university choral methods and conducting classes.

The book is divided into three parts. Part One, Rehearsal Techniques, *is a discussion of audition and rehearsal procedures, choral diction, and tone. Part Two,* The Score and the Conductor, *includes information about selection and programming of repertoire, score study, conducting techniques, and interpretation. Part Three,* Organization and Management, *includes chapters on choral department management, contests and festivals, organizing chamber ensembles, teacher relationships, student teaching, and securing a teaching position.*

The material contained in this book is the result of this author's research and experience with high school, university, and community choirs. The contents are also being used by former students and serve as the basis for this author's choral techniques course at the university level.

I wish to thank the following companies and professional associations for permission to use excerpts from their choral publications or to quote from their publications: American Choral Directors Association; Belwin-Mills Publishing Corporation; Mark Foster Music Company; Standard Music Publishing, Inc., and Concert Press; E. C. Schirmer Music Company; G. Schirmer, Inc.; Schott and Company; Shawnee Press, Inc.; Texas Education Agency; Walton Music Corporation; and Wenger Corporation.

I also wish to express my appreciation to Dr. Frederick W. Westphal who, as consulting editor, provided helpful comments throughout the preparation of this book. For his critique of the chapter on musical style and interpretation, I wish to thank Dr. John W. Grubbs, Associate Professor of Musicology at the University of Texas at Austin. Special thanks are due my wife, Nancy, for her continued encouragement and valuable assistance during the writing of this book.

I

REHEARSAL
TECHNIQUES

chapter 1.

selection and placement of voices

The choral audition has two primary purposes: (1) to determine membership and, (2) to place singers in sections. Auditions for a select ensemble will involve both purposes, whereas the audition for a nonselect training choir will be used mostly as a tool to place voices in sections. Other information of value is also gleaned from the audition, including: student attitudes, experience, general health, soloistic qualities, and other knowledge the director determines necessary.

Everybody faces auditions with a certain amount of trepidation, particularly young singers. Generally, the auditioning students have not had much private voice study or experience singing alone. The knowledge that the audition will determine their admission to an ensemble makes them even more nervous. There is always a feeling of insecurity knowing that they might not be selected.

Because of this, the director should bend over backwards to make the student feel as much at ease as possible during an audition. A friendly word or two at the beginning of the audition can help the student relax and decide that the audition is not going to be the ordeal he thought it would be.

Personal Data Card

It is necessary to obtain some information about the student, not only to aid the director in making an objective decision about the audition, but also to have phone numbers, addresses, and the like on file for future reference. A sample data card is given in figure 1. Often, local situations will warrant the inclusion of additional information and a variation of this card may be used.

It is best to use cards rather than paper for this information because they file easier and are more durable. A 4″ x 6″ card will serve well. As you can see, the card in figure 1 (p. 2) is minimal in the information requested about the student's personal or family background. Some directors recommend that

Name_____ Class_____
       last   first   middle

Address_____ Phone_____

Previous choral experience_____

_____

List instruments you play_____

- -
                    Do not write below this line

Range
                PR 1__2__3__4__5__6__Total__   Choir_____

                Quality_____Chorus_____

                Rhythm_____Girls Cho._____

                Intonation_____Boys Cho._____

                Part Assigned_____Pvt. Voice_____

Comments _____

_____

Figure 1   Personal Data Card

more information be obtained that can be used later to evaluate the student's possibilities regarding smaller groups chosen from the choir. At the outset, this information is unnecessary and clutters the file card, a card that you want to be as simple and direct as possible. This information, which will be necessary for only a small number of the students, can be obtained later when you need it, and on a form solely for that purpose. You can then obtain information about the student's other school activities, outside involvements, transportation, and any other pertinent information, when it is most appropriate and up-to-date.

Have a small filing case available where the audition cards can be filed. Keep each card until the student is no longer in school. A student may not be selected one year but may reaudition the following year. It will be worthwhile to be able to refer to his previous audition card and your comments on his earlier audition. A director will also have occasional students, who, for one reason or another, will sing in choir one year and not the next. The card should be kept on this student as he may return to sing the third year. The comments on the card will serve better than your memory as a reminder of the student's capabilities and contributions while a member of the choir.

It is generally not the practice to meet with all of the auditioning students to discuss the audition and the choir's goals and activities prior to the auditions. In many situations it will be helpful to type a brief description of the activities of the choir including: dates of the known concerts, possible number of extra concerts, smaller ensembles later selected from this group, fundraising campaigns in which students are expected to participate, required wearing apparel, trips, and your expectations of each student beyond the regularly scheduled rehearsals. This handout should be brief, to the point, restrained but truthful, in its demands placed on the student. However, indications of extra rehearsals can look quite foreboding in writing; whereas in reality, they may not require very much extra time at all.

The Audition for a Select Ensemble

The audition begins when the student enters the room. Remember, he has probably been waiting for several minutes while you finished the prior audition, and has had more opportunity to become nervous. Greet the student, take the audition card and quickly scan it to be sure it is legible and contains all the requested information. This is a good time to say something to the student to help him feel as comfortable as possible. It is a good idea to read his name aloud, helping you to learn to pronounce it correctly and to remember it. It also helps the student if you call him by name during the audition. All of this should take only about half a minute.

Ask the student to stand several feet from the piano, facing you, but unable to see the keyboard. This will allow you to have the student sing in various parts of his range without his knowing the actual pitches he is singing, therefore not being able to become psychologically thwarted by specific pitches he believes to be too high or too low for him. It will also eliminate asking him to move later when you come to the pitch retention part of the audition.

The exercise shown in figure 2, in the middle part of the student's probable range, works well for the first part of the audition. Let the singer gain some

Figure 2

confidence in his singing, keeping in the middle range, for eight to ten repetitions of the sequence.

This can be followed by the second exercise (fig. 3) which requires the singer to negotiate easy intervals (the triad), followed by step-wise notes, related to the first exercise.

Ah _____

Figure 3

After ten to twelve repetitions of exercise two, the third exercise may be used (fig. 4). It too is related to the previous exercises, but instead of beginning with a downward motion triad it begins at the root of the triad. The *yah* syllable will help the singer place more emphasis on the notes and create more intensity and volume in the voice. This is what you will want to hear at this point. You need to know the volume capabilities of the voice as

Yah,   Yah,   Yah _____

Figure 4

well as the quality at several volume levels. Ask the student to accent the first three notes of this exercise and maintain a forte level throughout. Move the student to the top and bottom of his range with this exercise.

Pitch Retention Test

The pitch retention test is one of the best determinants of the student's possibilities for success in a choral ensemble. It will tell you, quite accurately, of the student's potential to learn to sight-read and to learn choral repertoire. This method of auditioning is used by a number of leading high school and college choral directors.[1]

The sight-reading used at choral auditions had bothered this author for some time because one could never be sure that the mistakes made weren't caused by nervousness as well as lack of the skill of sight-reading. More

1. Similar tests were originally used by Louis Diercks, former choral director at Ohio State University and Eastern New Mexico State University.

importantly, it never gave any indication of the student's *potential* as a reader or learner. Over a period of some years, the pitch retention test was found to be a reliable guide toward the selection of choir members. It has been found that, when good voices with low scores on the PR were admitted, it was usually regretted later. On the other hand, when a student with little background with a high score on the PR was admitted, even in place of a more experienced person whose PR score was lower, that decision was never regretted. Any director will have to use a PR test for some time before he will place full confidence in it, but eventually he will be able to rely on it as an accurate guide to a student's potential as a choral singer. After using a pitch retention test the choral director may wish to eliminate sight-reading from the auditions completely.

The pitch retention test given in figure 5 has proved successful at both the high school and college level.

* for younger students the first five
notes of whole tone scale will suffice

Figure 5   Pitch Retention Test (transpose to suitable range)

When administering the test be sure that:
1. The room is free of other noises and distractions.
2. Waiting students cannot hear the test.
3. Each exercise is played only once, asking the student not to hum the notes as they are being played. If the student asks to have the exercise repeated, subtract a proportionate amount from his score.
4. The results are scored so a glance at the card later will provide you with all the information you desire. The sample card allows for six exercises and a total score. Each director will find it easy to determine his own method of scoring.
5. Each exercise is played accurately, with all notes played at the same volume level.
6. The piano has recently been tuned.

Some directors may wish to have students sight-read in addition to the pitch retention test. This author would recommend that these directors write several short exercises for this part of the audition. More reading problems can be incorporated in this manner and less time wasted than when a choral score is used. Choral music also requires a familiarity with a four-part score and can therefore be confusing to a beginner.

Auditioning Nonselect Choirs

Although you may intend to accept all of the interested students for a choir, it is still best to audition each of them. It may not be possible or even necessary to do this before the first meeting of the ensemble. If the schedule determines that the audition must be held during the first rehearsal, have the students come, one at a time, to another room for this brief hearing.

Assuming that these students have no prior choral experience, the audition will not need to be as rigorous as that for the select choir. Begin with a three note exercise in a downward progression (see fig. 6).

Start in the middle of the range and do not be discouraged if the student seems unable to sing even the opening pitch. Students that are completely inexperienced and very nervous sometimes won't match pitch except in a limited part of their range. It is necessary for you to find that usable part of the range and begin there.

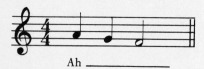

Ah ⎯⎯⎯⎯⎯⎯⎯

Figure 6

Use a stepwise ascending and descending exercise up to the fifth, as in figure 7, for the next part of the audition.

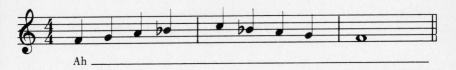

Ah ———————————————————————————————

Figure 7

The pitch retention test can be used, not to determine membership, but to provide you with an accurate indication of potential that you will later want to have. The pitch retention test may be modified to fit particular situations and age levels of the students.

Length of Audition

The total length of the audition for the select ensemble should be no more than ten minutes. You will often have students audition whose singing abilities are poor and it becomes apparent to you very early in the audition that you will not be able to use them. If they can be placed in another group, perhaps a training choir, the audition can be modified toward that goal. Even if this is not possible, it is still best to give the student a good hearing. If the audition is cut too short, the student will feel that he did not receive a thorough hearing and was unfairly eliminated. It is not necessary, however, to use the full time for this type of student. A modified audition can be used which will satisfy the student that he has been given the same chance that all other students received. This will also help point out to the student his own inadequacies and the reasons why he will not be selected.

When any audition is completed, thank the student and, if it wasn't made clear before, let him know when and where a list of accepted students will be posted. It is always best to post the results later, rather than attempting to make decisions on each student at the audition. You can't make any intelligent selections until after you have heard all of the students sing.

Categorizing Voices

Each voice that a director hears is different in some way from every other voice. It is necessary to place these into certain categories by means of range and quality. These two items determine in which section a voice is to be placed. Voices that are constantly changing and maturing may be placed in one section for a year, or even a part of a year, and later moved to another section as the change in quality and range indicate. High school voices should be reauditioned periodically because they are in a constant state of flux, and need close attention.

A brief description of the voice characteristics of each type is listed. A director could not place voices with this information alone. He must have heard a true tenor or alto, for instance, in order to know what the description really means. For those wishing more information, there are several excellent books on the voice listed on page 58 in chapter five and in the bibliography.

Figure 8

Soprano—lyric voice, light and bell-like. The 2nd soprano will have more depth in the lower part of the range.

Alto—heavier quality than soprano, more mellowness. The 2nd alto will have a deeper tone in the lower range and will sing notes below middle C with less pressure and more ease.

Tenor—lyric quality with brightness in the middle and upper range. The 2nd tenor will tend to have a thicker quality and be somewhat more dramatic.

Bass—a deeper tone, heavier and darker. The 1st bass will resemble the 2nd tenor quality but with a deeper, lower range. The 2nd bass will have a rich, deep tone with a resonant lower range.

It is obvious that these characteristics can overlap categories and that not all voices will seem to definitely fit into a given section. These categories really do not allow for the middle voice, one that directors will find in abundance among young singers; a baritone quality that hasn't the low range to sing bass or the top range to sing tenor; or the girl's voice that cannot sing the low alto notes nor the top soprano notes without straining. Some of these voices will be very pleasant and you will want to include them in your choir. The danger lies in the demands the director makes of them, not in which part they are assigned. They should be placed so they may move from part to part as the music necessitates and cautioned from attempting to sing the extreme notes in a given part. These voices can still be valuable choir members and profit from a good singing experience.

A word of caution about assigning altos to the tenor part is still necessary. Do not assign any altos permanently to the tenor part. Such an experience will harm the quality of the girls' voices and be detrimental to their future singing possibilities. It is preferable to never use altos on the tenor part, but it may be necessary on occasion. Use these spot assignments carefully, only when necessary, and do not always assign the same altos to the tenor line. It is far better to balance the chorus first, without relying on altos to help the tenors balance a girls section that may be too large. It is gratifying that fewer tenors are needed to properly balance the other parts. In fact, it has been this author's experience that fewer boys than girls are needed to balance a high school choir. This assumes that the quality of the boys voices is equal to that of the girls.

After you have determined which voices you will use in the choir, all other considerations pertain to the choral rehearsal. That is, decisions from this point on will directly affect the success of your rehearsals.

Seating Arrangements

Several seating arrangements are shown and the reasons for using each are given. During the first part of the academic year it is best to establish a specific seating arrangement and use it for some time before adding another one. This doesn't mean that individual changes cannot be made within each section. These changes may be necessary because of a discipline problem, inability to see the conductor, or an error in judgment when the person was originally assigned. After a month or so of rehearsals, an alternate seating arrangement is a good idea. This will provide some variety to the regular rehearsal, allow singers to hear new voices and perhaps new parts of the choir better, and adapt to certain repertoire more easily.

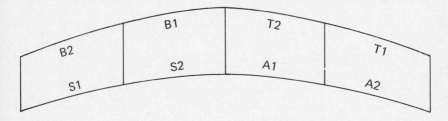

Figure 9

In the arrangement shown in figure 9, the outside parts are grouped together. The 2nd bass and 1st soprano, as outside parts, are lined up together emphasizing the polarity of the two parts, often an aid to good intonation. The baritone and 2nd tenor parts are next to each other so you can assign help to and from either part. The low tenor parts can be bolstered by baritones, who, in turn, can receive help on high baritone passages. The same thing is true of the 2nd soprano and 1st alto parts. The 2nd alto is also directly in front of the 1st tenor so several voices may be added when high tenor parts need assistance. A choral work in eight parts will work with this arrangement as will four-part music. This arrangement is highly recommended for advanced, well-balanced choirs.

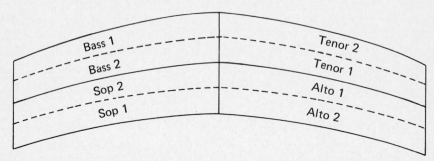

Figure 10

Another good arrangement for advanced choirs is diagramed in figure 10. It is similar to the previous arrangement, having many of the same advantages. It does not have the proximity of 2nd alto and 1st tenor as the first grouping but all the other advantages are present. An additional feature, however, is that the entire 2nd soprano section, for instance, is heard completely across the soprano side of the choir. The same is true of the other parts when it is necessary for them to divide. Another asset is the placement of the 2nd tenors and baritones, and the 2nd sopranos and 1st altos. When the choir is divided for eight parts a director will have made certain voice assignments to balance his particular choir. When music divides into three women's parts and three men's parts the eight-part division will not provide a satisfying balance. When this happens, a new assignment of voices is necessary and the second arrangement works well for this. The middle parts of both the women's and men's voices are next to each other allowing for a natural grouping into six parts.

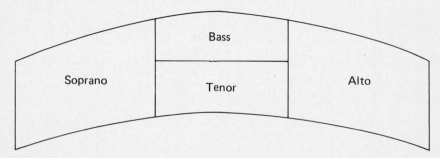

Figure 11

Placing the men's voices in the middle and front of the choir is a good idea when there is a weakness in the tenor and bass parts, or when there simply aren't enough of them (see figure 11). There is no need to worry about divided parts because this arrangement is best for a young choir doing two-, three-, or four-part music. Advanced choirs don't usually blend as well in this arrangement as when the men's voices are placed behind the women. If the tenors are few in number and weak, it may be necessary to place them across the front row, in front of the basses. If there are many more women than men, the women can continue a row behind, and even in front of, the men, thus placing the men in a pocket in the front center of the choir (see fig. 12).

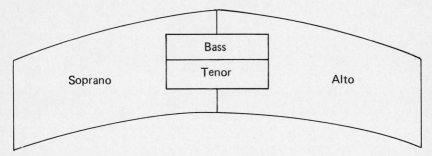

Figure 12

The mixed or scrambled arrangement is now being used extensively (see fig. 13). This grouping has the advantage of producing a homogeneous sound, and often providing a choir with a better balance.

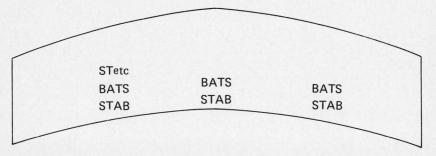

Figure 13

Average and good choirs will benefit from this scrambling as a method of encouraging the choir members to be independently secure on their part and allow them to hear each of the other parts easier. The intonation of a choir usually improves noticeably when a choir is first shifted to this arrangement. The new proximity to all the other parts will help each singer contribute toward a better ensemble intonation. This arrangement, however, will not cure intonation problems caused by poor vocal technique. Young, inexperienced choirs will rarely benefit from this grouping, since it demands more than the singers are capable of producing.

The mixed arrangement is best used for homophonic music, particularly that of the nineteenth and much of the twentieth century. Polyphonic repertoire may suffer from this grouping because of the clarity of line that the music needs can be lost in the scrambling of the sections.

Placing Individual Voices

Sort the audition cards, placing the best quality and potential reading ability in one group and the worst quality and potential reading ability in another group. This will leave you with the largest group consisting of good quality but poor potential as a reader, poor quality but good reading potential, and those that are mediocre in both areas. The potential reading ability would have been determined in the audition by the pitch retention test or by a sight-reading test if one was given.

There are several possible ways to place the voices. One is to place the best singers in the middle of the section (or on the insides of each section, making the center of the choir the core of the sound) in hopes that the sound will filter out to the rest of the choir. A distinct disadvantage is that the weaker singers on the outside may have more intonation problems than otherwise. Another often used method is to distribute the wealth throughout the choir, spotting the best singers around in the section.

A more desirable way is to combine the best attributes of both of the above, reinforcing one singer's weakness with another's strength. A singer whose quality is excellent may be placed by a good reader whose tone is not as good. Both will be aided by this arrangement. This premise may then be used to place all the voices in the section. Be aware of individual attitudes and place students whose attitude may be borderline next to an eager and enthusiastic one.

Be especially careful not to place voices on the front row whose quality (even though good) will make them stand out from the rest of the choir. It is best to put these voices in the middle rows where they seem to be of more help to the choir (if they are good singers) and the sound will be better absorbed.

During the first several rehearsals you may test the section sound by having the students sing in the medium range for blend and quality. The director can make any changes in the seating at that time to correct any errors in placement.

Do not underestimate the importance of proper voice placement. The entire musical success of a choir may often depend entirely upon voice placement. The balance, blend, and even the tone of a choir will likely change as different placements are used.

Discussion Questions

1. How would you demonstrate the best way to conduct an audition for a select choir?
2. Can you write several sight-reading exercises that would be suitable for high school students?
3. Should all students be allowed to sing in one of the choirs?
4. What attributes, other than musical, would you look for in a student as a possible member of a choral ensemble you would conduct.
5. Discuss the characteristics of the various voice qualities. Have students sing to demonstrate each quality. Which of the voices best characterizes each quality?
6. Which seating arrangements have been used in choirs in which you have sung? Which ones did you like the best and why?

SUGGESTED READINGS

Diercks, Louis H. "A Prognostic Approach to the Choral Auditions." *The Choral Journal* November 1962, pp. 9-11.

Ehmann, Wilhelm, *Choral Directing,* chap. 1. Minneapolis: Augsburg Publishing House, 1968.

Umberson, George. "Experimentalism and Pacing in the Choral Rehearsal." *The Choral Journal* March 1970, pp. 10-14.

chapter 2.

the first rehearsal

The first rehearsal is a very important one. It is the first meeting of the entire choir; their first encounter, as a choir, with a new director; and your first chance to hear the results of your selections. Even when the first rehearsal of the year is not the director's first rehearsal in a new school, the rehearsal is crucial. Student attitudes are important in a choir and the attitude established during the first rehearsal will carry into the first part of the semester.

Chapter one included a procedure for placing the voices in various arrangements. Determine which seating arrangement you believe will be best for this choir at this time. Each student's name may be written on a small piece of heavy paper and pinned to a bulletin board in the choral room. If each section is labeled on a different colored paper it becomes easy to place voices and know the section arrangement at a glance. This becomes particularly handy if you want to utilize a scrambled or mixed seating arrangement.

Once you have determined the seating for the first rehearsal, you must decide which will be the best way to inform the students of their place in the choral room. Whatever method is chosen, it should be one that will avoid confusion at the beginning of the first rehearsal. Exactly what you will do will depend on the size of the choral room (whether or not there is room for people to group in sections away from the chairs and wait to be seated), what hour of the day the choir meets (whether or not there is free time immediately preceding the hour which could allow some students to help with the seating), and the size of the group.

The following methods have worked in various situations. It is necessary to determine a method that will work in your particular situation. Although this seating may seem unimportant, it will be an indicator to the students of the manner in which you approach the choir, your concern that everything be just right for rehearsal, your ability to make the most use of available time, and the importance of this ensemble. All of these factors are psychological, on which much of the success of the first rehearsal hinges.

One method is to have the students group under signs already placed around the room—**tenors,** etc. Then call off the names and indicate where they are to sit. At the same time have two students (whom you have already assigned) ready to hand folders to the students as they are seated.

Another method is to place the student's names on the chairs and have the students find their own name. Folders can be distributed after the choir is seated.

The seating chart may also be placed on a bulletin board near the entrance of the room and a listing of folder assignments next to it. Each student can check for himself to determine where he is to sit, then get his folder, and be seated.

It is important that the students understand that they are seated in a particular place for a purpose. Often students will ask to sit next to a friend. They usually have not given any thought as to the reasons the choir is arranged as it is. In your announcements during the first rehearsal, impress upon the choir the reasons for the seating and that it will remain as it is until you change it for a good reason.

Preparing the Choral Room

The rehearsal room should be made as attractive as possible before classes begin. Usually every school district requires the teachers to report for in-service meetings several days before classes open. You can use part of this time to get your choral room ready for classes. Don't rely on the custodian to place the chairs as you want them. It will probably be necessary for you to do this. The bulletin boards should not be left vacant. Classrooms are often dull and lifeless looking rooms and empty bulletin boards add to this unattractive setting. It isn't necessary though, to spend many hours making bulletin boards. Your time could be better spent in other preparations. Several record jackets of choral groups can be effectively used, with some color backgrounds. If this is not your first year in the school, you can use pictures of last year's ensembles and some of the programs to liven up the room.

A simple, but colorful bulletin board will help dress up a classroom. The above suggestions are but two of many. It is important to do something attractive but not to spend much of your time doing it.

Selection of Repertoire

One of the most difficult tasks is the selection of music for this first rehearsal. This is particularly true if you are new in the school. Even though you have auditioned the students, it will be difficult to ascertain exactly their full capabilities. If the situation is such that auditions are not held prior to the first rehearsal, the situation is even more difficult. It is imperative that there be a variety of repertoire available during the first rehearsal, including easy and difficult music, sacred and secular, and accompanied and unaccompanied.

The quality of the students will not have changed between the audition and the first rehearsal. Keep in mind the level of students that you placed in the choir as you select the music for the first rehearsal. Too often, directors ignore the facts that were apparent at auditions and choose literature that the students are simply not capable of singing. A reason usually given is that, "I wanted to challenge them" or "I wanted them to know that the choir will sing harder music with me than they did before." These immature approaches to the selection of repertoire, of course, will cause many problems.

Choose six to ten pieces to be placed in the folders for the first rehearsal. All of them will not need to be rehearsed during the first rehearsal but students will be happier knowing the selections that they will be singing in the near future. Don't place anything in the folders that you do not plan to rehearse in the near future. Padding the folder with several extremely difficult pieces, for instance, that the choir cannot possibly sing will not gain the admiration or confidence of the students. It will soon become apparent to them that they cannot sing those works and they will question the judgment of their director. They may also decide that the pieces were placed in the folder only for "show."

The following guidelines will aid in the actual choosing of the music for the first rehearsal. The music for this rehearsal is not necessarily all the music the choir will work on during the first semester. New works can be added at subsequent rehearsals as the director determines the potential of the choir.

1. Choose one piece that the choir performed last year, particularly if this is your first year in the position. Look through the programs from the year before and select a piece that is not too difficult and that is substantial musically. At least one piece will be familiar to a large percentage of the ensemble, assuming there is a good return from the previous choir. This will give you an opportunity to have one piece available to determine what type of sound they can get on a piece with which they are familiar.

2. Select one very easy piece that is basically homophonic. One of the J. S. Bach chorales would do nicely. While the chorales are not always easy to totally realize musically, they are not technically difficult and can serve the purposes of this first rehearsal.

3. Have one piece in the folders that is unison or almost unison. This will give the director an opportunity to work on a solid unison tone within a piece of music rather than only in an exercise.

4. Choose one piece of some difficulty that the choir does not know. If the director has underestimated the capabilities of the choir, they will be concerned if all the music appears to be quite easy (even if they can't sing it with understanding). This work can be available to the director in the event that he has misjudged the choir's capabilities.

5. If possible, include two selections that you are interested in performing in their first concert. If the first concert for the ensemble is a Christmas performance, it would be good to introduce two of these pieces at the first of the year. It can give the students an idea of the type of music you will want to perform in concert. These Christmas pieces can be withdrawn after a few rehearsals and reintroduced in November when you want to begin serious rehearsals on them.
6. Include one folk-type piece that is well arranged. Avoid works whose text is in poor taste. Make this selection according to the same criteria used for every other piece.
7. Be sure to include compositions from more than one musical period. Give the students a little tonal variety always, especially during the first rehearsal.

Beginning the Rehearsal

The students are looking forward to the first rehearsal and, if the director is new, to meeting the director in a rehearsal capacity. They have not yet seen how the director handles rehearsal time or how he conducts. The responsibility for getting the rehearsal off to a good start rests with the director. It must be planned carefully and properly paced.

It is probably necessary to have a few words to say in the way of an introduction but these words should be kept at a minimum. Unless an audition was not possible, the students already know who you are and have met you. It is usually best to keep the remarks at the opening of the rehearsal short and get singing as quickly as possible. Remember, the students came to sing, not to hear you talk.

Consider the following:
1. The choir should be told that you are pleased that they were selected through audition to be in the group.
2. The development of a good choral ensemble is not a speedy process but that you are looking forward to working with them toward that end. This will infer that the students should not expect the choir to attain a polished tone during the first rehearsal, or to sound as good as they may have in the spring concert the previous year.
3. Briefly state your ideas of the performance responsibilities that lie ahead and give them some idea of the music you intend to do in the first concert. Students like to know immediately what is planned for them. Don't worry about being too specific but do not mislead the choir regarding your plans. Don't try to project plans that are unrealistic in an attempt to impress the students. They will see through this if it isn't true and will lose respect for their director. Ambitious plans should be thoroughly discussed with the administration *before* anything is mentioned to the students.

The most important thing is to get singing as quickly as possible. It is often best to say just a few words and then break into the rehearsal at a midway point and take care of other necessary announcements. The students will need a break at that time and will be ready to listen to what you have to say.

Pacing the Rehearsal

The first rehearsal should be paced so that it moves fairly rapidly. This time must not drag for the choir members. The suggestions given pertain especially to the first rehearsal but often apply to daily rehearsals and particularly to special day rehearsals. A full discussion of rehearsal pacing and planning will take place later in chapter three, *Daily Rehearsals*.

Know that a certain amount of time will be lost seating the singers and distributing the music. If the class period is sixty minutes, less five minutes passing time, you will probably only have thirty-five to forty minutes of actual rehearsal time.

It is important to let the students experience some of the rehearsal techniques that you will employ during every rehearsal. At the same time it is not necessary to try to teach them all you know during the first rehearsal. The choir should get the idea that rehearsals will be enjoyable, but that they are to be enjoyable working sessions with music, not fun and games. Be sure that the rehearsal is approached in a firm, business-like manner. This does not mean that the rehearsal should have a sombre appearance. It does mean that the students must learn quickly that rehearsals are serious studies in choral music and not the place for horseplay.

Opening Exercises

The following procedure could be used satisfactorily for the first rehearsal or a variation of it could be used.

After the students are seated and have the music, a few short warm-up exercises can be used to begin the rehearsal. These exercises should be considered as part of the rehearsal itself. If they are important enough to be included, they are important enough for serious attention. The students will be somewhat nervous about the sound during the first rehearsal. It will be easier for them to make the first sound in unison, rather than trying to read a new piece immediately. There is less chance of having a bad sound occur if an exercise is used first. Don't sing too many exercises, though. The tone in the opening rehearsal will probably be fuzzy and lacking in unity. Don't expect to solve all the tonal problems of the choir in the first rehearsal.

Begin the singing with an exercise using a unison hum or humming in octaves. The students can hear better when they are humming and can adjust to the pitch easier and follow any spoken suggestions you may make. One can change from the unison into a two-, three-, or four-part chord at a simple gesture from the director.

Figure 14

Move voices to parts at will, not metrically, changing hum to vowel as desired.

The exercise shown in figure 15 can be used to loosen the voice muscles and allow the singers to project a fuller tone.

Yah,   Yah,   Yah _____

Figure 15

Instead of using the exercises only for warm-up, try always to incorporate some tone building concept. Even in this first rehearsal, for instance, you can begin to instill the concept of growth in each note. Teach the students to sing forward, to stretch each note to its fullest capacity. A note that does not move forward, in terms of intensity, will lose some of its vitality. This concept will be discussed in detail in chapter five. Introducing this concept at the first rehearsal can be valuable to the ultimate success of the tone of the choir.

This introduction in the first rehearsal will also give the director an opportunity to improve the tone of the choir in the opening minutes of the first rehearsal of the year. It is not a superficial improvement either, since it is not gained at the expense of lasting musical techniques. The students will immediately hear the improvement of the tone and will also be impressed with the capabilities of a director who can obtain results even at the outset.

Do not overdo the warm-up exercises. Three to five minutes is enough.

Get to the music and continue to allow the voices to strengthen in the first piece. It should be remembered that virtually all of the choir has not sung, at least not intensely, for approximately three months. Do not try to push them too far, vocally, in these first rehearsals.

The First Piece

The first piece to be sung should be one of moderate difficulty with an English text. Use piano to reinforce the parts. Don't begin reading the piece by requiring the singers to use text. Young singers in a new choir, still trying to determine what their personal vocal contribution will be, should not be asked to attempt to read pitches, rhythms, and text at the same time. Instead, speak the rhythm for them. Give them an idea of the rhythmic flow. Have the pianist play some of the opening measures so they can hear the harmony. Initially, read it on a single vowel (or syllable such as *loh*). After one or two times through part of it, introduce the text. It is not necessary to read all of the piece in this rehearsal but this will depend on the length of the work, the complexity of the work, and the choir's reading capabilities. If all the piece is not read, the director should have the choir sing the part that will give them the best idea of the essence of the work. An easy piece can probably be sung in its entirety and a portion of it can be rehearsed in some detail. Don't feel compelled to read passages that are complex during this rehearsal unless the choir has outstanding abilities in sight-singing.

After the choir sings all of a piece, or part of it, some rehearsal time should be given to detailed work on a small section of the piece. Be careful in the selection of this piece or this part of a piece. Choose a portion of the piece that can be effectively rehearsed and is capable of some polish quickly. It is imperative that the students be able to see the results of your rehearsal methods. They need to know that even in the first rehearsal they have progressed under you as a director. You won't have to call their attention to it. If it occurs, they will know it.

Do not use this opening rehearsal to do tedious rehearsing. It will not be effective and it will kill the enthusiasm of the students. It is more important to keep the rehearsal moving and to keep the students interested and alert.

A Rehearsal Plan

A breakdown of the rehearsal plan would be something like the following:
1. Seat the choir and distribute the music.
2. Make a few brief announcements.
3. Use exercises for three to five minutes.

4. Read first piece of moderate difficulty and polish at least one passage musically.
5. Read the second piece which should be easy material, unison if necessary, or easy two-, three-, or four-part music.
6. A three to five minute break to be used for additional announcements.
7. Read part of a third piece which could be difficult.
8. Save enough time to return to the piece that contained the section that was polished. If the entire piece can be done with some success, sing all of it. If not, use the section that was polished somewhat, to end the rehearsal. It is important to end this rehearsal on a positive level. The last thing the students should have on their minds as they leave the room will be a musical sound, at least some realization that the choir can produce a good sound. They will know that they have accomplished something and will be excited because of it. Do not end the rehearsal with sight-reading or with too many announcements. It will be more beneficial to end the rehearsal singing than to end it talking.

Keep the rehearsal moving by having all announcements well planned so there is no stumbling around on the part of the director. Know exactly what you want to say and how you want to say it. Be sure that the impression you give the students is one of careful planning, organized leadership, and musical competency.

Accompanists

The accompanist is a vital part of every rehearsal. The following comments will pertain to every rehearsal, but will logically occur before the first rehearsal.

Determine who the capable pianists are as early as you can. If you are new to the job, check the programs from the previous year for the names of the accompanists. If they are still in school, get in touch with them. Ask the band and orchestral directors about accompanists. They usually know since they also use accompanists for instrumental soloists. If necessary, find out who the local piano teachers are and call them to determine if any of their students are possible accompanists. However, keep in mind that private piano teachers may not be aware of the requirements of a good accompanist. A student who works on one piano piece all year and plays it in a recital may not be capable of playing as a choir accompanist.

If capable students are available, they should be given the opportunity to play. If possible, and if there are several possible pianists, have them audition for you. Have them play a piano solo and one or two pieces of choral music which you can select. The accompanist should be able to sight-read to some degree, although this should not be the most important attribute. Actually, the accompanist will not sight-read very often. It should be a rare occasion when the accompanist and the choir will sight-read a work at the same time. When at all possible, the accompanist should be given a new piece several days before it is introduced to the choir.

During the audition, direct the accompanist in a choral piece to see how well he follows your direction. When possible, select two accompanists. They can divide the accompanying responsibilities. If they both sing, this will give them an opportunity to sing in the choir as well as to accompany it.

Once you have chosen the accompanist(s), set a time several days prior to the first rehearsal when you can spend approximately thirty minutes explaining the role of an accompanist in your rehearsals. This is the time when you should give the accompanist a copy of each piece that will be used in the first rehearsal. Comment on each piece regarding tempo, when you want parts played, and the place of each piece in the format of the first rehearsal.

The following items should be discussed with the accompanist.

1. Write out the exercises that you will use during the first rehearsals and have the accompanist practice them with you. Let him know how high or low you wish the exercises to go and what signals you will use to indicate a change of pitch direction.
2. The accompanist should give all pitches, in order, from the lowest part to the highest part. When chords are given in this manner, the root of the chord will be heard sooner (since it is often the bass). This allows singers to more readily associate the entire chord with their pitch as it is given.
3. Ask the accompanist to pay close attention to your directions so he can anticipate the place in the score at which you want to start.
4. Impress upon the accompanist that he can save valuable time in every rehearsal and that the time is important. An ineffective accompanist can continually halt the flow of a rehearsal. This can be very annoying to the choir and to the director.
5. Instruct the accompanist to play all separate parts from the vocal line rather than to continue to play from the piano reduction. The reduction will not include the proper voice leading. In works without a piano reduction, either have the accompanist write out the parts or have two pianists combine to play all the lines.
6. The accompanist should be at the piano as quickly as possible at the beginning of the rehearsal. You will want to begin rehearsals when most of the students are seated.
7. Let the accompanist know that his position is very important. Ask him to have you notified if he is ill, and notified in advance, of any scheduled trips that will take him from rehearsals. It is very distressing to elaborately plan to rehearse a work that needs an accompanist, only to find, after the

rehearsal begins that the accompanist is ill that day, or worse, that he is on a field trip that was planned a month in advance.

8. If the accompanist is capable, try to include at least one accompanied work in each concert that will give him an opportunity to play in public.

If student accompanists are not available, it may be necessary to hire an adult to play for rehearsals. This may require you to convince the administration that the expenditure is necessary. Make every effort to convince them that if the ensemble is to advance musically, you need a capable accompanist.

Discussion Questions

1. What ideas for improving the appearance of the choral room do you have?
2. What repertoire do you know right now that would be suitable for the first rehearsal?
3. Recall opening rehearsals when you have been a member of a choir What was done that could have been improved or omitted?
4. How can you justify the need of a capable accompanist to an administrator if capable students are not available?
5. When students are available, is it ever justifiable to have an adult play instead?

SUGGESTED READINGS

Davison, Archibald T. *Choral Conducting,* chap. 4. Cambridge: Harvard University Press, 1945.

Ehret, Walter. *The Choral Conductor's Handbook,* chap. 1-7. New York: Edward B. Marks Corporation, 1959.

Wilson, Harry R. *A Guide for Choral Conductors,* chap. 2. New York: Silver Burdette Co., 1950.

chapter 3.   **daily rehearsals**

One of the most important preparations for rehearsal is the prerehearsal analysis of the music. This analysis is presented in detail in chapter ten. Its importance cannot be overemphasized. One can have a well-planned rehearsal, but if one doesn't know the music thoroughly, all will have been in vain; the rehearsal will not be a success. **It is imperative that the director know the music thoroughly.**

Planning for Rehearsal

Planning for daily rehearsals is different than planning for the first rehearsal of the year. Some of the same principles are involved but every rehearsal now has a place in a chain of rehearsals that ends in one or more performances.

Know exactly which pieces are to be rehearsed and why. Most directors don't know the why often enough. Determine what must be accomplished with each piece and decide how that can best be done to save time and energy. Devise ways of teaching similar passages that occur in separate works. When possible write the two similar passages on the chalkboard before the rehearsal begins. Have the students learn the similarities and the differences. Have them sing both passages and then continue to rehearse one of the works involved.

A Rehearsal Guide

A rehearsal guide, such as shown in figure 16, can be used to establish balanced, consistent rehearsals. This kind of attention to planning will pay off for both the director and the choir. The director will find that the use of a rehearsal guide will discipline his approach to each rehearsal.

Sing the first four notes on an *oh* vowel, not fast. Add the last two notes and move the tempo up gradually.

Secondary purpose of warm-up

Strive for clarity of notes. (The theme [No. 2 of figure 16 is that used in Britten's *Wolcum Yole!,* Boosey and Hawkes.)

1st Selection

Wolcum Yole!—work to clean up the moving notes at both the text, "Wolcum Yole!" and "Be thou heavne King" passages. Apply the principle of diaphragmatic support to the moving notes. Work up to the soft section.

2nd Selection

"Break Forth, O Beauteous Heavenly Light," J. S. Bach, G. Schirmer.

Apply two-finger principle to the line (described in chapter five). Sing the phrases using an *oh* vowel with the two fingers in the mouth. Stress the amount of room needed to produce a free tone. Then use text, still striving for room in the mouth. Have students place index finger in front of the ear to detect jaw motion.

Continue to use text, emphasizing the growth principle, striving for the continued deepness of the tone, open throats, and growth in the tone.

3rd Selection

"Now Thank We All Our God," J. Pachelbel, Robert King Music Co.

Begin on the last section, sing on *pum;* stress the rhythmic activity and its relation to the cantus firmus. Use C. F. with text, other parts on *pum.* Emphasize the relationship between the C. F. and the other parts, including dynamic levels needed to achieve clarity of both.

4th Selection

"Psallite," M. Praetorious, Bourne Music Co.

Work for balance, blend, and style. Must not be too forceful, although rhythmic. Work for correct word stress. Be careful of Latin and German pronunciation. Have choir speak text.

If Time

Repeat *Wolcum Yole!,* recapping work done at beginning of rehearsal. If possible, continue to end of work.

Figure 16   Rehearsal Guide

If there is a chalkboard available directly in front of the choir, list the pieces that will be rehearsed in their rehearsal order. As the students are seated, they can begin to place the music in order, saving time later in the rehearsal. Rehearsal time will be conserved if the choir has permanently assigned music folders. Except in an emergency, rehearsal time should not be used to distribute music.

After the pieces have been selected for rehearsal, the following points will aid in determining the order in which they will be rehearsed.

1. Place the most difficult task of the rehearsal toward the beginning of the rehearsal. Either begin with it or precede it by a short work or only a small portion of a work, so the singers will be fresh for the most difficult work of the hour.

2. Don't rehearse passages in extreme ranges before the voices are properly warmed up.

3. Try to put different styles into the rehearsal, but don't mix the styles so there is no continuity and no carry over of ideas.

4. When possible, use two or more works that have the same kind of a problem.

5. Don't rehearse several pieces in a row that have a high tessitura or whose total vocal requirements are quite demanding. If this is done, the rehearsal will really be finished long before the director dismisses the students. If the singers have to sing too long in extreme tessituras they will become tired quickly and flatting will become apparent. The tone quality will also suffer and students will begin to force to try to regain the lost quality. There is only one result, a poor rehearsal.

6. Separate the most difficult pieces with easier ones. Do not have an entire rehearsal on just difficult repertoire. The singers senses will dull and much less is accomplished than desired.

7. Build variety into the rehearsal even if it is variety within only several works (choosing contrasting sections, etc.).

8. Don't always start at the beginning of every piece. Beginnings of pieces are often overrehearsed to the detriment of the rest of the work. Don't waste rehearsal time singing through sections that the students know. Go immediately to the place in question. It is often worthwhile to begin rehearsals in the middle of a work.

9. It is also desirable to have the students sing one piece in its entirety or a section of a longer work during the rehearsal. It should be remembered that the students will not always share your enthusiasm for part learning.

10. Place a short break in the middle of a one hour rehearsal. Confine the student talking to a few moments during the break before the necessary announcements.

Establish a Rapport

At the beginning of each rehearsal the director must reestablish a rapport with the singers. The singers come from a variety of situations just previous to choir. Some of them may have had a strenuous physical education class, or some a stimulating social studies discussion in which they are still engaged as they enter the choral room. Someone else may have just flunked a test or had an argument with a boy-friend or girl-friend. It is the task of the choral director to reorient these many different kinds of personalities with a variety of things on their minds, to choral music—to the rehearsal. Some prefer to start every rehearsal with some physical movements together on the premise that it not only loosens muscles and releases tensions, but that it also brings the group into a psychological unity—doing the same thing together, often interacting with one another. These can be worthwhile but perhaps would not have to be done every day. Anything that is done every day can easily become commonplace and then lose some of its value. The director, through his personal magnetism and ability to motivate students, can bring the group together to the mutual concern, choral music.

Pacing the Rehearsal

When the rehearsal begins, the director must maintain a pace in the rehearsal that is comfortable, a pace that moves along nicely but is not hurried. Directors are often admonished to keep rehearsals moving rapidly. Rehearsals can acquire a flustered, hurried atmosphere that is not conducive to good singing. The rehearsal should move fast enough to keep the singers alert without being tense.

Determine which seating arrangement you will want to use for the rehearsal. This will depend upon the place of this rehearsal in the overall rehearsal plan, and the type of music being rehearsed. If you have several standard seating plans, place the number or name of the one for that day on the chalkboard. Unless they are otherwise informed, students should plan to be seated in the number one arrangement.

The director must be aware of fatigue in a rehearsal. He must be ready to change the pace of the rehearsal or move to the next piece if he senses that the students are beginning to slip away from him. Signs that the students are tiring of a particular work are talking, less enthusiasm, inattention, and musically, a poorer tone, and lack of attention to pitch. There is a point with every ensemble when learning has stopped and the material has been belabored.

Don't be afraid to move around during the rehearsal. There is a difference between concert conducting gestures and those that may be used in a rehearsal. Step to the section in question if they are being rehearsed on a single part. Avoid getting into the habit of singing with the choir during rehearsal. The task of the director is to listen.

When it is necessary to rehearse a section alone, the other students are not participating. Some directors tell the other students to look at their parts and learn them while the other part rehearses. This is only partially successful. This may or may not keep the other students quiet which is usually the intent. Often it helps to have the other students hum their parts while the part in question uses text. This will still allow the director to hear the part that needs help, and will also keep the other students actively participating in the music, providing a harmonic foundation for the section being rehearsed. This also prevents discipline problems. Sectional rehearsing during general rehearsals is necessary, but it should be kept at a minimum.

Repetition with Meaning

It will be necessary to repeat sections, rehearsing the same thing a number of times. This can be tiresome to both the choir and to the director. Tiresome as it is, don't allow sloppy work. Insist from the start that the music be sung correctly. One cannot wait until the time to "polish" to correct all the "little" errors. These errors aren't really little, they are just easier to pass over during the earlier rehearsals. The longer that one rehearses the error, the more difficult it will finally be to correct it.

Constant repetitions in choral rehearsals that do not have a purpose will result in little advance of the work musically. It is repetition *with meaning* that will foster real learning. When it is necessary to repeat, call attention to the reason for the repetition, don't just sing it again. Incorporate the reason for the repetition with the direction to repeat. For instance, "Let's start again at letter *B,* and this time be more conscious of the gradually rising dynamics," tells the ensemble where to start and why the repeat is being made and what should be done with the music this time through. The statement, "OK, take it again from *B,*" brings a mental, if not vocal, groan. If the director cannot give an immediate reason for repeating, there isn't a reason.

Keep your own talking in the rehearsal to a minimum. The students came to sing. There will be specific times when you will want to tell the students something about the style of a given work or tell them about the composer. Make these talks brief and to the point. Don't ramble. Prepare your statements just as you would prepare a lecture for a class studying the work.

Tape record occasional rehearsals just to check your rehearsal guidance. Time the amount of talking done by the director and the number of minutes spent in sectional rehearsals (while much of the choir sat idle).

One of the real difficulties in a rehearsal is that of recognizing the real problems. Much rehearsal time is wasted by directors working on the wrong thing, trying to cure the wrong problem. Don't jump to conclusions. Listen critically and analyze the problem carefully, then determine what to do about it. In actual rehearsals this must be done very quickly. The choral director must anticipate as many problems and make projected solutions in his rehearsal guide. These will come about as a result of his score study and his knowledge of his own students. This is a facet of choral directing that needs to be developed over many rehearsal experiences.

During rehearsals there are many times when directors are tempted to show a group just how bad they really are. This negative attitude is an act of immaturity and will stifle any desire to improve. Instead, try to show the students how much more they can learn. It is better to teach by giving good examples rather than bad ones.

Special Day Rehearsals

There are certain days of the year that need special consideration. These are days of schoolwide activities that have the students' emotions aroused. For instance, homecoming, football games, most ball game days (particularly important tournament games), school elections, the day immediately preceding the Jr.-Sr. Prom, and other such days. The amount of attention that the director needs to give these kinds of days depends entirely on the participation and interest of the choir members. It is unfair to expect the usual concentration, for example, from a senior girl who is a nominee for Homecoming Queen on the day that the results are to be announced. Nothing will remove that event from her mind that day. The same can be applied to other choir members who are deeply involved in other school activities. The director must be flexible enough to accept these and be less demanding in terms of extended concentration. Keep the rehearsal moving faster than most, sing more pieces, and do very little part rehearsing. Sing through entire works as much as possible. This does not mean that one should not rehearse diligently. The students should always know that choral rehearsals will continue through all other student activities. One cannot eliminate rehearsals for every school event that involves choir members. However, a director can be considerate of this involvement and shape a rehearsal accordingly. This rehearsal will not likely be the same kind of rehearsal that one would expect of the same students two days before a choral clinic or concert.

Don't Waste Rehearsal Time

Utilize all available rehearsal time. Start rehearsals on time. Use the break as an opportunity to take care of announcements. Have a student take the attendance so the director can be rehearsing. If three minutes are wasted while the director takes attendance of a choir of sixty, he has wasted three minutes of all sixty persons, or 180 minutes (three hours) of time. Take a hard look at rehearsal time and use every minute that is available as economically as possible. It has been this author's observation that directors, whose groups do not meet every day, make better use of rehearsal time than directors who are able to have their ensemble once a day. The former is more aware of the value of his time and the time of his students.

Introducing a New Work

There are several opinions regarding the presentation of a work for the first time (a sight-reading). The reference to a *first presentation* was carefully made because this author feels that more choral music would be better received by choirs if the director adopted an attitude of presenting a new piece for singing and understanding, rather than simply sight-reading a new work.

One's attitude toward introducing a new work depends heavily on the reading ability of the choir. If a choir reads very well, many works can be read through and the choir will be able to get a fairly accurate idea of the music. If however, the choir reads at the level that most amateur choirs read, the sight-reading of a piece, unless it is quite easy, rarely represents an accurate view of the work.

When a new piece is presented for the first time, a director should have spent a good deal of time studying the score, and should have determined an approach that will provide the best reception of the piece. Remember, the choir should be sight-reading, but the director shouldn't be! It is assumed that the director would desire that all the students in the choir like every piece that is sung. This is not likely, but every effort should be made to provide each piece with a receptive atmosphere. If the work is worth the attention of the choir, it is worth the best possible reception. Often, when a work, in a style or harmonic idiom new to the students, is presented to an unprepared choir, the director finds that the students don't like the piece. It is quickly withdrawn and the director vows never to try that again; or, the director fights the piece through, battling student resentment all the way.

If a new style of music is to be presented, the director should lay some groundwork before the work is introduced. Otherwise, the chances for its success are poor. Discuss the composer (if possible), mention other works of his they may know about, and discuss the type of music that it represents. Try to give the students an idea of the harmonic style of the work. If, for example, a piece with electronic tape is to be introduced, it should be thoroughly discussed in advance.

It is also important, in the presentation of an idiom new to the students, to choose a work that expresses the conservative aspects of the idiom, and one to which the students will most quickly relate. An example of this would be to present a twentieth century work whose "dissonance" is conservative, rather than to introduce a Webern Cantata as the first twentieth century piece to be done.

Favorable impressions of a work are nice but equally important is an attitude of simple receptivity on the part of the students. The students will hardly be able to sight-read a score and be able to grasp the full musical value of a piece. They need to be taught to adopt a *wait and see* attitude. Impress upon the students that, at the first reading they won't know what the work really sounds like. It is not until they have sufficiently mastered its technical difficulties that they will begin to have an idea of the merits of a piece. All they can tell at a first reading is how the work sounds when sight-read by that particular choir, a reading that may be good or bad.

It is sometimes a good idea to play a recording (when available) of a work when it is being introduced. This is particularly an advantage when a work in a new idiom, or a score of some magnitude or complexity is being introduced. This can give the students a truer concept of the work and often greatly interest them in performing the work, wanting to sound as good as the record. When a recording is played at this point in the rehearsal of the work, there will not be a tendency to copy the recording. When recordings are played to *teach* the choir a piece, the choir usually sounds like a poor carbon copy of the record.

Methods of Introducing a Work

After a work has been selected for rehearsal use, and a rehearsal study has been carefully made, the director must then determine the best way to introduce the piece. Assuming that all the necessary groundwork for the work has been laid, the following guidelines should be applied.

1. Should the piece be sung through in its entirety? This question has already been dealt with. This author does not belong to the group of directors that insists that the best sight-reading consists of a sing-through to "give the choir an idea of what the piece sounds like." There is no necessity to always sing through a work. You are meeting the choir regularly and can establish a continuity from rehearsal to rehearsal, that will provide an adequate vehicle for learning a new work.

2. It is advisable, when at all possible, to find a portion of the work that can be brought to some stage of fruition in the first rehearsal, even if it is no more than one or two phrases.

3. Regardless of the complexity, the director should determine the thematic, harmonic, and rhythmic material that comprises the core of the work. The

analysis should reveal this and all the derivatives of these compositional traits. A good presentation of the main thematic, harmonic, and rhythmic material will greatly speed the learning of a piece.

4. It is usually best to avoid use of the text in the first reading unless the work is quite slow and the text is easy to read. If the text is printed between the staves of two parts for both parts to read, it is unrealistic to expect the singers to handle the pitches and rhythms while trying to find the text. It is more beneficial to have the singers read on a syllable. Avoid overusing the same syllable for reading purposes. *Loh* or *loo* will work very nicely for legato works, although *loo* becomes very tiring for tenors if the tessitura is at all high. The use of a light *pm,* with no *uh* sound between the *p* and the *m,* is also very useful. The latter is also effective in later rehearsals to clearly define rhythm and precision.

Discussion Questions

1. Recall your own high school rehearsals. How did the director manage to pull the students' minds together for rehearsals?
2. How many ways are there of wasting rehearsal time? List them and try to learn to avoid them.
3. Why is pacing so important in a choral rehearsal?
4. What time of day is best for choral rehearsals?

PROJECTS

1. Make several rehearsal guides based on four choral works.
2. Visit a local rehearsal. Take notes on rehearsal techniques and bring these back to class for discussion.
3. List several twentieth century pieces that would be good introductions to twentieth century music for a choir. Are there any twelve-tone works that are within the realm of high school singers?

SUGGESTED READINGS

Boyd, Jack. *Rehearsal Guide for the Choral Director,* chap. 6. West Nyack, New York: Parker Publishing Co., 1970.

Davison, Archibald T. *Choral Conducting.* Cambridge: Harvard University Press, 1945.

Green, Elizabeth A. H. *The Modern Conductor.* 2d ed. Englewood Cliffs: Prentice-Hall Inc., 1969.

Hillis, Margaret. *At Rehearsals.* American Choral Foundation, 1969.

Lawson, Warner. *Choral Directors Guide,* chap. 11. Edited by Neidig and Jennings. West Nyack, New York: Parker Publishing Co., 1967.

chapter 4.

final rehearsals and preparations for the concert

The last several rehearsals before a concert take on a new meaning for the choral director. The concert, for which he and the choir have been preparing, is almost upon them. The director will find that there are a number of details that must occupy this time. These details must not interfere with the planning for these last, very important rehearsals.

These final rehearsals will have new rehearsal goals. The director must be working to put the concert together. Note hunting should be a thing of the past. The singers should be ready now to do detailed work for as long as it takes to polish a piece. As much as is possible, the time should be spent in bringing together the various sections of works that have been rehearsed for so long as separate parts. The director should plan to rehearse in large segments, at least as large as the capabilities of the choir will permit. Although the director may have placed the sections together in his mind and be totally aware of how they should sound, the student has not. In the performance of a number of many smaller works, the student has probably not thought of the pieces as parts of larger groups of works as they will appear in the concert. The following timetable is an example of how one could utilize the last few rehearsals before the concert.

Five Rehearsals from the Concert

It is a good idea to choose a rehearsal about five rehearsals from the concert in which to do a straight run-through of the concert program. This rehearsal should be held on risers and in the performance hall, if possible. This will not only give the students an idea of the full program but it will also be a good barometer for the director. He can judge the state of preparation of the music and better determine how he can best use his remaining rehearsals.

If tape recording facilities are available, the rehearsal should be taped.

The director may then listen to the tape and pinpoint exactly every trouble spot. It is not usually advantageous to play this tape for the students. Their time can usually be better spent now in rehearsal. The director should listen to the tape objectively and mark the score where he hears mistakes, balance problems, intonation problems, etc.

Four Rehearsals Away

During the next rehearsal, spend all of the time working on the small points that were noticed on the tape. This rehearsal should take place with music in the rehearsal room. Don't waste time singing the music they know. All directors are faced with the temptation to have their choir sing the work they know best because it is the most enjoyable to listen to and to conduct. This is not good use of rehearsal time and particularly not at this point in the preparations.

It is sometimes advantageous to edit a few items from the tape of the previous rehearsal that can serve as brief demonstration models for work in this rehearsal. If one section of a piece, for example, is being flatted but the choir doesn't seem to be aware of it, play just this section for them. Then work it out and tune the section properly. Use the tape sparingly though.

Three Rehearsals Away

The director should continue to spot rehearse, checking the areas that were worked on in the previous rehearsal and any that were not able to be rehearsed then.

Two Rehearsals Away

At this point the director should return to rehearsing as much of the music as possible. After spot rehearsing in the previous rehearsals, one should attempt to put these places back into the musical scope of the work or works. The students need to be more conscious of the entire musical effort of the concert rather than the trouble spots in each piece. This rehearsal should take place on the risers again, and, if possible, in the performance hall.

Before the final rehearsal is discussed it would be good to bring up several points that are relative to the last several rehearsals.

If the ensemble's wearing apparel is easily available, it is often a good idea to use it for one of these last rehearsals, but not necessarily the last one. This is particularly true with younger students and if choir robes are to be worn. The director can use this as a means of checking to see that each robe is the correct length and that each is clean and free of wrinkles. It also gives the students an opportunity to learn how warm it may get on the stage in full concert dress. This is an important factor when the choir is robed, since the robe is worn over some type of normal street wear, adding another layer of clothing.

The emphasis to be on risers is made because the students will have a slightly different sound on the risers. If the rehearsal room acoustics are not better than average, or do not match the performing hall, the director will note a change in the sound on risers. Often, the rehearsal room does not adequately raise the back rows so the sound of these singers can carry well over the rest of the choir. When the students are suddenly placed on the risers, the director will often hear more of the back rows than he did in the rehearsal room. He may also notice a rough edge on their tone, a result of the singers continually singing louder than the rest to provide the director with the balance he desired.

The students also should become accustomed to standing on the risers for extended periods of time. Instruct the students not to let their knees become locked, as they stand, but to keep their legs free and be able to flex the knees occasionally. This will help prevent fainting. There are often one or two students who have a history of fainting and who must be watched closely. It is usually apparent who these people are. Tell the students to sit down on the risers if they begin to feel dizzy. Don't talk too much about fainting because this alone will cause some students to become slightly ill. Be sure to give the choir a break during the rehearsal and get them off the risers for a short time.

There are several areas of concern about which a director should be very conscious in these last rehearsals. This does not imply that they are not important up to this point, but that now they carry a special significance.

Dynamics

Intense, busy rehearsals up to this point may have allowed the dynamic level to climb, creating dynamics of loud and louder. Remember, all dynamics are relative. They can change for the same piece according to the type of hall in which the work is being performed. Listen carefully to the dynamic levels of the choir and be sure that they represent the volumes that were initially sought.

Attacks and Releases

Ragged beginnings and endings of phrases can contribute to an undisciplined and unmusical concert that is not satisfying to anybody. The responsibility for this precision rests solely with the director. The choir members, regardless of how hard they try, cannot begin and end the phrases together without the aid of a conductor. A renewed interest is necessary at this point in the rehearsals.

Balance

When a choir steps on risers the balance can change somewhat. The problem of the back two rows, usually the tenors and basses, has already been mentioned. Where, in a long series of rehearsals, a full *fortissimo* has been the goal, a director may now have to hold one specific section back in order to balance another section whose *fortissimo* does not reach the same level. For the sake of balance some section dynamics may have to be scaled down and a few scaled upwards. It must be remembered, if an alto section, for instance, cannot reach the *fortissimo* level of the rest of the choir, the director must scale the other section dynamics down to meet the altos best effort. It is impossible, but often tried, to bring the alto volume, in this instance, up to the rest of the choir. The range of dynamics must be geared to the section that has the least amount of dynamic range. Trying to raise a volume that cannot be raised with a good singing tone will only result in yelling. Acute listening by the students will also help in this regard.

Text

Extra attention to text should be given at this point also. If a choir will now make a renewed effort toward communication of the text, it will greatly aid the attempt at sensitive phrasing. Although the director has been working on choral diction in previous rehearsals, it is easier now with the notes learned, to concentrate more on the text. The good choral director has worked for a vocalization of the text that takes advantage of the syllabic stress. This stress is important to musical phrasing.

It has been too often observed that choirs place equal weight on each word or syllable regardless of its importance. It is recognized that, on occasion, some phrases are meant to be sung with the same heavy accent on each note with no indication of syllabic stress. This is a choral effect that is not the norm, however. Most choral music demands that few notes receive the same weight. If the director will call attention now to the stressed and unstressed words and syllables, the complexion of many phrases will change.

Phrasing

Sensitive phrasing is the one item most often missed in amateur performances. In the struggle to learn pitches and rhythms, choirs too often sing in a mechanical way that is quite unmusical. The artistic recreation of a composer's score demands nuances of shading that involves a constant give and take to form a musical phrase. Music is in a constant state of flux. It is always moving and is never still.

Tone Quality

In these final rehearsals a director must reemphasize the importance of a warm, vibrant quality. Sometimes students will be expending so much energy trying to meet the demands of the director that their attention to the vocal quality itself slackens. Keep the students constantly listening and trying to improve the quality of the sound.

The Final Rehearsal

The dress rehearsal is the name most often given to the final rehearsal. Some directors like to use it for a nonstop run-through, with everything as it will be in the concert itself. The overall idea is good except that it really isn't necessary to adhere completely to that plan. This rehearsal should include all instruments, if there are to be any, and should take place in the hall where the performance will be held.

When possible, sing through the pieces in their entirety, but don't hesitate to work on a section that causes difficulty. It is often advisable to begin this rehearsal with the piece that will probably need the most work. Don't let this rehearsal become too long. The singers will become unduly fatigued and it can reduce their effectiveness in the concert.

At this, and the other culminating rehearsals, do not verbally abuse the ensemble. Heavy criticism and cutting comments will not help to improve the group's performance. Usually they will react in just the opposite manner. The singers will also become intimidated and their performance will lack the spark and spontaneity desired. There is no point in throwing temper tantrums. Displays of rage and temper will create insecurity among the singers. Approaching a concert is a time when the closest bond between the singers and the conductor should be felt. The ensemble has arrived at its present state of preparedness as a direct result of your teaching. If you wish to be mad at somebody, wait until after the rehearsal and be mad at yourself.

At the last rehearsal a director should do all he can to bolster the confidence of the choir. Urge them toward better singing, but do so by leading them toward a higher goal of excellence, not by berating them because they do not sing as well as you want them to.

Before the rehearsal ends, give the choir all last minute instructions, reminding them of preconcert warm-up times, etc. Instruct them to get to bed early and conserve their energy on the concert day to insure maximum concert effectiveness.

Combining Ensembles for a Concert

High school concerts usually involve more than one ensemble because most high school choirs do not have the rehearsal time available to adequately learn a full program of choral music. Even if they did, it is extremely difficult for one ensemble of high school students to maintain the concentration necessary to present a lengthy, musical performance. The problem that results from combining groups is more of a logistical problem than a musical one, although the logistics affect the musical result. Let's deal with the musical considerations first since they should be the most important.

One of the most usual combinations of ensembles is a select concert choir, a less select mixed chorus, a girls' chorus, a boys' chorus, and one or two small groups such as a madrigal or chamber choir.

The largest musical problems involved are the quality gaps between the groups and the variety of repertoire they will perform. There will undoubtedly be a marked difference in the sound of the most select choir as compared to the second choir. In order to minimize this contrast in quality, the director should try to separate these ensembles on the concert program. This can be done by placing another ensemble of contrasting membership between them.

It would be better to hear the select choir followed by the girls' chorus, for example then the second mixed choir can follow the girls' ensemble. The difference in the types of voices will create a clear distinction for the audience and avoid comparison of the two mixed ensembles.

One possible ordering of the groups would be:

> Concert Choir
> Girls' Chorus
> Mixed Chorus
> Madrigal
> Boys' Chorus
> Mixed Quartet
> Concert Choir

The repertoire of the ensembles will also determine the concert order. The madrigal will undoubtedly sing a different kind of literature than the concert choir, and the girls' and boys' chorus repertoire also tends to be unique to those groups. It is difficult to put a concert together that has continuity when so many different kinds of ensembles are involved. Try to maintain a consistent element of progression in the program or a logical motion in the change of types of repertoire. Suggested programs are listed in chapter eight for this type of concert.

The logistical problem of putting several ensembles on the same concert program is not difficult if the ensembles never have to perform together. If the concert is given on a stage with curtains, the curtains can be drawn after each ensemble while the groups change on the stage. If the students are very quiet, part of them can move onto the stage while a smaller ensemble performs on the apron in front of a closed curtain. Other students can move on and off just before and just after the small ensemble's performance. The desired effect is to keep a concert moving and avoid the *track meet* effect that often occurs as a result of poor planning. At the same time, an audience prefers to have a few moments between groups to adjust to the next type of repertoire.

If the performance must take place in a gym or all-purpose room, and there is no room convenient to use as an offstage room, the students can remain in the gymnasium in seats reserved for them. If the risers are placed in the center of the floor, choirs can be seated on both sides and one choir can move to the risers as the other leaves.

Often, choral directors wish to combine the various ensembles into one large chorus to perform a final number on the concert, or to sing an extended work. When this is the case, the individual groups must have been well rehearsed. Because the quality of the groups is usually so sharply contrasted, the combining of the groups will often be less effective than anticipated. If such a project is undertaken, the groups must rehearse several times together and, because of school schedules, this rehearsal will usually have to take place outside of school time.

The selection of the combined work must be carefully made so it does not overchallenge the less select ensemble(s). Unfortunately, too many directors believe that these students will be raised to a higher level of performance. The opposite is true, however. The quality of the top ensemble is lowered somewhat by the addition of the less select students. Simply because there are more students involved does not raise the caliber of the lower students. It is true though, that the students in a less select ensemble may be given an opportunity to sing a piece that would be too difficult for their group alone.

Adding Instruments

On the occasions when instruments are added to a program the director should meet with the instrumentalists several times before they rehearse with the choir. The exact number of rehearsals will depend on the quality of the instrumentalists. Semiprofessional or professional players, playing parts of medium difficulty, will not require more than one rehearsal to establish tempos, etc., but average-to-good high school players will require several rehearsals in order to understand their role with the chorus.

When the instrumentalists are placed with the choir for the first time neither group should have to endure prolonged rehearsing of the other as a single unit. This kind of rehearsing should have taken place before the combined rehearsal. These combined rehearsals should start on time and end on time. Allow time for tuning and warm-ups, as well as for assembling the groups in the proper order on the stage. If it is necessary to bring several groups of varying sizes together, plan the rehearsal to use the largest group first, and release people as you progress to smaller ensembles. Don't keep 200 singers standing idly by while you work with two soloists for an extended period.

Concert Checklist

1. Secure a date on the calendar. Be sure it is listed on the official school calendar to protect it.
2. Reserve an auditorium for the concert and for final rehearsals.
3. Have tickets printed if they are to be used.
4. Plan the printed program and get it to the printer by the deadline date.
5. Plan the publicity. The following types of publicity can be utilized to draw a sizable concert audience:
   Newspaper releases (include pertinent photos)
   Radio releases
   Television releases
   School announcements
   Notices to other schools in the area
   Posters
   Help from parent organizations
6. Send complimentary tickets to:
   Board of Education
   Superintendent
   Principal
   Music Supervisor
   Teachers that helped in some way
7. Have the president of the choir send personal letters of invitation to people that are special to the music program (newspaper editor, Board of Education, Superintendent, civic club presidents, etc.).
8. Appoint a stage manager. He should be someone who can control the stage lighting, pull curtains, shut off air circulation fans that are noisy, and see that the stage is ready for the concert.
9. Check wearing apparel. Be sure that all students have the correct accessories. (Same type and color of shoes, no gaudy jewelry for girls, etc.)
10. Post on bulletin board and tell students the time they will meet for a pre-concert warm-up. High school students will perform best if they meet together at least forty-five minutes before the concert.

Discussion Questions

1. What kind of behavior from the conductor will spark the best response from a choir? The worst response?
2. Recall the format of dress rehearsals you have attended. What would you have eliminated? What was good about them?
3. Why is the wearing apparel of an ensemble important to their performance?
4. Should all music be memorized for concerts?
5. Should the conductor use music for the final rehearsals and the concert?
6. Should any pieces be dropped from the concert program as late as the final rehearsals?
7. How long should the dress rehearsal be? How long can high school students sing with intense concentration?

SUGGESTED READINGS

Simons, Harriet. "Problems to Anticipate in Preparing Your Chorus for Another Conductor." *The Choral Journal* May 1970, pp. 16-18.

Wilson, Harry R. *Artistic Choral Singing,* chap. 2. New York: G. Schirmer, Inc., 1959.

Zipser, Burton A. "When Chorus and Orchestra Get Together, Harmony or Discord?" *The Choral Journal* July-August 1968, p. 18.

chapter 5. **choral tone**

The characteristics of a good solo tone are also characteristics which are desirable in a good choral tone. It is not possible to thoroughly teach voice in a choral rehearsal, but it is possible to incorporate certain fundamental aspects of vocal technique in these rehearsals. These techniques will be basic principles in obtaining a choral sound that is pleasant and one that is properly produced.

Diaphragmatic Breathing

Proper breathing is important to good singing. Most students breathe in a shallow manner that is inadequate for the purposes of singing. It will sustain life however, and be usable for normal speech. It is necessary to point out to students that breathing from the diaphragm, rather than clavicular breathing, is desirable for the following reasons:

1. A singer can take the necessary amount of air without tightening muscles in the throat.
2. A singer can get more air by breathing from the diaphragm.
3. A singer can control the air once it is inhaled. The air must be released in a continuous supply for sustained singing.

Diaphragmatic breathing requires correct posture for singing. There is no need for elaborate diagrams to illustrate good posture. The singer should stand erect, but not ramrod straight. The weight should be evenly distributed on both feet and the singer should carry the weight on the balls of the feet. The chest should be high and the shoulders slightly sloped, not hunched up in an attempt to "square" them. In effect, an erect but nonmilitary stance will be the result of a good singing posture. When students are seated they should be told to sit forward in their chair and not use the back of the chair. An instruction to sit in a position that will allow them to stand immediately without shifting their weight will give the students an idea of the physical alertness that is desired. This will be a position of erectness from the hips up with both feet on the floor.

As a general rule, young people must be taught to breathe from the diaphragm. It is a teaching that requires insistense, because it involves changing a habit of long standing. Actually, a serious student of high school age should be able to consistently breathe from the diaphragm after two or three lessons (rehearsals). There are many exercises that can be used, but none will be of much value unless the student really wants to change. Three exercises are listed below that seem to be most universally successful.

The first is the panting exercise. Ask the students to pant very rapidly and, as they do so, to place one hand on the abdomen, just below the rib cage. After this is done a few times, ask them to gradually slow the panting down to about one breath (one inhalation and exhalation) per second.

A second exercise asks the students to bend over at the waist with the hands on the bottom of the rib cage, fingers spread apart. Have the students inhale deeply. The singers will breathe from the diaphragm because that is the only way one can breathe in that position. After taking the breath, have the students stand erect, hands still on the rib cage and blow the air out in a steady stream, making a hissing sound. The ribs should come in slowly as this occurs. This hiss can later be changed to a singing tone.

A third exercise is that which combines the breathing with pitches and rhythms. This is more difficult and should not be used with beginning choirs. Have the singers sing the pitches and rhythms in figure 17, *staccato*, bouncing the diaphragmatic muscles on each note. Every note should have an *h* in front of it. This strengthens the rib muscles and gives the singers a better capability to later sing cleanly articulated runs.

Fundamentals of Voice

Every choral conductor should have a thorough understanding of the human voice. If he hasn't studied voice privately, he should do so.

A vocal sound is produced by the exhalation of air causing the vocal cords to vibrate. The vocal cords are probably better labeled vocal folds or bands because their make-up is more characteristic of our understanding of those terms. These folds lie across the throat, stretching from the thyroid cartilage at the front, to the arytenoid cartilage in the back. Since the larynx is a muscle, it reacts exactly like other muscles that are better known to us, that is: it is controlled by the individual; it can become so tense that it will not respond properly; it needs continued exercise to be brought into a desirable state of conditioning; it is controlled by the mind; and, it can be damaged by physical abuse (improper use).

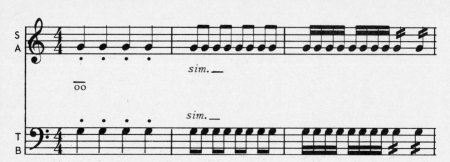

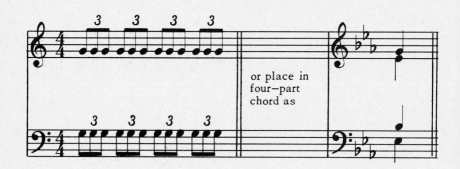

Figure 17

Although pitch is determined by the tension of the vocal folds, it is more difficult to pitch the voice than probably any other instrument. The pitch must begin in the singer's mind. He must be able to mentally *hear* the pitch before he can sing it. Any average person can be taught to play some notes on a piano, for instance, and those notes will always be correctly pitched if the piano has been properly tuned. It is also true that a string player will be able to produce the correct pitch by an accurate placing of the finger on the string and a bowing technique that will allow the string to vibrate properly. A singer has no outward, physical method of placing pitch. One cannot rely on pushing down valves, covering holes, or striking keys to produce the correct pitch. Unless a singer has absolute pitch he will need a given pitch as a reference point or must be given the actual pitch that he is to sing.

The singer produces the pitch by applying the correct amount of breath pressure so the vocal cords will vibrate at the proper tension for the given pitch (a process which is done unconsciously by the singer). This does not insure the singer of a good tone but will only produce the correct pitch.

Resonation

The tone can become deep and rich when the tone is properly placed in the natural resonating chambers. These resonating chambers are the larynx itself, the pharynx, the mouth, and the nasal cavity. The trachea and chest are also considered to be resonators by some people. Since they are located below the larynx and the singer has no control over them, in terms of resonation, they are of little importance to this discussion.

The pharynx consists of the upper part of the throat directly above the larynx. In order for this resonating cavity to be of value to the singer, the throat needs to be open. The pharynx changes somewhat because of its relation to the mouth and the formulation of vowels.

The mouth is a resonating chamber and is the one that can be constantly altered. The tone and the vowels are colored by the shape of the mouth. The tongue and soft palate (velum) play a large part in the act of singing. The tongue must be relaxed and remain low in the mouth. It is recognized that it will be higher when singing an *ee* vowel, than when singing an *ah* vowel. However, it should always be relaxed.

The soft palate should be raised so the back of the mouth is in an open position. When the soft palate remains lowered, the tone does not have the resonance of the upper cavities that singers find add pleasant qualities to the tone. When one yawns, there is a point just before the yawn actually takes place that is a good position for singing. Once into the yawn itself, of course, one will find a constriction of the throat that is not conducive to good singing.

The nasal area cannot be changed by the singer. However, the tone will not resonate properly unless the previous suggestions are followed. It is true that teachers constantly attempt to teach singers to direct the tone forward and high into the head, particularly into the mask of the face. While this is good imagery, the fact is that one cannot direct the sound vibrations in any direction inside the head. What really happens is that a properly produced tone will resonate where it is *allowed* to resonate. Like water that will seek its own level, the vibrations will seek all resonating chambers that are open to them. The teacher's real goal is to create ideal conditions in which proper resonation can take place.

The Choral Tone

An ideal choral tone is one that is pleasant to listen to, is capable of a ringing *forte,* is equally as capable of an intense *pianissimo,* and is warm and vibrant. Good choral technique is compatible with good studio voice technique. Many choral directors are also, or have been, studio teachers, and good ones.

The voice teachers that attack the choral director for punishing voices seem, somehow, less likely to attack the opera director who may demand even more punishing vocal work. Good voice teachers will not attack choral techniques that are based on good vocal habits. Unfortunately, the teaching of voice is not very standardized and disagreements seem to be as constant between voice teachers as they are between voice teachers and choral directors. Several good reading references are listed for the student at the end of this chapter.[1]

The Vibrato and Choral Singing

Some discussion of the vibrato needs to be made because this is one of the points at which voice teachers and choral directors often differ. A vibrato is an essential part of the life of the tone of a choral ensemble. A slow and wide vibrato is not acceptable in a good choral tone and should not be acceptable as a good solo tone either. The tremelo, or fast bleat, is also not desirable in either the soloist or choral group. A well-controlled tone with a pleasant vibrato should be acceptable to anyone.

Some problems seem to arise when a choral director rightfully desires a tone for stylistic purposes with a minimal vibrato, or occasionally, for an effect, without any vibrato. This is no different than the soloist who will want to minimize the vibrato or even use none at all, to sing a text describing a "stark, desolate place."

Real problems and legitimate ones are created by the choral director who attempts to achieve a so-called *straight tone*. This person can abuse voices in an attempt to imitate certain choirs that have a reputation for such a tone. It is the imitation of these choirs, even by their graduates, that does the most harm. The college singer may have enough maturity and sometimes enough vocal technique to be able to cope with such demands. The young high school singer does not. In his eagerness to please the director, he will go beyond the point that his technique and support will carry him without strain. There is no doubt that a quick blend can be obtained through the use of this straight tone. It creates the false security of having achieved something. It will not however, have the capabilities of singing a true *forte* or the warmth to be interesting. It is a white tone with little capacity for beauty. It is used by only a few choirs in the country now, and is on a downward trend.

The following guidelines will help a choral director achieve a desirable choral tone that will also benefit the individual singer's vocal growth.

1. Directors can refer to the National Association of Teachers of Singing *Bulletin* for consistent and usable information on the voice and the teaching of voice.

Warm-ups

Some choral directors use vocal warm-ups at the beginning of a rehearsal because they believe the warm-ups will make the student's voice ready for intensive rehearsal. Some of these directors use the same warm-up exercises in every rehearsal and strive to obtain maximum results with their use.

Other choral directors use warm-up exercises only because they think they are supposed to use them. They do not have a planned use for them but use them because they don't know what else to do to start the rehearsal.

The use of vocal exercises only to free the student's voice and ready him for rehearsal is a poor use of rehearsal time. While it is true that these two factors are important, it is equally as true that much more can be gained through the use of this time. Try to incorporate some rhythmic, melodic, or harmonic elements from the music that is being rehearsed into some of the opening exercises. This does not mean that this must be done with each exercise or all of the time, but that one exercise can be slanted to a particular rehearsal problem. This can be done with just a little planning and the use of a chalkboard.

One example of this is a passage that this author used as an exercise to develop cleanly articulated runs for several weeks before the music from which it was taken was even distributed. It was apparent that it (and one other similar passage) would cause rehearsal problems because both were to be sung at a moderately fast tempo, and by the basses, often the least flexible section of the choir.

dis - per ⸺⸺⸺⸺⸺⸺⸺⸺⸺⸺ sit

Copyright 1963, Walton Music Corp., used with permission.

Figure 18

The passage given in figure 18 was placed on the chalkboard twice and sung by all voices on several vowels and syllables. It was even sung once or twice on the text "dispersit." This was done at various moments in several rehearsals to change from one style to another style of repertoire, or as a beginning exercise. After the second time it wasn't necessary to write it for the students. When it was finally introduced later as part of a work, it had already been learned and needed no further attention. When this is done, no mention will need to be made of its existence in any piece. The students will be aware of it when it occurs in a selection, or it can be mentioned when the piece is introduced.

This use of actual music in exercises can be done with many pieces of music and in a variety of ways. It can save valuable rehearsal time and make learning easier and more enjoyable for both the choir and the director.

Several general exercises are listed that can be used to open a rehearsal or can also be used any time during the rehearsal. Each of them is discussed briefly. Although the exercises are notated in one key, they can be transposed to any key and moved by half or whole steps through various parts of the student's range.

A few general comments about the use of exercises is needed first. It is best not to use the same exercises every day. No matter what they are, they can become boring. Mix the exercises, but mix them so, over a period of one to two months, the ones that are basic to the development of a good tone occur in a steady cycle. Don't hesitate to use exercises at points in the rehearsal other than the beginning. After some strenuous singing, exercises can let the singer relax the throat and, once again, unify the choral tone.

Which exercise to use depends on the point the ensemble has reached in its choral development. Some directors remark publicly that, ". . . no matter what choir I conduct, I always use these two exercises, ..." Any conductor who makes this statement is ignoring the capabilities and differences of singers. It makes no more sense than saying, ". . . no matter what choir I conduct, I always use the same piece of music." There are some choirs at the college level that can achieve a desirable choral tone through choral repertoire without the aid of exercises per se. This is probably not true of high school choirs, however.

There is also no reason that some rehearsals cannot begin without exercises. If the director chooses carefully, the students can free the throat and warm up the voice using a piece of music instead of a vocalise. One doesn't have to use the text of a piece all the time, but can have the choir sing the parts on any given vowel. In this manner the director can rehearse the notes and rhythm of a piece and still get the voices warmed up.

The Warm-up as a Tune-up

Another important aspect of the opening part of the rehearsal is that of tuning up. The warm-up is a tune-up also. Sometimes the students do not need to have the voices *warmed-up* but they do need to *tune-up* to the refined use of their voices within a choral ensemble, toward a unified goal. This aspect should not be ignored because it is the part that helps to reorient students to the rehearsal. The moment a student begins to refine the use of his voice, to listen to the vowel color, to listen to the voices of others, and to contribute to a choral tone that has beauty and warmth, he will have turned his mind on to the choral rehearsal.

Work for a choral tone that has ringing resonance and a deep, rich warmth. This is much easier to say than to do. It is the tone that most choral conductors are aiming for. This tone will not happen accidentally, although one will occasionally have students who, without any prior training, sing with a tone that is very close to that desired. Usually these students cannot maintain the tone consistently throughout their range; good voice training will help gain that control.

Choirs need both the forward resonance and the depth. Several exercises can be used to help acquire both. Figure 19 is an exercise that can be used to develop a focused tone with a forward placement. Have the singers accent

hehm - ee

Figure 19

the *h* and go immediately to the hum. Each singer should make the abdominal muscles tense at the attack. Cue the singers to move slowly from the *m* to the *ee*. Tell them to try to maintain the ring or buzz of the *m* in the *ee*. This is a good exercise for the first part of the year when extra attention will also be given to diaphragmatic breathing.

Another similar exercise that serves much the same purpose as the above is shown in figure 20.

ning - nee

Figure 20

Let the first note be held on the *ng* sound. Change smoothly to the *ee* and hold as long as desired. The first note should not be accented but should be started with a clear attack. After you are convinced that you are getting the best possible sound on the *ee,* let the students sing from *hm* or *ning* to *ee* and then to *ay* (*eh,* avoiding the second part of the diphthong in *ay*). The next step is to add an *ah* vowel to both of the above—from *ee* to *ay* (*eh*) to *ah*. This is the most difficult transition to make. Most often the forward *ping* in the tone is lost when the *ah* is begun. The tone seems to fall down in the mouth as the *ah* is reached. Some imagery will be valuable here. Try to suggest the image that the vowel "stands up" in the mouth, that it is then alert and has forward resonance. The tone needs to follow a path up the back of the mouth, over (following the roof of the mouth), and out, just below the upper teeth. This can be illustrated on a chalkboard as in figure 21.

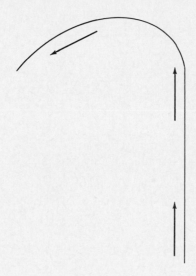

Figure 21

A visual expression of the tone can be quite helpful to students. Impress upon the singers that, at the uppermost point of the curve, the soft palate exists and must be raised. Have the students sharply inhale through the mouth. They will feel cold air strike the soft palate. It is this area that needs to be high when a singing tone is produced.

Another way to give the singers an idea of the space needed inside the mouth is to ask them to imagine that they are startled by something and involuntarily say "oh!" with a sharp inhalation. That shape will also provide the space for a nice singing tone. All of the above suggestions are particularly good to use at the beginning of the year.

The following exercises can be used all year to formulate and maintain a consistency of vowels and a color line in the vowel sounds.

Figure 22

The exercise, figure 22b, works well to provide more depth in an *ee* vowel that has nice resonance but needs to be richer. The *oo* that precedes it can be fed ever so slightly into the *ee* to create a rounder and deeper tone.

The exercises in figures 19 (p. 51) and 20 (p. 51) work particularly well with ensembles that have breathiness, often a characteristic of young girls' voices. The exercises in figures 22a and 22b can help transfer the focus of the brighter vowels into those that are most likely to be breathy, the deep vowels.

Often young choirs can gain a forward focus and even eliminate some of the breathiness but not gain the depth needed to provide a full singing tone. Several exercises will help achieve more depth in the tone.

Figure 23

When singing the exercise in figure 23, be sure that the students drop the jaw sharply on each new syllable. Have the students place their index fingers just in front of the top of the ear lobe and drop the jaw. (Always tell the choir to "drop the jaw," never to "open the mouth." There are many ways to open the mouth but only one way to drop the jaw.) They will find another "hole in the head" at the hinge of the jaw bone. When the tip of the index finger can fit into the depression, the jaw is down and the throat open. Be sure that this happens on each repetition of *yah* and remains that way on the melisma. The tendency will be to bring the jaw up during the five note descending passage. Also emphasize that the tongue must be flat in the bottom of the mouth, with the tip of the tongue touching the lower front teeth.

Another similar exercise that is good is given in figure 24. Be sure that

Yah,　　　Hah _____

Figure 24

the students keep the jaw down after the first note. Even have them hold the jaw down with their hand, if necessary, as they sing the *yah*. The accent on the second note is a diapragmatic accent with a sharp *h* preceding the vowel sound.

Both of the preceding exercises emphasize a lowered jaw. It is always necessary to reiterate that point. Inexperienced students are reluctant to actually drop the jaw as far as it must be dropped to obtain a good tone. Too often the jaw is dropped only slightly and is very tight. This tension contributes to poor intonation as well as a poor tone. It also precludes the possibility of good diction.

Another exercise that can be used anytime during the year is one that asks the students to place the index and third finger of the hand inside the mouth while singing. This should be done with the thumb *down,* preventing the students from raising the head. Have the students vocalize on an *oo* or an *oh,* being sure that the tongue does not arch in the mouth. The following two patterns (figs. 25 and 26) work well for this exercise. Note the crescendo on the first note, again reinforcing the concept of growth in the tone.

The exercise in figure 26 helps students discover an openness and con-

oh _____

o͞o _____

Figure 25

sistainst throughout an octave. Again, placing the two fingers inside the mouth, sing the pattern. Note the accent on the top tone which will help that tone be full and keep a steady rhythm in the passage.

Oh _____

Figure 26

When the two finger exercise is used the lips must not be drawn tight against the teeth. The lips should protrude slightly from the teeth when singing. All of the exercises should be moved to different pitch levels and the last one should be used to the upper and lower limits of the ranges.

The following exercises (fig. 27) can be used to train the singers to match vowel sounds and listen carefully in order to sing in tune. They also help a choir achieve a balance and blend at various dynamic levels. When these are used, ask the singers to sing them at all volumes (not necessarily all during the same rehearsal period).

Figure 27

Some directors like to have a progression of chords available that the choir can sing anywhere to do some preliminary testing of voices in a new concert hall or to bring the singers attention back to a unified vowel and tone. The progressions given in figure 28 have been used with success.

Growth in the Tone

During the discussion of the first rehearsal, and previously in this chapter, the concept of growth in the tone was mentioned. This concept which is

Figure 28

referred to as *growth* or *stretch* of a tone is important to a warm, lyric choral tone. The word *lyric* has been added at this point, and is very important. It is the one quality that many choirs do not have. It is also the one quality that is so important to the teaching of private voice. The rising, spinning quality in a voice that seems to be lightly balanced on a steady column of air, is characteristic of a free tone that has the quality known as *lyricism*. More beautiful singing can be gained lyrically than can be gained by attempting to create powerful masses of sound. A lyric voice can have a *forte* and still produce an intense, vibrant soft tone. In fact, intensity and vibrancy are two necessary qualities of a good, lyric tone. This tone must be approached with a free throat and a solid foundation of diaphragmatic breathing. The growth in a tone may be visualized as:

Figure 29

If this concept is overdone, it can result in a mushy tone. But if used with understanding and common sense, it will allow a choir to develop a warm tone that has strength and beauty. It also makes a choir more alert to the molding of sensitive phrasing.

Have a choir sing in unison on *mee, may, mah, moh, moo,* letting each half note grow to the beginning of the next. Place the choir in a four-part chord and do the same thing. Listed in figure 30 is a chant-like melody that is easily used to develop warm, sensitive phrasing.

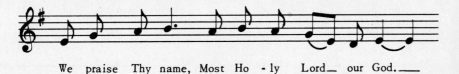

We praise Thy name, Most Ho - ly Lord— our God.—

Thou —— the giv - er of life, ————

Oh Lord ———————— on —— high, ————

We praise ——————— Thy ——— name.———

Figure 30

Each note must be stretched as it is sung, even for its short duration. A sense of a sigh can be the feeling at the ends of the phrases, with the release coming as though one stopped just before the end of a sigh. There is no "falling off" as in a sigh, but the release will seem to float on the breath. These releases can be just as precise as those that come from a clamping off of the tone. Releases should be attained by an inhalation of air. This will guarantee stopping the tone and again save the voice from abuse.

Treat the beginnings of phrases here, and in most literature, as clear beginnings but not as *attacks*. Too much choral music is attacked and not sung. Many choral phrases require a beginning that starts "on the breath." There is a slight exhalation of air an instant prior to the attack. This is not enough to aspirate the first note but enough to take away sharp accents and bludgeoning openings. This use of the breath also helps the singer open the throat and protects him from vocal abuse. It should be noted that there are times when phrases must begin with a sharp attack. There will also be times when the release must even be accented to satisfy a stylistic trait, but most of the time this is not the case.

Note that the melody in figure 30 is free of metrical indications. It should be sung as a chant should be sung, free of the accent of metrical rhythms and the flow of the melody shall be governed by the text.

Much good choral singing is dependent on the ability to sing chant well. If the choir can develop the ability to sing unison chant, or chant-like melodies with sensitivity, this ability can be quite readily transferred to choral music in parts.

A properly produced tone will be capable of more beauty, better intonation, and better diction than a tone that is incorrectly produced. The beauty of choral music lies first in the choral tone. It is necessary to also sing the text so that it is easily understood, and to sing in tune, but if the tone is not pleasant, the audience will not be moved and the music will not have been communicated.

Discussion Questions

1. Why do high school boys generally try to expand the chest area when taking a deep breath? Can a director correlate diaphragmatic breathing to athletics? Will an athlete benefit from diaphragmatic breathing?
2. How can students determine which tone in the choir is the one closest to the ideal that the director desires?
3. How can recordings of different choirs—professional, college, and high school—help in the developing of a choral tone?
4. How can a tone remain beautiful and still communicate a text that describes something less than beautiful?
5. Will the tone change for each musical style? Can the tone remain basically the same with some slight changes?
6. How does the director determine when to change the tonal color of a choir?
7. Which is most important, tone or text? Is one always more important than the other?
8. How can a director devise exercises to teach certain musical problems in choral music?

SUGGESTED READINGS

Bragg, George. "The Adolescent Voice." *The Choral Journal* May 1971, pp. 10-11.
Kagen, Sergius. *On Studying Singing.* New York: Dover Publication, 1960.
Lehl, Allan. "Developing Choral Leadership through Solo Singing." *The Choral Journal* March-April 1969, p. 21.
National Association of Teachers of Singing Committee. "The Solo Voice and Choral Singing." *The Choral Journal* December 1970, pp. 11-12.

Swan, Howard. "Style, Performance Practice and Choral Tone." *The Choral Journal* July-August 1960, pp. 12-13.

Thomas, Kurt. *The Choral Conductor*, pp. 44-50. New York: Associated Music Publishers, 1971.

Van Camp, Leonard. *Choral Warm-ups for Minds, Ears and Voices*. New York: Lawson-Gould Music Publishers, Inc., 1973.

Vennard, William. *Singing, the Mechanism and the Technic*. Rev. ed. New York: Carl Fischer, Inc., 1967.

chapter 6.

choral diction: english and latin

Although choirs perform in many languages, English and Latin are the two languages sung by almost every choir. English, because it is the spoken language, and Latin, because of the vast number of motets and masses in our choral heritage. Since there is insufficient room to discuss all languages choirs may encounter, these two were chosen because of their obvious importance to us.

English

There are so many details to the study of English diction that one chapter cannot possibly cover the subject. It deserves an entire book by itself. The purpose of this chapter shall be to call attention to the principles of good diction and to some of the traps that are inherent in the English language.

Choirs are almost always involved in communicating a text to an audience.[1] When this is the case, it is rewarding when the audience can understand the words. This intelligibility will come through consonants that are short and clean, and through correctly formed vowels that are uniformly pronounced throughout the choir. Although there are some exercises aimed directly at diction it is rarely necessary to work in that manner. A choir director is always working on diction no matter what other purpose may also be in his mind. For instance, when a director is working on tone, he is dealing with vowels. His choir will not develop a satisfying tone or sing in tune until they are singing the same vowel sound. So, no matter what the concern, diction is always part of it. The key to good tone, good intonation, and good blend lies in a single, unified vowel sound. In the course of this chapter,

1. In some instances of avant-garde literature the choir does not attempt to communicate a text. There are also pieces of traditional music in which the choir may communicate the sense of the text rather than a literal transmission of it.

several techniques will be suggested that will help a choral director achieve the best possible diction with his choir.

Singing diction should be nonregional; it should not reveal the native state of the performers. It may take a major effort on the part of the concerned choir director to convince his students that the sounds they make in everyday speech will be undesirable when elongated in a choral work. To "sing as we speak" would only be a correct instruction if we all spoke the same way and if we all spoke the English language correctly. The facts are that we do not speak the language the same way (note the differences in pronunciation between the southern area, the southwestern area, the midwestern area, and the northeastern area). There are still further subtle differences inside each of these areas. The director must also impress upon the students the difference between sustaining a sound on pitch and quickly passing over it in normal conversation.

Figure 31 lists the *International Phonetic Alphabet Symbol* (IPA) for the vowels and consonants. This chart includes single vowels, diphthongs, triphthongs, and consonants that combine to make one sound. Learn to use the IPA symbols and be able to apply them to choral texts. This is the best possible way to insure consistent and correct pronunciation. Anything less than a concerted and disciplined approach will result in erratic diction.

Letter	As in the Word	IPA Symbol
a	lap	|æ|
a	date	|ɛɪ|
a	father	|ɑ|
e	met	|ɛ|
e	meet	|i|
e	here, dear	|ɪə|
er	never	|ɚ|
i	mist	|ɪ|
i	night	|ɑɪ|
ir	fire	|ɑɪə|
o	go	|oʊ|
o	obey	|o|
o	top	|ɑ|
o	for, Lord	|ɔ|
o	lose	|u|
oo	took	|ʊ|
oo	boot	|u|
ou	our	|ɑʊə|
oy	boy	|ɔɪ|
ow	now	|ɑʊ|

Figure 31   International Phonetic Alphabet Symbol (IPA)

Letter	As in the Word	IPA Symbol
u	up	$\|\Lambda\|$
u	use	$\|ju\|$
u	burn	$\|\mathfrak{z}\|$
b	bat	$\|b\|$
c	precede	$\|s\|$
c	cat	$\|k\|$
d	date	$\|d\|$
f	full	$\|f\|$
g	George	$\|dz\|$
g	get	$\|g\|$
h	home	$\|h\|$
j	judge	$\|dz\|$
k	king	$\|k\|$
l	love	$\|l\|$
m	marry	$\|m\|$
n	no	$\|n\|$
p	people	$\|p\|$
q	queen	$\|kw\|$
r	ride	$\|r\|$
s	sing	$\|s\|$
s	easy	$\|z\|$
t	top	$\|t\|$
v	very	$\|v\|$
w	want	$\|w\|$
x	apex	$\|ks\|$
x	exert	$\|gz\|$
y	you	$\|j\|$
z	zone	$\|z\|$
ch	church	$\|t\int\|$
ng	bring	$\|\eta\|$
sh	wish	$\|\int\|$
th	there (voiced)	$\|\eth\|$
th	thing (unvoiced)	$\|\theta\|$
zh	azure	$\|\mathfrak{z}\|$

Figure 31—Continued

Before any of these vowels can be correctly pronounced, they must be correctly identified. This is a problem for many directors since it is apparent that some choirs make a directed and unified effort toward a wrong pronunciation of some words. One example of this is the word *sing* $\|s\imath\eta\|$. One often hears it pronounced as $\|si\eta\|$ which is incorrect. There are many choral directors who ask their students to modify $\|s\imath\eta\|$ toward $\|si\eta\|$, and even ask them to use an $\|i\|$ sound on occasion. The knowledgeable director expects his choir to sing with a brighter $\|\imath\|$ sound and does not actually want the sound of $\|i\|$.

It is the director who misapplies the technique of brightening the vowel (that doesn't know when to stop), whose choir sounds strange on the concert stage. Good diction should not sound strange. When good concert diction is achieved, an audience should recognize it as refined English. Certainly no one would expect gutteral or dialectal speech on the stage.[2]

Figure 32 applies the IPA symbols to the single vowel sounds, and lists several examples of these vowels in use. Practice speaking the sound of the words and writing them with the proper IPA symbol. This will help each director establish a consistent approach to diction that will have a lasting effect on the sound of the choir.

Two possible symbols have been purposely omitted, |ɒ|, a short *o* sound and |a|, an intermediate sound between |æ| and |ɑ|. The first |ɒ| is generally not used in the United States. The words to which it is applied, *hot, top,* etc., are usually pronounced as |hat|, |tap|. This pronunciation is more practical and consistent with our usage. The latter |a| is also not practical since we don't usually make the sound between |æ| and |ɑ|. All of the words to which this symbol is applied may be pronounced either |æ| or |ɑ|.

IPA Symbol	As In	IPA Spelling
|i|	me, thee, fee	|mi, ði, fi|
|ɪ|	gift, listen, shrill	|gɪft, lɪsən, ʃrɪl|
|ɛ|	wed, led, hair	|wɛd, lɛd, hɛə|
|æ|	sad, cat, manner	|sæd, kæt, mænə|
|ɑ|	father, hot	|faðɚ, hɑt|
|ɔ|	lawn, gone	|lɔn, gɔn|
|ʊ|	wool, full, took	|wʊl, fʊl, tʊk|
|u|	moon, soon	|mun, sun|
|ɝ|	mirth, learn, turn	|mɝə, lɝn, tɝn|
|ə|	around, aloft, never	|əraʊnd, ələft, nɛvə|
|ʌ|	up, cup, abrupt, love, come	|ʌp, kʌp, əbrʌpt, lʌv, kʌm|
|o|	omit, obey, proceed	|omɪt, obeɪ, prosid|

Figure 32

Figure 33 lists diphthongs with their IPA symbols. In all cases but one, the first vowel sound is the one that should receive the emphasis.

2. There are some obvious moments when choirs should use a dialect—spirituals, some folksongs, etc.

IPA Symbol	As In	IPA Spelling
|oʊ|	know, mow, go	|noʊ, moʊ, goʊ|
|ɛɪ|	may, taste, faith	|mɛɪ, tɛɪst, fɛɪθ|
|ɑɪ|	might, fight	|mɑɪt, fɑɪt|
|aʊ|	cow, now, sound	|kaʊ, naʊ, saʊnd|
|ɔɪ|	boy, soil	|bɔɪ, sɔɪl|
|ɪu|*	music, few, dew	|mɪuzɪk, fɪu, dɪu|

Figure 33

In order for the word to be correctly pronounced and ultimately understood, the first part of the diphthong must be held as long as possible during the duration of the note. The second vowel sound should be placed at the very end of the note. The transition between the two sounds should be quick but smooth, and never abrupt.

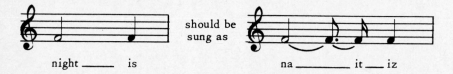

night ____ is   should be sung as   na ____ it ___ iz

Figure 34

This principle, as illustrated in figure 34, should be applied to other words. This is only a metrical illustration and does not intend that the second part of the diphthong should take on rhythmic significance. It is important that the vowel be formed deep in the mouth, and that this deep vowel be maintained until the very last moment.

The exception to this is the |ɪu| diphthong, which is marked with an asterisk on the chart in figure 33. In this instance the first vowel sound is quickly sounded and the second vowel sound is elongated.

Formation of Vowels

There are special requirements that are peculiar to each particular vowel sound. All of the vowels, however, share some of the same requirements for good production. These are:

1. A relaxed jaw
2. A relaxed tongue
3. Proper room in the mouth

These three conditions, upon which good vowel formation depends, are those that are most frequently absent from choral performances. Any choral director that has served as an adjudicator will attest to the common failure of singers (both solo and choral) to drop the jaw and open the throat. These are important enough to be dealt with individually.

A Relaxed Jaw

A tense jaw will prevent any singer from making a consistently pleasant tone. Young singers find it difficult to solve this problem without help. There are several reasons for this. The first is that everyday or conversational speech does not require one to provide much room in the mouth. Most Americans, young and old, move the jaw only slightly (some not at all) when they talk. Young people then, when asked to drop the jaw, open the mouth only a small portion of the amount actually needed to produce a good singing tone. They feel certain, because the mouth is open approximately twice as much as for normal speech, that their mouth must be gaping wide. A director must show the students that the room needed for really good singing is much more than they initially assume. Young people are also self-conscious about opening their mouths too far thinking that it will make them look funny or appear silly. Of course, this is ridiculous because people expect singers to open the mouth when performing. The same people don't think it's ridiculous when a violinist tucks the instrument under his chin, placing his head in an awkward position. Neither will they consider a singer ridiculous who opens his mouth the proper amount to sing.

Ask the students to drop the jaw rather than to open the mouth. (This is discussed further in chapter four, *Choral Tone*). There are many ways to open the mouth but only one way to drop the jaw. When the jaw is "dropped," the lower jaw will go down and in toward the throat. When the jaw is open comfortably it will be free of tension and will seem to be hanging open. Singers can drop the jaw too far and place tension on the throat but this is rare. The opposite is more likely to be the case. The face muscles should also be loose and the lips should be relaxed and free of tension. The jaw position will necessarily change when producing the various vowels but it should be kept open as much as each vowel will allow.

A Relaxed Tongue

The tongue will also change position according to the vowel being produced. As is true with the jaw, the tongue should also be relaxed. Any tension in the tongue and connecting muscles will produce a tight tone and impure vowel sound. In all cases, the tip of the tongue should touch the back of the lower front teeth. All of the vowel sounds can be correctly produced from this position. Do not allow the students to let the tongue "bunch up" or be pulled back into the mouth. If this happens, the tone will become throaty or mushy, because the inside of the mouth as a resonating chamber is greatly altered. The vowels themselves will also be distorted. This will also place more tension on the larynx and cause vocal fatigue.

If excessive attention is called to the role of the tongue, a few students may become too conscious of it and more, rather than less, tension will be the result. The tongue, however, is not a reflexive muscle. It can be consciously controlled by a singer. Most average high school students will not have a tongue-tension problem. It usually occurs in a student who, for some misguided reasons, is striving to produce a "deeper and bigger" tone, not realizing that he is really only diffusing the good qualities of his natural voice. This may come about as a result of poor teaching, but can just as often be caused unwittingly by the student himself, in a naive attempt to emulate a mature singer.

Proper Room in the Mouth

A relaxed jaw does not necessarily insure that each vowel will have the proper amount of room for its best production, nor is the opposite true. It is necessary to have both and to understand the amount of room needed to adequately produce each vowel.

The |ɑ| (ah) vowel will need the most room and the |i| (ee) vowel the least. Other vowels will be correctly formed with space somewhere between these two extremes. The formation of the five primary vowel sounds (see fig. 35) are discussed in the following paragraphs.

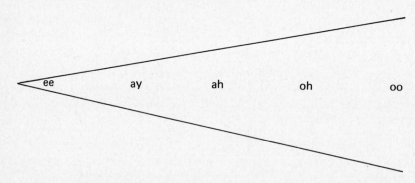

Figure 35   Five Primary Vowel Sounds

|ɑ| (ah)

The correct mouth position for the *ah* vowel is one that will place the jaw in its lowest position. The lips should be relaxed and just slightly away from the teeth, revealing part of the middle upper front teeth. The tongue should be lying in the bottom of the mouth, slightly grooved in the middle, with the tip touching the back of the lower front teeth. The vowel is formed deep in the mouth with the soft palate raised. This vowel is often distorted into an |ʌ| (uh) sound because the jaw is not low enough.

The sounds |æ| as in *bad,* and |ʌ| as in *up,* can also be produced with only slight modification of this opening. The tongue will come up slightly on the |æ| vowel but the jaw and lip position should remain the same. A good vowel sound will be obtained if the students shape for |ɑ| and sing |æ|. Instruct them to place (fill) a vertical opening with a horizontal vowel. Some choirs mistakenly attempt to avoid this vowel. This is wrong. In the first place, the vowel cannot be avoided because it occurs too often as a part of our language. Some choral directors pronounce |æ| as |ɑ| in nouns or important words, but not when the vowel occurs in other places in the sentence. This is just as wrong as the choir that sings the vowel with a careless and shallow production, creating a sound often known as the midwestern twang.

The |ʌ| (uh) vowel sound is produced from virtually the same jaw, lip, and tongue position as the |ɑ|. There will be a slight movement upward of the middle of the tongue. Do not substitute the |ɑ| sound for that of |ʌ|. The |ʌ| vowel can be artistically produced. Substitution of |ɑ| for |æ| and |ʌ| vowels will only result in affectation.

|ɛɪ| (ay)

The jaw must come up just a little in order to produce this sound. The tongue will also come up slightly, but the tip of the tongue should remain just behind the lower front teeth. The lip position will also be modified somewhat. The corners of the mouth will be extended outward just a little. Of course, this position will be desirable for the pure |ɛ| sound as well as for the diphthong.

|i| (ee)

The |i| vowel requires a further modification forward, bringing the jaw up to its highest position. There will be less room in the mouth for the |i| vowel than for any other vowel sound. Too often this room is so small that the sound is very piercing and thin. There should be approximately enough room between the teeth to admit the width of one finger.

It is with this vowel, particularly, that care should be taken to prevent any tension in the jaw. This is important with all vowels, but the position of the jaw makes it even more important on an |i| vowel. Have the students place their hands on their face to be sure the muscles of the face are not tight and the lips are not drawn tightly against the teeth.

The tongue will be in its highest position, but the tip of the tongue should still remain just behind the lower front teeth. Students will find it helpful to let the edges of the tongue touch the back upper teeth on the |i| vowel. This will aid the singer in maintaining room in the mouth and prevent them from chopping off the tone.

|oʊ| (oh)

This vowel is more toward the back position (see fig. 35) than any of the previous vowels. The lips should be forward, away from the teeth. The jaw will be slightly higher than for the |ɑ| vowel, although it is good to teach the students to leave the jaw in the |ɑ| position and to bring the lips forward and round them.

The tongue will rise only a very small amount. Some students will tend to curl the tip of the tongue back in the mouth when forming this vowel. Again, guard against this by keeping the tip of the tongue touching the lower front teeth.

|u| (oo)

The position of this vowel is at the other extreme from the |i| vowel. It is the most closed and the darkest vowel. The jaw will come up somewhat from the |oʊ| position, but the change should be quite small. The lips will form a smaller, more forward position than the one assumed for the |oʊ| vowel sound.

The back of the tongue will come up slightly, but its movement will probably not be noticed by the singer. If the student is instructed to leave the jaw as close to the |oʊ| position as he can and move the lips forward for the |u| sound, the result will be a deeper vowel with good forward focus.

The |ʊ| (as in *full*) can be placed into the same position as the |u| vowel. The lips will not be pushed quite as far forward but the position otherwise, will be essentially the same.

Vowel Modification

The human voice is capable of expressing many emotions. The voice can easily express sorrow, anger, surprise, gaiety, etc. It is because the voice has these capabilities that we may modify certain vowels to help create the sound of the emotion we are trying to express. This modification, or coloring of vowels, if carefully done, will expand the expressive capabilities of the choir. A choral ensemble is an instrument of great diversity in the hands of an imaginative choral conductor.

The choral director should not be timid about using his musical ear as a guide to the modification of vowel sounds. At the same time, any coloring must be done with taste, and with a concern that all of the choir is doing it together and to the same degree.

Range Considerations

Certain modifications are necessary in all voices in the extremes of the ranges. For example, tenors will produce a tone that is more consistent and a vowel pattern that is more even if he modifies the top tones on an *ah* vowel toward an *aw*. Conversely, in the lower range, he will maintain a better sound by brightening the vowels and bringing them forward. The result of the modification in these instances is that the tone of the singer remains more consistent throughout the entire range.

Darkening Vowels

Young voices tend to sing with too much shallowness and brightness in the tone. Modification of the brighter vowels to a darker vowel will actually bring the voices to a desired vowel somewhere in the middle of the tonal color range. Often the |i| (ee) vowel, for example, is shallow and piercing. Generally more room in the mouth is needed to give the vowel a deeper sound. In addition, the choir may be instructed to shape more for |u| (oo) and sing |i| (ee). Do not shape quite enough toward |u| (oo) to make the German umlauted |u| sound, however.

Choirs can successfully shade a vowel by thinking one vowel while singing another. The same effect can be obtained by implying one vowel while singing another. It is also quite easy to ask a choir to "feed a little *oo*" into an |i| (ee) vowel to help the depth of the tone.

When one asks for a darker color one should not confuse this with asking for a darker quality, or what is usually known as *throatiness*. The vocal production can remain the same but the color of the vowel will be changed.

Another vowel that often lacks any true placement in young singers is the |ɪ| (ih) vowel. If it isn't properly placed it will sound blatant and will also affect the intonation. By placing some of the vowel |u| (oo) into this sound, it will have a better shape and produce a more pleasant tone.

Choirs tend to sing a lot of words without much thought. One of the results of this is a lack of continuity in the vowel production. Some words will be dark, others bright, and others somewhere in between these two extremes. In order to create a more musical and flowing line, a conductor must have the ability to slightly alter vowel sounds. When one trims the harsh edge off a vowel sound or modifies one vowel to match others in the line, one will begin to hear the refinement in the tone that is desired.

Figure 36 lists several vowels that often need modification with young singers. Judicious use of this chart will be an aid to a choral director. If the technique is overdone, it will, as will the extreme or misguided use of any method, have adverse effects on the sound of the ensemble.

Vowel	If too Bright, Modify	If too Dark, Modify
*ah	toward aw	toward a more forward position
*ee	with oo	by bringing it forward
*ih	with oo	toward ee
*æ	with ah (shape for and sing)	
ay	with more eh	bring the eh forward
oh	toward aw	toward oo
aw	toward oh	toward ah

* These vowels create the majority of problems for most choirs.

Figure 36

Consonants

Although the vowels provide the beauty in singing, these sounds would be meaningless without cleanly articulated consonants. The consonant provides tonal energy and makes the vowel come alive. Consonants need to be articulated quickly, making way for the next vowel sound. At the same time, the consonants must not become so explosive that they seem to obliterate the choral tone.

In order for the words to be clearly understood, the consonants also need to be exaggerated more than is the case in normal speech. The word *top* is an example. If it is sung as it is normally spoken and if this sound could be described visually, it would look like this |tAHp|. In order for it to sound like *top,* as desired, it must be sung as |TɑhP|. This relationship between the consonants and vowel will provide a clearly understood text. This does not mean that consonants have to be so exaggerated that they become unmusical. They must be exaggerated only enough to make the word understood.

There are two general types of diction, or styles of singing that a choral director will teach. These are *marcato* and *legato* diction.

Marcato diction is sharply defined with explosive consonants, and often, accented vowels. It is a strong diction reserved for forceful, declamatory texts. This diction would be appropriately used in such works as portions of *The Last Words of David* by Randall Thompson (fig. 37).

The opening of this work, as in figure 37, is a good example of the power that is sought with marcato diction. Not only are the consonants exaggerated but the vowels also receive a heavy accent. Legato diction, misapplied in this instance would destroy the forceful nature of this opening statement.

Legato diction, on the other hand, is a smooth linking together of consonant and vowel. Many choral works involve the use of legato diction. *O Vos Omnes,* by Juan Esquivel, is but one example.

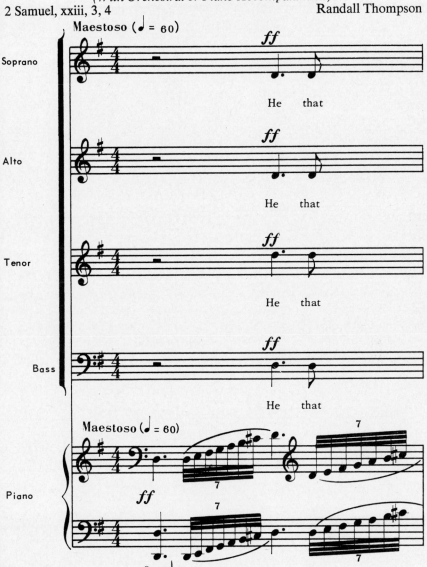

To Dr. Serge Koussevitzky
The Last Words of David
For Four-Part Chorus of Mixed Voices
(With Orchestral or Piano Accompaniment)

2 Samuel, xxiii, 3, 4   Randall Thompson

Figure 37

Figure 37—Continued

Figure 37—Continued

Figure 37—Continued

O Vos Omnes
(For Holy Saturday or general use)
For Four-Part Chorus of Mixed Voices
a cappella

Juan Esquivel (16th century)
Edited by Robert L. Goodale

Figure 38

Figure 38—Continued

O Magnum Mysterium

For Four-Part Chorus of Mixed Voices
a cappella

Tomás Luis de Victoria
Edited by Alice Parker
and Robert Shaw

Figure 39

Figure 39—Continued

Each note should be tied to the next with no space between them. This is somewhat difficult for young singers to do. They often allow the intensity to drop off in the tone toward the end of each note, creating a space between notes. Again, the principle of growth in the tone will help achieve a smooth, flowing line.

The consonants |m| and |n| take on special significance in legato diction. They may be elongated somewhat, being sounded as a *hum* slightly before the consonant is articulated. These sounds help carry a well-shaped tone through to the next vowel. The excerpt quoted in figure 39 is but one case where this technique may be applied.

Many choral works, of course, combine marcato and legato diction. The director needs to determine which type of diction will be appropriate to each phrase and emphasize that fact to the choir. Figure 40 is an example of a work that incorporates both types of diction in an alternating manner.

It is also necessary to sing *staccato,* but this isn't as much a style of diction as it is a special type of light, quickly articulated diction that might be categorized at the very extreme end of marcato diction. Staccato diction will rarely be used as an effect in choral singing.

(For Nancy)

Hodie Christus Natus Est

For SATB

Gordon Lamb

Figure 40

Figure 40—Continued

Special Diction Problems

There are a number of traps in the English language for the choral singer. The traps most often encountered are listed below. Directors should look for these in choral works and anticipate them for the choir.

|S|— The |s| (or |c| when it is a sibilant) is not a singer's friend. The sound can be excessively loud, and in a live room, virtually shatter the musical line. Instruct the choir to minimize the |s| sound. Some directors assign one of every three or four singers to articulate the |s| in any particularly bothersome passages. This is not necessary if the nature of the sibilant sound is brought to the attention of the singers. The |s| should be articulated as quickly and as quietly as possible to minimize the hissing sound. The director should also recognize that the |s| is often to be pronounced as a |z|. Be sure the |z| is formed further back in the mouth than the |s|. Otherwise, the meaning of some words will be changed—music, wrongfully pronounced, could come out to be |mu-sick|.

|D|— The |d| deserves mention because some choirs pronounce a |d| as a |t|, presumably because they believe it is necessary in order for the |d| to be heard. This is not necessary and is confusing to an audience intent on understanding the words. For example, "Dear, dear, what can the matter be" becomes "Tear, tear, what can the matter be." Or the word *heard* may sound like *hurt*. "I hurt the Lord's voice" is significantly different than, "I heard the Lord's voice." There are instances when the |d| is rightfully pronounced as a |t|, for example *taxed, wrapped.*

A |d| is formed further back in the mouth than a |t|. The |d| should be clearly formed but the *uh* that often follows should be eliminated. The |d| may receive some of the forward articulation of a |t| when it is necessary to project the consonant over an ensemble of instruments. In an unaccompanied work, however, this is not necessary and is undesirable.

|R|— The American |r| is a constant thorn in the choral director's side. It seems to be one consonant that young singers always project. It is a most unmusical sound and needs careful attention. When the |r| occurs before a consonant it can be omitted and the word will still be understood. The word *heard* would be pronounced as |hɛd|, as opposed to most normal speech habits, which pronounce the word as *hrrrd*. Often choral directors ask the students to sing |hɛd|, and *imply* the |r|, on the premise that ten percent will put the |r| into the word anyway, giving it plenty of |r| sound. Actually even this is unnecessary. Simply omit the |r| before a consonant or when it occurs before a pause.

When an |r| occurs before a vowel and needs to be articulated, as in the word *America,* let it be quick and, in this instance, part of the third syllable, rather than the second. When it is sounded during the second syllable it takes on the characteristic of doubling itself because it will receive another sound as the singer proceeds to the next syllable. On a number of occasions a flipped |r| will be most appropriate. This is particularly true in Latin texts.

Prefixes

There are a number of prefixes that are commonly mispronounced. Those that are abused the most are the ones that include a *re-* or *de-* and sometimes *be-*. A common rule to remember is that words like *re*new and *re*assure are pronounced as *ri* (ree) because they are a reiteration of the original. To renew means to make new again, and to reassure means that one will be assured once more. A word such as *repose,* which means to lie quiet and calm, is pronounced as |rɪpoʊz| (rihpoz) because one is not "posing" again. The same is then applied to words like deliver, which is pronounced |dɪlɪvə| (dihliver) because it is *not* the surgical removal of one's liver. "When Thou tookest upon Thee to *de*liver man," if wrongly pronounced, takes on an entirely different meaning. Not only should these words not receive a long ee |i| sound, but the prefix is not stressed. Directors will find that when the prefix is properly pronounced, the word stress is automatically better and the music will flow more easily.

Y (when final)—The final *y* should be pronounced |ɪ| as in the word *hill,* not as |i| in the word *me.* This correct pronunciation will also help the musical flow by again not giving added emphasis to a syllable that should not be stressed. When the final *y* is prolonged by the music, as it often is, it should still be pronounced as |ɪ|. Some brightening or implying of |i| may serve to ease the director's conscience if he has mispronounced it for some time.

There are instances when one will want the choir to separate, rather than link together, certain combinations of English words. These situations will occur when the same vowel must be reiterated and when the combination of consonants and vowels make the text unintelligible or alter its meaning. An example of the first is, "I see evil." The two *e's* need to be separated and a new *e* started at the beginning of the word "evil." This will avoid a slurring together of the *e* sounds, as "I seeevil."

The second problem, that of two sounds that blur the meaning of the text or alter it, may be illustrated by the combination, "her beautiful eyes" and "your ear." If these words are not separated they will become: "her beautifullies" and "yourrear."

Final |T| and |S|— These two consonants as the final sound in a phrase or selection are often too loud. It seems to be the one place where the director remembers to work on diction. These two consonants can be extraordinarily loud at this point and therefore be unmusical. Make the pronunciation of this final consonant appropriate to the phrase of which it is a part. An explosive

|t| or |s| at the end of a very soft legato passage will ruin any previous attempt at a musical line.

Listed in figure 41 are some of the words most often mispronounced in choral music. There are more to be sure, but if one becomes aware of these words, one may begin to notice other words that need special attention.

Word	Commonly Mispronounced as	Should be
alleluia	allayluy*uh*	|allɛluja|
and	ahnd	|æɴd|
any	ihny	|ɛnɪ|
beautiful	beeooteeful	|bɪutɪful|
behold	beehold	|bɪhoʊld|
can	kin	|kæɴ|
carol	kehruhl	|kærəl|
deliver	deeliver	|dɪlɪvə|
divine	deevine	|dɪvɑɪɴ|
glory	glawree	|glorɪ|
honor	hono*hr*	|ɑɴə|
Lord	Lo*hrd* or La*hrd*	|Lɔd|
many	mihny	|mɛɴɪ|
marry	merry	|mærɪ|
new	noo	|ɴɪu|
our	are	|ɑʊə|
poor	po*hr*	|pʊə|
pretty	pri*dee*	|prɪtɪ|
redeemer	reedeem*r*	|rɪdimə|
shall	shell	|ʃæl|
spirit	spea*ruht*	|spɪrɪt|
when	wen	|hwɛɴ|
where	we*ar*	|hwɛə|

Figure 41

The chart in figure 42 includes voiced and unvoiced consonants in pairs. These pairs are valuable in learning the proper pronunciation for the consonants, which, in turn, will allow the word to be understood. Voiced consonants must be pitched and must occur before the next vowel is to be sounded. If they don't, the choir will constantly seem to be dragging. The choir should anticipate the vowel with the pitched consonant. Unpitched consonants do not take the length of time as those that are pitched, and consequently may occur closer to the beginning of the vowel sound.

Students may note the difference between voiced and unvoiced consonants by placing their hands over their ears and pronouncing all of the consonants. The voiced consonants will be heard inside the head but the unvoiced consonants will not be heard.

Voiced	*Unvoiced*
b	p
d	t
g	k
z	s
v	f
j	ch
th (with)	th (thin)
w	wh
s (treasure)	sh (shoot)

Figure 42   Voiced and Unvoiced Consonants

Most criticism of diction centers around the following points:

1. Failure to sing a pure vowel, or to extend the correct vowel sound of a diphthong
2. Failure to articulate the initial and final consonants
3. Failure to pronounce words correctly
4. Poor word stress

The first three points have been discussed and the problem areas have been pointed out. The final point is important to the overall conveyance of a text. Communication of a text involves more than correct and perfectly sung diction. The words of a piece of music can be rendered so exactly as to destroy completely the musicality of the work, and make it sound quite artificial, almost sterile. Equally as important as good diction (correct formation and pronunciation of the words) is the understanding that each word or syllable should not and cannot have equal weight. This may seem to be so fundamental as to not need discussion, but this author, and many other clinicians and adjudicators, constantly find it necessary to comment on this aspect of clinic and contest performances.

Although examples like the following have been used for years to illustrate this idea, they are still valuable. Read the following sentence in a conversational tone with your own personal inflection.

Make a joyful noise unto the Lord.

Then underline the syllables that received the most weight. Go back and read it a second time to see if you can give the text yet another interpretation by stressing still other words. By this time it has been realized that more than two interpretations of the text are possible. In fact, there are many. This is also true in choral music. The weight or stress given by a choir to words will influence its communication to an audience. It will also have a direct bearing on the choir's ability to sing artistically shaped phrases. Don't allow the choir to give equal weight to each syllable unless that is the desire of the composer.

Two people really give the text its interpretation; the composer and the conductor. The composer, by his underlay of the text, demonstrates his preference regarding the stress. The example given in figure 43 shows that the composer has given rhythmic and melodic importance to "make," "noise," and "Lord."

make   a   joy - ful   noise   un - to   the   Lord. _____

Figure 43

The conductor may further emphasize these words and fully realize the composer's intent by instructing the choir to stretch (apply the growth principle) particularly to these words. They should not be accented, but the choir should "sing into them," which will create the effect of inflective stress. This will prevent a harsh rendering of the text, and will also help obtain a lyric vocal line.

In the following setting of the same text, the composer has indicated an entirely different inflection (see fig. 44). The intent here is to present a setting of the text in which all syllables have virtually the same importance. This emphasis is a rhythmic one and, with the use of percussion, reveals the "joyful noise" portion of the text.

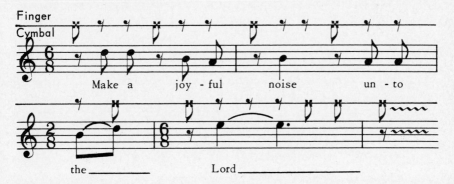

Figure 44

In this setting the conductor needs to stress the rhythmic vitality. The word "Lord" does receive extra attention by the composer. Because of its length and its syncopation, it will not be necessary for a choir to further emphasize it. The composer sufficiently "built-in" its emphasis.

The choral director will be most successful in his attempt at correct diction if he will mark each text with the IPA symbols. He should read the text aloud several times, using the pronunciation that he would use if he were singing it. Finally, he should sing the text as the composer set it, singing each part and carefully noting any awkward stresses as a result of rhythm, melodic leaps, or harmonic emphasis.

Liturgical Pronunciation of Latin for Choral Singing

The Latin language offers the singers the advantage of singing only the five fundamental vowel sounds. None of the vowels has a second sound (diphthong). A director must take extra care to be sure that the choir does sing a pure vowel and that they do not treat the Latin language the same as they do English.

One should also be apprised that the pronunciation of the Latin language, as it appears in figure 45, is the pronunciation used when singing. It is often referred to as, Italianized or church Latin. It will, and should, differ from the Latin language as taught in the classroom by the Latin instructor. It is usually necessary to preface the first work in Latin with remarks to that effect for the benefit of some students who are currently, or have been, enrolled in a Latin class.

The life of the Latin language is in the pure vowels. They need to be consistently pronounced as indicated in figure 45. Again, the IPA symbol is used along with an English word that contains the appropriate vowel sound.

Latin Vowel	As In	IPA Symbol
A	father	$\lvert\alpha\rvert$
E (also AE and DE)	red	$\lvert\varepsilon\rvert$
I and Y	feet	$\lvert i\rvert$
O	for	$\lvert\mathfrak{o}\rvert$
U	noon	$\lvert u\rvert$

Figure 45

A (AE and OE)—these vowels should *always* be pronounced as indicated in figure 45. They should never receive a second sound, such as in the word *may* $\lvert m\varepsilon\mathrm{I}\rvert$. They are not diphthongs and do not have a second vowel sound. This vowel sound is one of two that are mispronounced the most by choirs. While the vowel is to be pronounced as $\lvert\varepsilon\rvert$, it may legitimately have more brightness than we give that sound in English.

I, Y—these vowels are *always* pronounced as $\lvert i\rvert$. The word *in* is mispronounced by many choirs as |ın| (ihn) rather than as |in| (een). "In excelsis" is a text so often sung by choirs that it should be noted that the letter *i* (*in* and *-sis*) receives the pronunciation of |i| in both instances.

O—this is the other vowel that is mispronounced so often. It is *not* to be pronounced as though it were an |o| in the English word *go*. It does not receive the second vowel sound of that word, the |ʊ| vanish. The tone must be maintained on the first of the English sounds, the |o|, until the next consonant or vowel is sung. Have the choir sing the |o| as they normally would, but do not let them change to the |ʊ| vanish. Ask them to release by taking a breath at your signal. Give the signal somewhat prematurely to prevent them from sounding the |ʊ| vanish. The Latin *o* receives the pronunciation as in our word *awe,* with no trace of a second sound.

U—this sound should never be pronounced as the |ʊ| in *full* or with a preceding |i| sound, as in *you*. It is always pronounced |u| as in *noon*.

Other vowel combinations such as *AU, EI, EU,* and *OU* must be dealt with individually. The *AU* should be pronounced as the *ou* in the word *house.* The first vowel should be maintained until the very last moment when the second vowel is sounded, just before passing to the next syllable.

EI, EO, EU, OU, and *UI* are not diphthongs and each vowel is to be pronounced as though they are two separate vowels which they really are. Do not confuse them with diphthongs. The exception to this is the instance when *UI* is preceded by an *O* as in *oui*. The correct pronunciation is as in the English word *we*. One goes directly to the |i| vowel sound.

The vowel sounds in Latin are never changing. They must receive a consistent and correct pronunciation. Some of the consonants, however, receive more than one pronunciation depending upon their use. The following list of consonants gives all of their possible pronunciations and the situations in which these pronunciations are needed.

C—before *e, i, y, ae, oe* is pronounced as the *ch* in church. In all other cases it is pronounced as a *k*. The double *c,* as in *ecce* is also pronounced as the *ch* in church.

G—before *e, i, y, ae, oe* is pronounced as in the word *gentle*. In all other cases it is pronounced as in the word *get*.

H—this letter is mute, except in *Mihi* and *Nihil* where it is pronounced like a *k*.

J—is pronounced as the *y* in *yes,* and is combined into one sound with the following vowel.

R—the *r* should be flipped.

X—is pronounced as *ks*.

Z—is pronounced as *dz*.

EX—if *ex* is the beginning of a word and followed by a vowel, it is pronounced as *egs*. When combined with a consonant, it is pronounced as *eks*.

TI—when *ti* is followed by a vowel it is pronounced like *tsi*. **Exception:** This is not true when the *ti* is preceded by *s, t,* or *x.*

TH—*th* is always pronounced as a *t* because the *h* is mute.

CH—*ch* is always pronounced as a *k.*

GN—the combination *gn* receives the pronunciation similar to the *ni* in *dominion.*

SC—*sc* before *e, i, u,* and *ae* is pronounced as *sh* as in the word *ship.* In all other cases it is pronounced like *sk.*

Several Latin texts that are sung with regularity are given along with the proper pronunciation. If the suggested pronunciation is consistently followed, a choral director will find that the tone in a Latin work will improve and that the choir will also sing the English vowels with more purity and with a better tone.

The IPA symbols will not be used to indicate the Latin pronunciation because they resemble the Latin words so closely. Instead, phonetic sounds are used for the pronunciation guide.

Latin	*Pronunciation*
	Hodie Christus Natus Est
Hodie christus natus est	Aw-dee-eh kree-stoos nah-toos ehst
Hodie salvator apparuit	Aw-dee-eh sahl-vah-tawr ah-pah-roo-eet
Hodie in terra	Aw-dee-eh een teh-rah
canunt angeli	kah-noont ahn-jeh-lee
Laetanture archangeli	Leh-tahn-toor ahrk-ahn-jeh-lee
Hodie exultant	Aw-dee-eh eg-zool-tahnt
justi dicentes	yoo-stee dee-chehn-tehs
Gloria, in excelsis deo	Glaw-ree-ah een ek-shehl-sees deh-aw
Alleluia	Ah-leh-loo-yah.
	Agnus Dei
Agnus Dei qui tollis	Ah-nyoos Deh-ee kwee tawl-lees
peccata mundi	peh-kah-tah moon-dee
miserere nobis	mee-seh-reh-reh naw-bees
dona nobis pacem	daw-nah naw-bees pah-chehm
	Ave Verum Corpus
Ave verum Corpus natum	Ah-veh veh-room Kawr-poos nah-toom
de Maria Virgine	Deh Mah-ree-ah Veer-gee-neh
Vere passum, immolatum	Veh-reh pahs-soom, eem-maw-lah-toom
in cruce pro homine	een kroo-cheh praw aw-mee-neh
Cujus latus perforatum	Koo-yoos lah-toos pehr-fawr-ah-toom
fluxit aqua et sanguine	floo-kseet ah-koo-ah eht sahn-gooee-heh
Esto nobis praegustatum	Ehs-taw naw-bees preh-goo-stah-toom
mortis in examine	mawr-tees een ehgs-ah-mee-neh
O Jesu dulcis! O Jesu pie!	Aw Yeh-soo dool-chees! Aw Yeh-soo pee-eh!
O Jesu fili Mariae	Aw Yeh-soo fee-lee Mah-ree-eh

Discussion Questions

1. Look at several texts that include one or more of the diction problems indicated in this chapter. How many problems can you find in one piece?
2. Experiment with vowel modification. How can you modify vowels to match the character of the text?
3. What local speech patterns are not conducive to good singing diction? What methods can be used to eliminate these patterns in choral singing?
4. Can you apply the IPA symbols to choral texts?
5. What choirs do you know whose diction is good? What choirs have you heard whose diction was not so good?
6. Consider your own choral experience. Can you remember the manner in which choral directors applied the rules of diction in a rehearsal?
7. How many more words can you add to the list of those words that are most often mispronounced?
8. Can you sing the Latin texts using pure vowels rather than diphthongs? How can you best demonstrate these vowels to others?

SUGGESTED READINGS

Hillis, Margaret. *At Rehearsals*. New York: American Choral Foundation, 1969.

Marshall, Madeline. *The Singer's Manual of English Diction*. New York: G. Schirmer, 1953.

Montani, Nicola A., ed. *Latin Pronunciation According to Roman Usage*. Philadelphia: St. Gregory Guild, Inc., 1937.

Vennard, William. *Singing: The Mechanism and the Technic*. Rev. ed. New York: Carl Fischer, Inc., 1967.

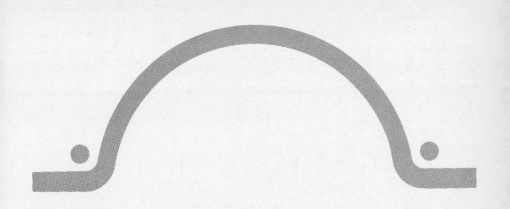

II

THE
SCORE
AND
THE
CONDUCTOR

chapter 7.

selection of repertoire

The selection of repertoire is probably the most demanding and time-consuming task facing a choral conductor. The decision to program a particular work is one of the most important decisions he can make. He must choose music that will best represent our vast choral heritage. He must further be sure that the work will be musically interesting and satisfying to his choir. The conductor must also ask himself many other questions about each work he examines. These questions and their answers are the basis for the criteria for selection suggested later in this chapter.[1] A few comments, however, are necessary before the specific details of selection can be approached.

A conductor's musicianship is reflected in the repertoire he chooses. Each program is an indication of the depth of the conductors understanding as well as a fairly accurate barometer of his choir's capabilities. This is fairly accurate only because most high school choirs are capable of doing just about what their conductor can teach them to do. Of course, it is true that an inexperienced choir will not be able to reach the same heights as one where a tradition of choral singing is present. All things being equal, however, the performance of a high school choir better demonstrates (to a trained ear) the capabilities of the conductor rather than the individual or corporate capabilities of the choir.

A most critical facet of the performance occurs at the initial selection of the music. Often choirs do not perform as well as they might because the repertoire is too demanding for their level of technique and understanding. Repertoire must be chosen that (1) you, as a conductor, can effectively teach to your choir; (2) can be a challenging musical experience to the choir; (3) can offer an opportunity for the chorister to learn more about choral music; and (4) can be successfully performed.

1. Portions of this chapter have been printed as articles by this author in the November 1971 issue of the *Choral Journal,* and in the *Guide for the Beginning Choral Director,* ed. by Gordon H. Lamb, published by the American Choral Directors Association. Permission for their use has been granted by the American Choral Directors Association.

The quality of the repertoire is vitally important. While it is true that voice training goals may be as easily achieved in the performance of inferior music, it is equally as true that the student will not gain aesthetically from the experience. Quality is too often equated with difficulty, yet there are many examples of excellent choral writing that can be rated as easy or medium-easy. These include works by such excellent composers as Schein, Schutz, Praetorius, Aichinger, Gibbons, Farrant, Hassler, Tye, Pitoni, Brahms, Distler, and many others.

When making selections for a program, one must carefully appraise the difficulty of the works involved. It won't be possible to successfully perform an entire program of difficult material. Instead, a conductor will want to choose music that includes one or two difficult pieces and one or two easy works. The bulk of the program will probably be repertoire that lands in the medium category but may have an added emphasis, such as medium-difficult or medium-easy. Naturally, all of these categories are relative, depending on the choir, the conductor, and the situation. However, these categories can be moved up or down the scale of difficulty and the overall premise will remain the same; the bulk of the program will probably be in the medium category *for that choir.*

Nonmusical Considerations

While the general considerations are important musical bases for the choice of music, it is also true that factors other than musical ones often enter into the selection of music. These may include music for specific occasions, rehearsal time, lack of instruments, lack of reading skills by the choir, mediocre or poor accompanist, lack of funds to purchase desired music, and still others that are peculiar to any given situation.

Another most important factor to consider, in addition to the amount of time that has to be spent searching for repertoire (which is considerable) is the type of time that must be used in this search. This refers to the fact that not only is this task extremely time-consuming, but that most of it must be done on the choral director's own time, outside of his normal teaching day. Most schools allow a small portion of each day for planning but, in reality, most of this time is spent either complying with the latest paperwork request from the principal's office or spending some deserved moments relaxing in the teacher's lounge.

The Choral Director's Unique Role in Education

The choral director's situation in the educational systems is quite unique. The high school teacher in mathematics, science, or English, for instance, usually has his program planned for him either by means of a schoolwide curriculum, departmental syllabus, or more often than not, by a text that will carry him through the school year. They are expected to cover the material in question during their specified number of class periods. Such is not the case in the choral music department. A choral portfolio of materials that can serve as a text for the year has not yet been designed. This leaves the choral director to plan an entirely new curriculum for each school year, and he has to do ninety-five percent of it on his own time! If this seems a bit staggering to a young teacher, it should. To have the sole responsibility to plan the educational goals for the year, to determine the means by which one hopes to achieve those goals, and then to step in as the teacher is, indeed, a most unusual educational challenge and opportunity. In short, the choral director in a secondary school is usually a curriculum coordinator, budget supervisor, teacher and finally, conductor.

Building a Reference File

Because time and energy are important to a busy director, it is best to determine a method to develop a reference file. There are various ways that this can be done, including the obvious procedure of keeping the copies that you are interested in, and throwing away those that you do not care to use. This is actually not a method, but the beginning of a method of cataloging information for future use.

It is first necessary to find music, and there are several ways to do this. One is to have your name placed on the mailing list of music publishers and dealers. (Addresses of publishers and major dealers are available in Appendix B.) Publishers are most happy to place copies of music in the hands of people who will want to buy their product. Of course, this means that you will receive many selections in which you will not be interested. Situations change, however, so you will do well to examine all good music regardless of your immediate needs.

Attendance at workshops and clinics allows one to take advantage of reading sessions that offer music often selected by other directors. These sessions provide selected, rather than unsolicited, repertoire and some of them are most worthwhile. Also available at many of these sessions are repertoire lists. The disadvantage of lists is that you have no music to examine. However, you can take advantage of someone else's research, and order reference copies of every work in which you are interested.

Conventions offer many of the above opportunities plus many concerts. These concerts, by carefully selected ensembles, will usually contain interesting and stimulating repertoire. Conductors are aware of the make-up of professional convention audiences and want to put their best possible repertoire on display. Again, it is best to order a copy of each piece with which one is unfamiliar.

In addition to the above sources, several professional organizations offer lists of recommended repertoire. Several publications are available from the Music Educators National Conference, the American Choral Directors Association, and the American Choral Foundation. (Addresses of these organizations are also in Appendix B.)

If you follow the suggestions made above, you will receive 500 to 1,000 copies of music a year. It would be foolish to keep every copy of music. The sheer bulk of it becomes a burden and you will not be interested in studying or performing all of it. Filing the copies in a cabinet does nothing to aid you in future searches for literature. Six months (or years) later you will have to sort through each file, copy by copy, to find music that you wish to perform. This duplication of effort is too costly in terms of time and energy, and is a contributing factor toward poor planning on the part of some directors.

The procedure that follows is one based on some years of use and was found to be practical, thorough, and useful for future reference.

It is much easier to have the information you desire in a card file than to look at all of the reference copies. The card contains all of the information

Title_____Pub._____

Comp. or Arr._____Key_____

    Difficult_____   Length_____

    Medium_____

    Easy   _____

Acc.   _____

          S   A   T   B

Comments_____

_____

_____

Figure 46   Reference Card

you desire for the moment, is portable, and can be taken from home to the office, etc., and will actually stimulate you to better examination of the music the first time. Later, for example, when you want to develop a group of four Renaissance motets for a Lenten season concert, you can do a quick card search, pull the cards on these pieces, know the approximate length of the work, the voicing, and the difficulty level as you have determined it. You may choose eight or ten possibilities and then pull the actual music for these pieces and choose the four that you wish to perform. The card may look like the one printed in figure 46 or vary from it to suit your personal desires.

Complete a card only on the pieces that you consider worthy of future use. In addition to general choral works, these may include seasonal pieces, specific occasion works, and several pieces placed in a special category—perform as soon as possible.

Figure 47 is a sample of the manner in which a card may be completed on a specific choral work.

Your comments need to be specific enough to remind you of the qualities of that particular work. It is also best if you record your impressions of the piece ("very well written," "one of the best settings of this text I have seen," "the advanced choir will like this one") and your indications of specific performance use ("would work well at the end of a group," or "good opener"). Remember that the comments you write must be those that will best recall the work to your mind when you review the card.

The cards can be filed in alphabetical order by title or by composer. Filing by composer has the advantage of a more chronological ordering without actually formalizing it as such. You will recognize Victoria as Renaissance, for instance, but *O Magnum Mysterium* has been set by many composers. Filing by musical period is usually not as good because the lines separating the periods are not as clear.

The remainder of this chapter consists of a set of criteria on which the judgments of selection of repertoire can be based. Once a director becomes accustomed to applying these criteria to each new piece he views, the process will become automatic and time-saving. In addition, it will enable him to choose music that is most appropriate for his ensembles.

Overall Characteristics

Do the overall characteristics indicate that the piece is within the performance realm of your ensemble? Is it technically within the grasp of your singers? There are many fine pieces that technically lie outside the grasp of many choirs. The notes may be so difficult to learn that the choir will never be able to get beyond this initial stage with the piece.

Can your choir achieve the type of choral sonority necessary for a musical

Title <u>Yea, Though I Wander</u>   Pub. <u>Augsburg Pub. Hze.</u>

Comp. or Arr. <u>Georg Schumann</u>   Key _____

Difficult _____   Length <u>c. 3:00</u>

Medium _____

Easy   _____

Comments Melodic beauty and harmonic interest make it outstanding. Written in two sections with extended ending. Each section begins with one voice, and adds each voice to full choir. C demands *ff* singing with all ranges medium except Sop. high A. Text underlay at B awkward

(reverse side)

at tenor opening. Harmonic modulations smooth *Demands*—bass, low   , solid, & secure intonation.

The slow tempo requires good control. Alto tessltura low. Difficult because of choral sonority necessary for success.

For general use—pleasing to any type of audience. Excellent work.

Figure 47

performance of the work? There are many works whose technical demands place them within the reach of high school singers, but whose artistic merits also warrant performances by college and professional choirs. Although high school students will not have the richness of tone that maturity and advance training brings, they can have a musicality and precision that excellent performances anywhere will have.

Ranges of Each Part

The following guide to vocal ranges indicates the *normal limits* of high school singers. These ranges may appear to be quite conservative, but this author has found that notes that exceed these range limits often cause singers to breach a good choral tone and create ensemble difficulties. One will find that, when a piece of music is very close to fitting within these limits, the overall sound of the choir is considerably better than when this is not the case. Choirs will always sound best when the notes they are asked to sing fall comfortably within the capabilities of the singers.

This does not mean that all selections must be tied to these limits, but that *most* of the singing should fall into these categories.

Figure 48

An example of a twentieth century work in which all the parts remain within the limits set above is *Hodie Christus Natus Est* by Gordon H. Lamb (see fig. 48).

If the ranges do exceed these limits it is important to note how often it happens and the manner in which these extreme notes are approached. It is also important to observe what vowel is sung on these extreme notes. When an extremely high note, for example, occurs on an *oo* vowel, it can pinch the tone and be difficult to sing with any real quality.

Are these extreme notes exposed or firmly supported by the rest of the choir? What volume level is indicated? For instance, a high B-flat for the sopranos at a *pianissimo* level, unsupported by the rest of the choir, has the possibility of being a disastrous moment.

Are the extreme ranges reached in several, or all parts at once? When this is the case, young, immature voices are rarely able to overcome this obstacle and fulfill the musical expectation of the work.

Is the tessitura high in any part (particularly the tenor), or low in any part (particularly the alto)? If either of the above is the case, can other voices be added to the part without destroying the choral sonority, or damaging voices?

Finally, is the piece possible to perform except for one part, which is just too high or too low? Don't be trapped into a poor performance by rationalizing that the strong parts will cover the inadequacies of the one in question, or that maybe your students can handle it after all. Instead, keep looking for repertoire that will come closer to fitting the capabilities of your ensemble.

The Composer's Craftsmanship

It is important for you as the potential conductor to appraise the musical content of each composition. It will be necessary to examine the harmonic flow, the rhythmic life, the part writing, and the composer's treatment of the text.

First, observe the scope of the work. Determine the style in which the work was written and its overall form. In a shorter work, this is usually not difficult. When examining a longer work, an indication of the number and type of movements will be sufficient.

Text

If after looking at the musical characteristics of the work, you are still interested, look more carefully at the text. Because choral music is literally text-tied, it would have been impossible to ignore it before this point anyway. Now however, you should examine it closely and consider the following points.

1. Is it worthy of being set to music?

There are many poems that read very well and are quite meaningful but either do not lend themselves to being set to music or, occasionally are so complete in themselves that a musical setting is superfluous and meaningless. At the same time there are certain pieces of prose or poetry that seem to be waiting for the "right" composer. Because of a composer's style of writing, certain types of texts seem to be more desirable for him to set than others.

2. Has the composer done justice to the text?

If the composer has achieved an artistic setting, the text will seem to be carried along by the music. If he hasn't, the joining of the text to the music will seem forced, laborious, and commonplace. Examine the setting carefully to determine if the composer has followed the normal accents of the text. When the composer has not followed the normal stress, be sure that his result is artistic and satisfying.

3. Is the text suitable for performance by high school students? Be sure that it is the type of text that high school age students will understand and be able to artistically project.
4. If the text is a translation, is the translation so different metrically that it no longer fits the original music? Are obvious musical stresses now placed on unimportant words or even on unaccented syllables? When this is the case, the work is better left alone, unless you have access to a translation that will enhance the original score.
5. Has the underlay of the text in each part been done with care regarding the syllabic stress?

Composers will often place fragments of the text in several voices while one part carries the entire text. It is important that this be examined also, to determine that such fragmentation enhances the setting and aids in the ultimate expression of the text. An example of the successful use of text fragmentation is presented in figure 49.

Part Writing

Does each part "sing well?" Sing each part, if not through the entire piece, at least through several sections of the piece and examine all of the part writing. While you are doing this, you can observe and mark those intervals that are most difficult to sing. If you encounter difficulty with some intervals, you can be sure that your students will also find those sections to be problematic. Later, in a rehearsal analysis you should do a detailed study of each part and mark all points of possible difficulties.

It should be mentioned that some avant-garde works may not contain melodic passages in a traditional sense. Each piece will still have an orderly quality about it that is apparent or, at least, that can be ascertained. A conductor must still examine each voice part carefully, because good part writing is necessary to any good choral composition.

The Rhythmic Life of the Work

As you observe the rhythmic life of the piece you may note patterns or other rhythmic uses that appear to be a foremost quality of the piece. You can also note any complications that are caused by the rhythm. Most choirs falter first rhythmically rather than melodically when reading a new score. Rhythmic complexity will cause more problems than melodic intervals, and will plague a director longer in rehearsals.

If the work contains shifting meters, try to determine if the composer has chosen the most direct and simplified meter changes that best convey the meaning of the work. You may now wish to make some preliminary nota-

VI. Orchard
Verger
For Four-Part Chorus of Mixed Voices
Rainer Maria Rilke   *Unaccompanied*
English version by Elaine de Sincay   Paul Hindemith

Figure 49

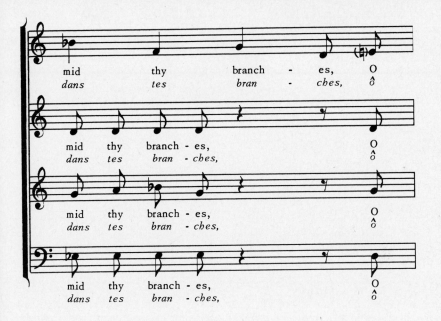

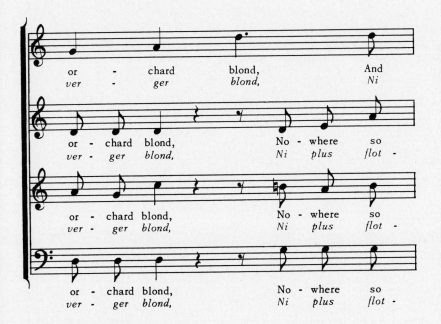

Figure 49—Continued

tions on the score for your future study regarding the conducting patterns you will want to use. In many contemporary compositions with shifting meters and tempos, a conductor will not necessarily want to conduct the number of beats in a measure as indicated in the time signature. The composer may indicate an ordering of rhythmic relationships in the measure which will also alter the type of gestures the conductor will use, as in *Rejoice in the Lamb* by Benjamin Britten. It is good to make some initial observations now that will later be reviewed as you study the work in greater detail. A concern now regarding the conducting problems of the piece will also aid you in making a better initial review of the composition.

The Harmony

The harmonic language of a composer is due, in part, to his training, cultural heritage, and personal preference. Some composers are most comfortable when composing within the bounds of tonality, while others are equally as comfortable outside those bounds. There is no reason to doubt the validity of either as long as the results are satisfying musically.

It is important to determine the harmonic language of each composition you examine. This is not particularly difficult with music prior to the twentieth century. Examine twentieth century works closely, checking to see that the composer remains consistently within a particular idiom. Ludwig Lenel's choral setting of the chorale, *Christ Is Arisen,* is an excellent example of a selection conceived carefully within a particular harmonic idiom, and remains true to that idiom throughout the work.

The harmonic rhythm of a work is essential to its successful performance. It should be logically conceived and proceed naturally within that structure.

The harmonic progressions of a piece are vitally important to its musical flow, and ultimately to its performance. Consequently, it is necessary to study the harmony during the first review of a work. Ask yourself the following questions. Do the harmonies proceed naturally, or do they seem forced and strained? Has the composer resorted to the use of any musical cliches? Does the composer's use of harmony enhance the setting of the text? All of these questions need to be answered in the initial examination of the score. It is also true that a later and more thorough review may find a work to be lacking in some respect, which was not revealed at first inspection.

Will the Piece Withstand Intense Rehearsal?

Does the piece have sufficient quality to withstand a long period of intense rehearsal? Any choral ensemble must spend a certain amount of time with any work in order to achieve a musical performance of the piece. This amount of time will obviously vary depending on the situation. If the choir becomes weary of the music before performance, the spontaneity that good performances enjoy will be impossible. Norman Dello Joio's *A Jubilant Song* contains both easy and difficult sections, and bears up well during the rehearsals necessary to successfully perform the work.

If the work is a relatively simple piece that has artistic value, such as M. Praetorius' *Psallite,* can you bring the piece through rehearsals in small doses to allow your choir to learn it and not tire of it?

Memorization

Can the piece be memorized without undue stress? If not, can your choir use music in performance without so tying themselves to it that musicality and precision are impossible. As a rule of thumb, the more amateur an ensemble, the less able they are to use music without gluing their eyes to the score. When possible, memorization will help considerably toward better performances.

Arrangements

If the piece is an arrangement, is it arranged in a manner that complements the original intent of the song? Often folk songs are altered by the arranger. When adapted in this manner, some songs are made more appealing than the original. Sven Lekberg's adaptation of *Weep, O Willow* is an example of a good adaptation. The slight changes that Lekberg made enhance the original without losing any of the folk character of the song. Some adaptations, however, destroy the initial flavor of the song and, generally, these settings are better left unperformed.

There are many choral arrangements of folk songs, including spirituals, that are overarranged. These are arrangements in which the melody has not been altered, but the choral setting is often complex. The simple beauty of a spiritual can well be lost in a multitude of parts in a setting that has been overarranged.

Programming

Will the piece program well? There are occasions when you will want to use a piece but it will not program well with the other selections. When this is the case, avoid the temptation to program the work simply because you want to use it. Every year there are a number of choral directors who, when asked why they are performing a certain work, reply, "I've always wanted to do it, and this year I'm going to do it!" Either be sure that the piece fits easily with the rest of the program or wait until you can choose other music that will fit with it. Remember, there is always another year and another opportunity.

Difficulty

If it is a difficult piece, is it worth the rehearsal time necessary to perform it well? Conversely, if it is not particularly difficult, will it stand up during the many rehearsals before the concert? These questions are quite important in the selection process. A piece mustn't be too difficult but it also should not be too easy. An error in either direction brings about its own type of choral repercussions.

If either error is made, in which direction is the error most compatible? It is best if every decision were correct and each piece contained enough complexity to keep the singers interested through the final rehearsals, but not so complex that the ensemble cannot realistically expect to perform it with control and artistry. There are other instances, to be sure, when you wish to offer a musical opportunity to your choir for educational reasons and the performance becomes secondary. When possible, it may be well to sing and study such a work, but not perform it. Every piece that goes into the folder does not have to be placed on the concert program.

Changing a Composition to Fit Your Choir

Does the composition require significant alteration for your choir to achieve a successful performance? While it may be true that some compositions can be edited by a conductor in order to achieve a "better" performance with a particular choir, the extent of this editing is important. To rearrange the voicing of a chord or two is one thing, but the rewriting of melodic lines or simplifying of difficult rhythms is quite another. If you begin changing the composer's scoring, you may find yourself in the position of the do-it-yourself carpenter, who cuts off the long leg of the chair only to find that it now seems to be too short. Changes in one section of the work may necessitate changes in other sections. There is often no end to this type of tampering. Be judicious in any rescoring of compositions. If the piece has to be changed significantly in order for your choir to perform it, you probably should have waited for another year and another choir to perform the work.

The list of compositions in Appendix A has been carefully selected for their adaptability to high school voices. They vary from easy to difficult in their range of complexity, but all have been used with great success with high school choirs. This is not meant to be a definitive list of all of the best choral repertoire available. Instead, it should be considered as a representative list and the core of a high school choral library.

Discussion Questions

1. Which of the selections that you performed in a high school choir do you believe would meet the criteria discussed in this chapter?
2. Which works that you have performed do you believe would not meet the criteria discussed?
3. Test your own present knowledge of repertoire. How many works can you list from each period that you believe would be suitable for a high school choir?
4. Try to obtain a copy of each selection listed in Appendix A. How can you best examine this music to reach a preliminary understanding of it?
5. How can you begin a reference file that will contribute later to your teaching needs?
6. How much of the college repertoire that you have performed is suitable for high school voices?
7. Assume that you are the conductor of a high school choir. What pieces would you choose to rehearse and perform for the first year and why?

SUGGESTED READINGS

Boody, Charles G. "Choral Programming . . . The Annotated List." *The Choral Journal* July-August 1968, pp. 19-21.
Decker, Harold. "Choosing Music for Performance." *Choral Directors Guide,* chap. 5. Edited by Neidig and Jennings. Parker Publishing, 1967.
Lamb, Gordon H. "Selection of Music for the High School Choir. *The Choral Journal* November 1971.
——. *Choral Director's Guide to Repertoire for Mixed Choir: An Annotated Bibliography.* West Nyak, N.Y.: Parker Publishing Co., 1974.
Lamb, Gordon H., ed. *The Guide for the Beginning Choral Director,* chap. 4, pp. 19-27. American Choral Directors Association, 1972.

chapter 8.

building a concert program

The choral concert can be a rich musical experience for all concerned—the students, the director, and the audience. Every concert needs to be thoughtfully planned more than several months in advance to be the right kind of experience for everybody.

It is easy for any director, new or experienced, to become so involved with the immediate stumbling blocks of his department that he loses sight of the long range goals for his department. Stumbling blocks refer to such things as a service club performance, a PTA request for a short program ("don't go to any trouble"), a dance sponsored by the choir to raise money, the director's extra work on faculty committees, his work as adviser to a class, and other similar responsibilities.

All of these responsibilities in addition to a full teaching load, make it difficult to devote enough time to programming considerations as they relate to the long range goals of the department. It is very easy to succumb to these pressures and choose music for a coming concert too quickly and make these choices on criteria of little merit. One must project the concerts of a department according to the goals that have been made for the department as well as meet the immediate demands that are placed on the department by the community.

Three-year Plan

Administrators criticize secondary instrumental and choral programs for lack of sound curriculum, and often rightly so. Counselors and principals sometimes tell students that they should not repeat choir since it is the same thing twice. In effect, they are saying, "You have taken the course once and received a good grade. What would be the point in taking it again?" It is precisely this attitude that a choral director must be prepared to counter. He can do so by establishing a sound choral curriculum which shows a study of choral literature through rehearsal and performance. Once the curriculum is developed, it should be placed in the school handbook and school curriculum guides.

The choral curriculum should show that students will, over a three-year period, study, rehearse, and perform both sacred and secular music from the:

1. Renaissance period
2. Baroque period
3. Classic period
4. Romantic period
5. Twentieth century

This goal can be accomplished by the following procedure.

1. Make broad determinations of the general periods you wish to cover and the manner in which you intend to cover them.
2. Select a number of compositions that you believe are representative of those periods. In this stage of the selection, choose more pieces than you intend to rehearse or perform. After broad determinations have been made, examine as much choral music as you can that fits these areas. Make a file for each period to be studied. As you find music in which you are interested, place it in the appropriate file.
3. After a preliminary examination of the music, make some determinations as to which works will be "rehearsal only" works; those that will be studied and rehearsed but will probably not be performed. This might include works that are too long for performance by high school students or works that you would consider to be too difficult for your choir to present in a public performance. However, the students may gain appreciably from the rehearsal and study of these works even if they cannot eventually perform them.
4. Determine the manner in which you will introduce and study this repertoire. Ask yourself, "How can the musical characteristics of the style be presented so the choir will quickly learn the performance traits necessary to the realization of the music?"
5. If the students are to study a style with which they are unfamiliar, choose works that will be good introductions to that style. A work that is representative of the style but not so difficult that it is inaccessible to the students would be a good introduction. Several of Benjamin Britten's earlier works would be good choices for an excellent choir wanting to sing twentieth century music. However, choral works that are extremely dissonant would not be good introductory pieces.

Types of Concerts

There are several formats that are widely used to present choral ensembles in concert. There are also certain times of the school year when choral concerts seem most appropriate. Almost every choral department presents a Christmas concert and a spring concert. Some schools schedule a Thanksgiving or patriotic concert in November. These times are logical because of the special nature of the concerts. It is convenient that Christmas occurs late in the first semester, allowing time to adequately develop a concert repertoire.

The following concert programs illustrate possibilities for the choral conductor.

The concert of Christmas music on Program One represents utilization of repertoire from several periods while allowing the best choir to study two periods in some depth, the Baroque and the twentieth century.

Program One

How Brightly Beams the Morning Star	*J. S. Bach* (1685-1750)
Cantate Domino	*G. Pitoni* (1657-1743)
Blessing, Glory and Wisdom	*G. G. Wagner* (1698-1756)
Sing Unto God	*G. F. Handel* (1685-1759)
Now Thank We All Our God	*J. Pachelbel* (1653-1706)

Concert Choir

Ceremony of Carols	*B. Britten* (1913————)

Girls' Choir

O Come, O Come Emmanuel	*English Carol*
Fum, Fum, Fum	*arr. Shaw-Parker*
Psallite	*M. Praetorious*

Mixed Chorus

He Is Born	*arr. Wagner*
E la don don, Verges Maria	*ed. N. Greenberg*
Riu, Riu Chiu	*ed. N. Greenberg*

Madrigal

Jubilate Deo	*B. Britten*
Festival Te Deum	*B. Britten*
Alleluia! Christus Natus Est	*R. lo Prestl*

Concert Choir

Another Christmas concert might include repertoire such as that found in the following program.

Program Two

Orietur Stella	*J. Gallus*
O Magnum Mysterium	*T. Victoria*
Quem Vidistis	*R. Dering*
Hodie Christus Natus Est	*J. Sweelinck*

Concert Choir

Allon Gay Bergeres	*G. Costeley*
My Dancing Day	*Shaw-Parker*
Christ Was Born on Christmas Day	*Shaw-Parker*

Madrigal

A Virgin Unspotted	*W. Billings*
The Shepherds Carol	*W. Billings*
Pat-A-Pan	*arr. De Vito*

Mixed Chorus

Winds Through the Olive Trees	*F. J. Pyle*
Lullee, Lulay	*arr. Davis*
A La Nanita Nana	*arr. Luboff*

Girls' Chorus

Glory to God in the Highest	*R. Thompson*
Three Christmas Songs	*J. Jarrett*
What Is This Lovely Frangrance?	*H. Willan*
Christmas Cantata	*D. Pinkham*

Concert Choir

General Concerts

General concerts (those that are not tied to a specific season or event) allow one to consider a wider range of repertoire. Two possible spring programs are listed below. Each provides certain opportunities of study for the singers and each has its own appeal from a performance and listening standpoint.

Program Three

Spring Concert

Jubilate Deo	*Lassus*
Lauda Anima Mea Dominum	*Lassus*
Christus Factus Est	*Anerio*
Suddenly There Came a New Sound from Heaven	*Aichinger*

Concert Choir

Three Madrigals	*Diemer*
Three Hungarian Folk Songs	*Bartok*
Holiday Song	*W. Schumann*

Mixed Chorus

One Day While Walking By	*De Wert*
Weep O Mine Eyes	*Bennet*
Come Tune Your Voice	*Gastoldi*

Madrigal

The Falcon	*Gerrish*
Orchard	*Hindemith*
Walking on the Green Grass	*Hennagin*

Chamber Choir

Like as a Culver	*Stevens*
My Spirit Sang All Day	*Finzi*
Four Slovak Folk Songs	*Bartok*
A Jubilant Song	*Dello Joio*

Concert Choir

The following program leans heavily on music of the twentieth century. The first group of compositions are linked to the twentieth century pieces by their transparent texture and attention to word stress. These two characteristics are also descriptive of the Micheelsen and Distler works. Groups II and III offer the listener an opportunity to hear German sacred music and two works in English that represent still another tradition in sacred choral music of the twentieth century.

Group IV presents four secular settings by American composers. These works are intimate settings easily performed by a large choir or by a chamber choir. Group V is a work of greater length. This particular work represents an involvement of the choir with the actual writing of a composition. The opportunity to rehearse and perform a work written especially for a choir is a very stirring experience. This work, while secular, is less personal than the preceding group and is more universal in scope.

Program Four

The University of Texas at Austin
A Cappella Choir
Gordon H. Lamb, Conductor

I

Ascendit Deus	*Jacobus Gallus*
Ave Regina Coelorum	*Orlando Lassus*
O Vos Omnes	*Juan Esquivel*

II

Es Sungen Drei Engel	*Hans Micheelsen*
Ich wollt, dass ich daheime wär	*Hugo Distler*
Lobe den Herren, den machtigen König der Ehren	*Hugo Distler*

III

Behold, I Build an House   *Lukas Foss*
The Path of the Just   *Knut Nystedt*

IV

All Day I Hear   *Paul Fetler*
I Will Make You Brooches   *Karl Korte*
Three Years She Grew in Sun and Shower   *Albert Lee Carr*
Three Choral Vignettes   *Gordon H. Lamb*

V

Years Prophetical   *Sven Lekberg*

Commissioned by the A Cappella Choir
The University of Texas at Austin
Text by Walt Whitman

Concerts such as the preceding ones provide a variety of repertoire for the students and the audience. There are times, however, when one may wish to present a concert based on a theme or based entirely on the music of a certain period or style. Such themes as "Music around the World" or "Music of the Americas" are among the most often used. While these concerts can be successful, it is true that they are often lacking musically. The director is usually hard pressed to find several choral works that express a specific event in a given point in time. He then chooses not on the basis of musical merit but on text or by default. (He can't really find what he wants, but he settles for a piece to fill a slot.)

Points to Consider

The following points should be considered when planning a program:

1. Group pieces according to a musical as well as textual idea.
2. Choose works that are musical entities and need no assistance to stand alone.
3. Choose works that will be musical complements to the pieces before and after.
4. Choose works that will be interesting and stimulating to an audience.
5. Choose works that will be interesting and stimulating to the students.
6. Be careful not to program pieces consecutively that are in the same key. Key changes are refreshing to an audience and to the choir. They will also prevent the choir from psychologically becoming sluggish in a key and allowing the pitch to sag.
7. Pace the program so each group or portion of the program peaks.

Special Programs

Choral directors will receive invitations to perform at various community functions, including meetings of local civic groups. Programs of this type require planning that is different from that required for the regularly scheduled concerts.

The length of the program will change for each particular situation. Keep the program to the specified length that you and the group's representative have previously agreed upon.

Taper the program to fit the audience. The repertoire that one might use for a men's luncheon meeting could be far different than the repertoire one would choose for a meeting of the Music Club. This is one of the reasons that an ensemble that performs a varied repertoire is valuable to a choral department. The same group can emphasize a certain portion of its repertoire for one occasion and another portion for another occasion.

As a general rule, twenty- to thirty-minute programs are a good length for these special performances. A twenty-minute performance after a banquet (that included a speaker) will be long enough to make the performance worthwhile and short enough to prevent the audience from thinking that it was too long. Requests for ten-minute performances must be viewed differently. Is it worth the rehearsal time and the time and effort to take the ensemble to the performance area for a ten-minute performance? Occasionally, these performances may be quite important because they are for a group that is a staunch supporter of the choral department. Often they are not important and can be declined with an offer to come at a later time for a full performance.

Several possible programs are listed below; one each for a mixed choir, boys' chorus, and girls' chorus. Although the mixed choir is listed as a chamber choir, the group may perform a variety of serious and light repertoire. (See chapter twelve for more information regarding this type of choir.) All three programs are less than thirty minutes in length and contain both serious and light music.

Program for the
Downtown Businessmen's Club Banquet

Central High Boys' Chorus

I

Vagabond	*Ralph Vaughan Williams*
Pasture from "Frostiana"	*Randall Thompson*
Amo Amas I Love a Lass	*arr. Bartholomew*
Simple Gifts	*Aaron Copland*
Song of Peace	*Vincent Persichetti*

II

If I Got My Ticket, Can I Ride?   *arr. Shaw-Parker*
Hunter's Song   *arr. De Courmier*
The Water Is Wide   *adapted Luigi Zaninelli*
Hey, Look Me Over from "Wildcat"   *Cy Colman*

**Program for the
Area Education Association Meeting**

Central High Chamber Choir

I

Cantate Domino   *Hans Hassler*
Sing to the Lord   *Christopher Tye*
Four Slovak Folk Songs (2)   *Bela Bartok*

II

Solo or Madrigal Performance

III

Three Madrigals   *Emma Lou Diemer*
All Under The Willow Tree   *Albert Lee Carr*
Sit Down, Lord   *arr. Gordon H. Lamb*
Selections from "West Side Story"   *Leonard Bernstein*

**Program for the
Area Bankers' Association Christmas Banquet
Central High Girls' Chorus**

I

Selections from "Ceremony of Carols"   *Benjamin Britten*

II

Three Mountain Ballads   *Ron Nelson*
Linden Lea   *Ralph Vaughan Williams*
Fancie   *Benjamin Britten*
Selections from "The King and I"   *Richard Rodgers*

There will be occasions when an organization will request a performance only one or two days before the program is to take place. There is only one way to prevent this from happening—refuse to accept any performances that are not requested a certain number of days in advance. If an ensemble has a repertoire developed, a two-week deadline is satisfactory. Once local groups understand the deadline they will plan accordingly and everything will run smoothly. Normally, late requests are due to poor planning on the part of the organization's program director.

Discussion Questions

1. What compositions would be good introductions to performance of music of the twentieth century?
2. How many concerts a year should be planned?
3. How can a conductor achieve variety and unity in the same concert?
4. What periods program best together?
5. How can a choral conductor outline the curriculum of his department for the administration?
6. Should serious works be performed for civic groups or should these performances be limited to "light" music?
7. Examine several choral programs. What makes each unique? Which is the best programming? Why?

chapter 9.

conducting techniques

The art of conducting has become a more refined and exacting art over a period of many years. Yet conductors differ considerably in the gestures that they use and, to a degree, in the fundamental beat patterns. Beginning conductors are often confused as to the necessity of a four pattern, for instance, that requires the second beat to be to the left of the first. It is true that if a conductor can spend enough time with an ensemble and the music is not complex, he could keep them together and probably obtain a musical response with gestures that are altogether foreign to the usual conducting patterns. However, if he wishes to conduct more than one ensemble, prepare his students to also perform under the baton of other conductors, or conduct complex scores, he will find that standard conducting patterns will serve him well.

A clear understanding of the basic conducting patterns is necessary before one can expand them into a personal conducting style. Without a solid technique, a "personal style" will be quite meaningless—arm waving without a purpose. After the basic fundamentals are mastered, students will want to adapt them to their own conducting personalities and musical temperaments.

The ability to reproduce the patterns physically, is easily within the grasp of any average person with normal coordination. Interpretation of the music, however, lies far beyond the mere reproduction of the beat patterns. A good technique is of value only to those who study and understand the musical score, who establish a good rapport with their ensemble, and are able to transmit the ultimate beauty of music with sensitivity.

Posture

The posture of a conductor is just as important as the posture of a singer. It should not be ramrod stiff, nor should it be so loose that the gestures have no energy. The same element of dynamic tension that is so important to the buoyancy of singing is applicable to conductors. The conductor should adopt a position of alertness that is inspired by energy but is not muscle-bound.

The feet of the conductor should be separated, the heels approximately six to eight inches apart. The knees should be flexible, not stiff. The weight should be distributed evenly on the balls of the feet. The conductor should lean slightly towards the choir. (The upper part of the body should be carried high.) The head should be held slightly in front of the shoulders, but without assuming a hunched position. A hunched position will appear extremely awkward to the choir and to the audience. It will also interfere with a good conducting style.

The arms are the part of the body with which beginning conductors are most concerned. The body posture must be such that the arms can operate freely and most naturally. How high should they be raised? The answer, "high enough to be seen clearly by the ensemble and low enough to be comfortable," may seem vague but it is true. The conducting plane (the level at which the arms operate) will vary depending upon the ensemble's size, its position from the conductor, and upon the conductor himself. The median of the conducting plane should normally be just below the heighth of the shoulder. Only in extreme instances should any beats go below the waist. Very few beats will rise above the head, except that the top of the last beat of a measure will, on occasion, go almost above the head.

The size of the beat will be determined by the style and tempo of each piece of music. Fast tempos demand smaller gestures as do most soft passages. The gestures for loud passages will be large and more dramatic. Exceptions will be made in musical situations that warrant excessive gestures. A chorus of six hundred festival singers will undoubtedly demand broader gestures than a choir of forty or fifty people.

Use of a Baton

Every conductor should learn to conduct with a baton whether one is used for all performances or not. Choral conductors will find that a shorter baton (approximately 10″ to 12″) is desirable for most situations. A longer baton might be warranted for conducting festival choruses or performances or large choruses and orchestra.

Although fewer choral conductors seem to use a baton than instrumental conductors, there is no reason why a baton should not be used for choral conducting. It is perfectly acceptable to conduct accompanied or unaccompanied repertoire with a baton. The conductor who does not use a baton regularly will find that the use of a baton will tend to force him to better conducting habits. Unnecessary gestures made with the hands are impossible with a baton. Usually the conducting technique improves considerably by the use of a baton.

Conductors are also encouraged to alternate between the use of the hands and the baton during rehearsals. Some compositions will seem most comfortable with a baton and the conductor will want to continue its use into the performance.

Many choral conductors use the baton when conducting works that involve instruments with voices. The addition of instruments alone does not necessarily warrant the use of a baton any more than the absence of instruments denies the use of the baton. The decision is a personal one and should be based on the music being performed and on the comfortability of the conductor and the ensemble.

Holding the Baton

Conductors, both beginning and experienced, often find it difficult to hold a baton with comfort. It is a slender instrument which causes many people to try to grasp it with the finger tips rather than with the entire hand. This kind of a grip creates tension in the hand and wrist and quickly becomes very uncomfortable. The conductor should grasp the baton so the handle fits into the palm of the hand and the fingers curl around the baton. The thumb should be on the left side of the baton at a point where it would touch the forefinger at about the first joint. Actually, it will not touch the forefinger because the thumb will touch the baton first. Figure 50 shows the proper basic grip.

Conductors must experiment with several batons before they will find one that seems most comfortable to them. Batons that have small wooden or cork handles are recommended over those that have plastic or rubber balls on the grip. The former are comfortable to more people and usually weigh less.

The Preparatory Beat

Before the basic patterns can be negotiated, the conductor must learn how to begin the conducting gestures. One should raise the hands almost as if one were going to catch a very large ball (a ball slightly larger than a basketball). The hands will come to a point slightly lower than the shoulders and the forearms will be pointing inward from the elbows, rather than extending straight forward. The elbows will then be the farthest points at the side of the body. If one is not using a baton, the fingers should be curved just a little to avoid any stiffness in the hand and to present a better appearance both to the ensemble and audience.

Figure 50

When the music begins on a count of the measure, the preparation beat itself will usually be one count in advance of the first sounded note. There are occasions when a conductor will use two counts in preparation to clearly establish the tempo for the choir, and to avoid any misunderstanding of the count on which the choir will begin to sing.

The preparatory beat must be given in the same style, mood, and tempo of the first phrase of the music. It is a vital part of the music and its importance should not be minimized. The first gesture by the conductor conveys something to the choir—either energy, style, mood, confidence and tempo, or indifference and lack of leadership.

The preparatory beat and the downbeat should always indicate the mood of the song. If the piece is to begin *pianissimo,* at a moderate tempo, the preparatory beat and the down beat must be given in a manner that will convey that information to the choir. Your motions should reaffirm the character of the music, and remind the ensemble of the attitude toward the work that you and they share.

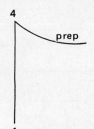

Starting on the First Beat

If the first beat of the measure in a 4/4 passage is the first sound, the fourth beat of the pattern will be used as the preparatory beat.

Figure 51

Starting on the Last Beat

If the last beat of the measure is the first beat on which sound begins, the previous beat of the pattern will be used as a preparation. For example, if the first sound occurs on the fourth beat of a 4/4 measure, the third beat of the pattern would be the preparatory beat (see fig. 52).

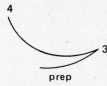

Starting on Other Beats

The same principle is followed when the music begins on a beat other than the first or last. If the piece begins on the second beat of a 4/4 measure, the first beat of the pattern becomes the preparatory beat.

Figure 52

In this case the starting position of the hands may vary slightly so the movement from the position to the first beat is only one downward motion. If the hands move upward before the preparatory beat, it will give the effect of two preparatory beats, as, "four, one, sing." This can be confusing to an ensemble which has been told, and expects, only one preparatory beat (see fig. 53).

If the first sound of the music occurs on the third beat of a 4/4 measure, beat two becomes the preparatory beat. Be sure the first motion is to the left

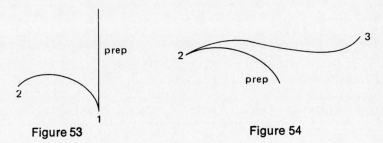

Figure 53   **Figure 54**

and is (as always) in exactly the same tempo and character as the first and ensuing beats (see fig. 54).

Starting on Fractions of Beats

Music that starts on a fraction of a beat causes special problems for the conductor. These may occur at the beginning of a piece or later, after a pause or fermata. If the rhythm is stopped after a fermata, the next entrance must be treated just as the beginning of a piece.

The principle of the preparatory beat, which is to indicate an entire beat previous to the first sound, remains the same. Since the first sound in the following example begins on the last half of the third beat it is impossible to give a preparatory beat that starts *exactly* one full beat before that note. The problem here is that an indication of only the third beat as a preparatory beat does not convey *one full beat*. It is most difficult for the ensemble to determine where the halfway point (the first note) of that gesture would occur since they have no idea as to its ultimate length. For this reason it seems logical (and safer) to use the second beat and the first part of beat three as the preparatory beat. The ensemble will be able to determine exactly when the eighth note should occur because they have seen (and felt) one entire beat of the rhythm. They were able to count "2 and 3," during the preparatory gestures.

the ev - er - last - ing life, ____   the ev - er - last - ing

Figure 55

It is true that after many rehearsals, a conductor might be able to indicate only beat three and the ensemble would start together. It is recommended that conductors avoid doing this in performance, however, unless it has been done often in rehearsal. Such a change would be dangerous in a performance when the ensemble is nervous and could misinterpret a new gesture such as this.

There are occasions when the preparatory beat will not need to show the tempo or rhythm of the first phrase. This would occur when the first note has no rhythmic implications to any following notes. For example, when a work begins on a hold as in figure 56, the preparatory beat does not need to indicate

Psalm 90
For Mixed Chorus (SATB), Organ and Bells

Charles Ives

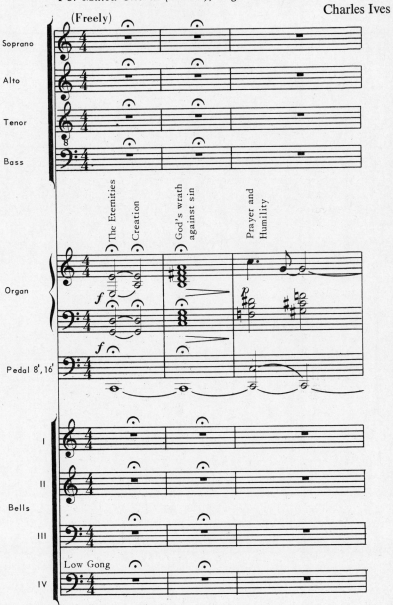

Figure 56

Figure 56—Continued

the rhythm since the note is static. One must convey the character of the music however.

It is recommended that a conductor mentally "conduct" several measures of each piece before he begins it. This will help him establish the tempo and renew the rhythm in his mind. He may even indicate the beat itself to the ensemble by using the forefinger and thumb of the left hand in front of his body, hidden from the audience. This can be effective for a choral conductor who is conducting his own ensemble of thirty to fifty singers.

The Release

The release should be considered as one more gesture in a sequence of gestures that interprets and reminds the ensemble of the musical essence of the score. If considered in this manner, the release gestures will be given in the same character as the preceding gestures. If the music is slow and soft, the gesture of release should be subdued and generally, not large. If the music requires a very loud ending with a flourish, the gesture of release will need to be a pronounced and striking one.

Figure 57

Like the first beat, the ensemble needs to have some preparation for the release. Unless the release gesture has some preparation, the ensemble will not respond together. One beat before the tone is to stop, the release gesture should begin. A normal release is usually done with both hands to obtain the utmost precision. Although both inward and outward motions are used, the inward motion is suggested as the preferred one.

Often a choral conductor wishes to indicate a final consonant at the point of the release. This can be done with a slight flick of the fingers, or some other precise motion. If the composition ends with a vowel, the conductor should be careful that his motion does not cause the singers to clamp the jaw closed to stop the tone. Works that end in a vowel sound should be ended by the singers taking a breath, leaving the mouth in a singing position. The tone is stopped by taking in air.

The Beat Patterns

The most important thing to learn about the indication of the beat is that the beat must be clear to the ensemble. In order for this to exist, the conductor must make one beat, the downbeat, slightly more important than the others. The ensemble cannot determine beats two, three, or four if they are not sure which beat is beat one. The downbeat should be the only beat that is made at the center of the base of the conducting plane. Some conductors describe all beats as arriving at the same point as the downbeat. This action blurs the beat distinction for the ensemble and weakens the first beat of the measure.

Clarity is of utmost importance in a conductor's gestures. The ensemble is relying on a conductor for many things but most importantly, for a clear indication of the beat. In any work, but particularly in a work with complex rhythms, the ensemble is most interested in knowing where beat one is. Orchestral players are probably the most critical of the choral conductor whose gestures are so mushy that they cannot determine the beat. Occasionally, when a conductor hears that the precision is slipping in a performance, he will quickly stop any extraneous motion with his hands and concentrate on giving the ensemble nothing more than the simple beat pattern. This pattern must be the core of every conductor's conducting style.

The Rebound

The conductor's beat must have some sort of rebound in order for the ensemble to be able to discern the *ictus,* the exact moment when the conducting gesture indicates the rhythmic pulse. The rebound should not be too high or it will confuse the motion toward the next beat. The exact distance will depend upon the style and tempo of the piece. In faster tempos the rebound will be short and quick, whereas in slower tempos it may be a little higher and slower.

The following beat patterns are the ones that will be used in almost all conducting situations. There are some examples of new music that involve combinations of these patterns or are so different that new patterns must be created by the conductor to fit the music.

All of the patterns assume that the conductor is conducting with the right hand. The left hand is reserved primarily for gestures other than time-beating. To avoid confusion as one conducts various ensembles, the left-handed person should use the right hand to conduct the patterns given below. Practice each pattern until it becomes comfortable to you. Do not attempt the combination practicing suggested later until you have practiced each pattern separately.

The Two Pattern

The most fundamental of the patterns is the two-beat pattern (fig. 58a.). In fast tempos this pattern is simply up-down. When the tempo is slower, the pattern will be as indicated in figure 58b.

Figure 58

All of the patterns then evolve from this basic two-beat pattern. The first beat of the meter or measure is always down and the last beat (the last beat indicated) is always up.

The Three Pattern

The pattern for three beats in a measure is given in figure 59. The conductor is reminded to be sure that the third beat is in an inward and upward direction and does not become lazy. This is the beat that amateur singers will tend to rush, causing rhythm and tempo problems.

The Four Pattern

The four-beat pattern is shown in figure 60. In the four pattern, beat two goes to the left rather than to the right as in the three pattern. Again, one is reminded to be sure that the downbeat is given its place of importance at the center of the base of the conducting plane. Some four patterns are described as having all beats occur on the same level except for beat four. It is felt that this will blur the distinction of the downbeat. Therefore, the second and third beats are described as being slightly higher than the downbeat.

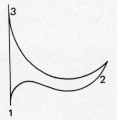

Figure 59

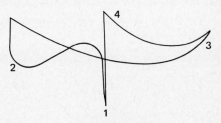

Figure 60

The Six Pattern

The 6/8 meter has been conducted in two different patterns for some time. Both patterns are given in figure 61. Both of these patterns are used widely by conductors. Figure 61a is most often referred to as the German six pattern. Figure 61b is usually labeled the French six pattern. The latter has certain advantages, particularly when 6/8 alternates between six beats and two beats. Pattern b differs further, in that: (1) beat four, usually the secondary beat in a 6/8 measure, receives a gesture of commensurate strength; (2) the last beat of the measure is a very weak beat and here only receives a small gesture, whereas the pattern in figure 61a has a very large motion accompanying the last beat; and (3) this pattern can be easily modified to become a two-beat pattern, most desirable for the many pieces in which a fast 6/8 has only two beats in a measure.

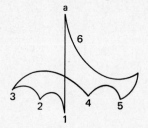 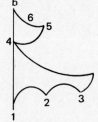

Figure 61

Which of the two patterns is used will depend upon the personal choice of the conductor. This decision will be based on the type of music being conducted and his own comfortability in the pattern.

The Nine Pattern

The nine-beat pattern, is a modification or subdivision of a three pattern. The fourth beat of the nine pattern is not as far to the right as the two beat of the three pattern, allowing the indication of beats five and six with ease. The pattern in figure 62 also allows a conductor to transfer from nine actual beats to three beats, which occurs in some instances.

The Twelve Pattern

The beat pattern for twelve beats in a measure is shown in figure 63. This pattern is used when a conductor actually indicates the twelve beats in a measure. There are many occasions when 12/8, for example, is actually conducted as a four pattern. The pattern in figure 63 is a modified four pattern with two smaller indications after the principal beats.

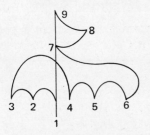

Figure 62

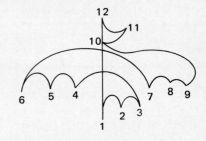

Figure 63

The two added beats after the downbeat are made to the conductor's right, so no more than three consecutive beats will be given in the same direction. This division of the downbeat is *opposite* of the division of the nine-beat pattern for just this reason. The nine pattern is a modification of a three pattern. Since its second principal beat is to the right, the added beats to the downbeat must be to the left.

Asymmetrical Patterns

Music that is written in asymmetrical (irregular) meters is most often conducted in a modification of one of the previously described patterns. The patterns for irregular meters are not as standard as the other patterns because they are not used as much. These patterns usually adapt easily because most of the 5/4, 7/4, and other similar irregular meters are combinations 3 + 2 (5/4), 2 + 3 (5/4), or 4 + 3 (7/4), 3 + 4 (7/4), etc. There are other combinations but the above are found more frequently. There are also instances in which irregular meters are truly pure 5/4, 7/4, or 11/4 measures. These instances are in the minority, however.

Several possible ways to conduct five beat measures are given in figure 64.

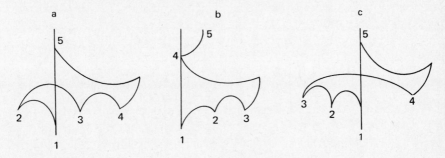

Figure 64

The pattern to use is the one that is most appropriate to the music and most comfortable for the conductor. (Also see the discussion of fast tempos, p. 131.)

A seven-beat measure has the same type of implications as the five-beat bar. The patterns in figure 65 are usable in most situations. One may encounter other more unusual orderings of the rhythmic relationships within the measure that will demand a different pattern. The conductor must deal with these instances individually and modify the patterns as needed.

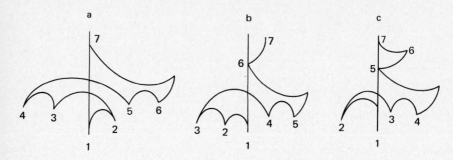

Figure 65

Pattern a is a modified and divided four pattern with the last gesture eliminated. It is quite effective for measures that are not combinations of 3 + 4 or 4 + 3. It is effective, for instance, for 2 + 2 + 2 + 1. Patterns b and c work well for the combination measures. (See also the discussion on fast tempos.)

Practicing the Patterns

The following suggestions are made for those beginning to learn the basic conducting patterns and for experienced conductors who wish to review the fundamental gestures. It is recommended that all conductors, from time to time, review the fundamentals of conducting to insure that their conducting does not stray so far from the fundamental gestures that they destroy the clarity a conductor needs. One should not confuse imprecise gestures with "personal style."

1. Practice conducting the various patterns at several tempos until the patterns are comfortable. The use of a metronome can help to maintain a steady pulse. Practicing in front of a mirror will give a person a good opportunity to actually view his own gestures and correct undesirable personal idiosyncracies.

2. As you practice conducting a particular beat pattern, sing a song or a part of a choral work that is in that meter.
3. After the patterns are comfortable, combine them in the following manner: three measures of two, three measures of three, three measures of four, three measures of five, three measures of six, and three measures of seven. Then practice two measures of each and one measure of each.
4. Practice the patterns with the left hand inactive, after the first downbeat. When the left hand is inactive it should be held across the waist with the fingers slightly curved. It is then in a position of readiness for cueing or other conducting gestures.

Fast Tempos

Fast tempos create situations when the patterns previously mentioned must be modified. A fast two will become nothing more than a one beat. A moderately fast tempo in a three meter may prevent a conductor from conveying all three beats comfortably. In these instances, the second and third beats may be implied by a rounded gesture after the downbeat. A very fast three meter will be conducted in one. Fast tempos in four will be conducted in two unless the tempo is so extremely fast that even a two pattern is impossible.

There are times when a conductor will question whether he should be conducting in two instead of four, for instance, or in one instead of three. Sometimes a tempo will seem to be too fast to conduct in three but slightly too slow to conduct in one without losing control over beats two and three. There is never one simple answer for these questions. Each example must be dealt with on its own merits. The following questions can be asked, however, to aid a conductor in making the best decision for his ensemble.

1. If all the beats are given, will the gestures add undesirable "punch" to the piece?
2. What pattern will be most clear to the ensemble?
3. What pattern (which gestures) will best control the rhythm?

There is a marked difference in a piece that must have the rhythmic feeling of two rather than four. Conductors must look "inside" the score to determine these situations.

Works that contain fast tempo conducting problems:

1. *Liebeslieder,* op. 65, Brahms, Lawson-Gould
2. *Hodie Christus Natus Est,* Willan, Carl Fischer, #A-575
3. *Glory to God,* Randall Thompson, E. C. Schirmer #2470
4. "This Little Babe" from *Ceremony of Carols,* Britten, Boosey and Hawkes

5. *The Lamentations of Jeremiah,* Ginastera, Mercury Music Corporation, #MC–103
6. *Praise Ye the Lord,* Fetler, Standard Music Publishing Co., #A26MX1

Divided Beat Patterns

The normal beat patterns will not seem sufficient to control the rhythm when the tempo is quite slow. It is then that one must use a divided beat pattern. The diagrams in figure 66 indicate the normal division of beats within duple, triple, and quadruple meter. These are the meters in which the conductor will find most of the necessity for division of beats. Any other beat patterns can be modified from those listed.

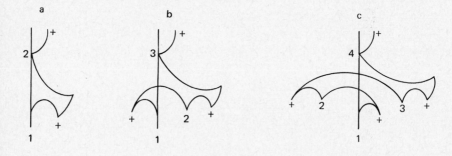

Figure 66

Conductors should be certain to maintain a stronger gesture on the principle beats. One must also be careful not to make the gestures of beats two and three so far to the left and right that the last half of those beats becomes difficult to indicate comfortably.

The musical example from Mozart's *Missa Brevis in F* is an instance when a conductor may conduct a divided pattern (see fig. 67).

It should be stated though, that a conductor will not use a divided pattern often. It is reserved for the true moments when the music can only be controlled by dividing the beat. If this technique is used where it is not needed, the music will become somewhat choppy from a continuous pulsing of notes that should not receive a stress.

There are also times when a conductor will wish to divide the beat to indicate a slowing of the tempo. This may occur at a point of a ritard or allargando. The conductor should again take care not to divide the beat to indicate the weak portion of the beat when it is not necessary. Occasionally, conductors attempt to give too many indications of extra notes by subdividing the beat in an attempt to help the singer sing the notes at the right time. Some

Agnus Dei

Edited by Arthur Mendel   Wolfgang Amadeus Mozart

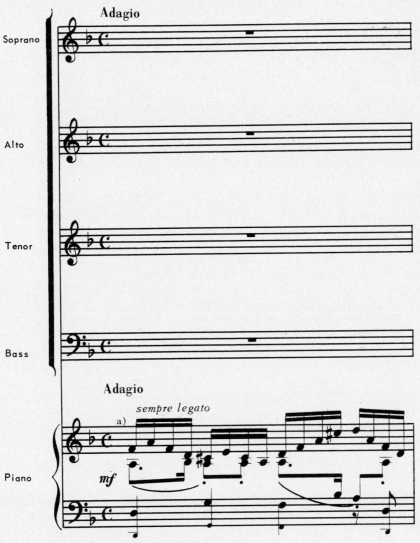

a) Bring out the middle voice.

Figure 67

Figure 67—Continued

Figure 67—Continued

Figure 67—Continued

Figure 67—Continued

Figure 67—Continued

Figure 67—Continued

Figure 67—Continued

conductors have even attempted to conduct the first two notes of the national anthem, presumably in an effort to be sure that each note is sung. The same is also attempted with "of Thee" of *My Country 'Tis of Thee.* This type of conducting only leads to nonmusical performances and to ensemble confusion.

Works that contain examples of divided beats:

1. *Missa Brevis in F* (Agnus Dei), Mozart, G. Schirmer
2. "Crucifixus" from *Mass in B minor,* J. S. Bach, entire work published by G. Schirmer, single octavo published by Bourne Publishing Co., #750
3. "Kyrie" from *Coronation Mass,* K. 317, Mozart, Breitkopf and Hartel

Unmetered or Free Rhythms

Chant or passages that do not have rhythmic or metric indications create special conducting problems. Two examples are given in figure 68 that illustrate both situations. The first illustrates a passage in which the meter is purposely omitted, preventing any misunderstanding of a metric pulse. The conductor should be reminded not to arbitrarily divide the passage into measures. This would undo the composer's intentions. In these instances the stress will be governed by the text. The most important words will receive slightly more weight (stress, not accent) than the other words. Avoid any metric pulse that will give the effect of a standardized meter.

al - le - lu - ia ____ al - le - lu - ia, ____ al - le - lu - ia. ____

Figure 68

The example in figure 69 is a chant in which the composer has placed all of the text over a single whole note. This prevents the association of any rhythmic values to the text itself. In this instance the conductor will find the best solution by repeatedly singing the words himself until he finds the combination that he feels will be most comfortable, most musical, and indicative of the composer's desires.

Works that contain examples of free rhythm:

1. *Psalm 90,* Ives, Mercury Music Corporation.
2. *Psalm 67,* Ives, Associated Music Publishers
3. *Hodie* (*Ceremony of Carols*) Britten, Boosey and Hawkes
4. *Magnificat and Nunc Dimittis,* Willan, H. W. Gray #2044

Psalm 90

Charles Ives

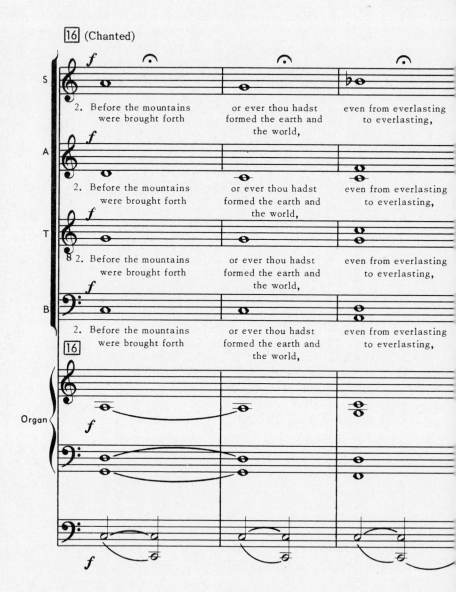

Figure 69

Displaced Rhythmic Accents

The beauty of music is that it often does the unexpected. A composer may alter the accent of a particular passage to achieve interest. The conducting gestures may also change for that passage. A different ordering of beats than those previously discussed is illustrated in figure 70.

Often a composer indicates the rhythmic ordering of the measure in the manner shown above. This is an aid to the conductor's score study since he knows exactly what rhythmic relationships the composer intended; there is no room for speculation.

The passage (fig. 70) should be conducted with three gestures in the 8/8 measure and two gestures in the 4/8 measure. Any attempt to conduct all of the eight beats at this tempo would be ridiculous.

The conductor will find that a modified three pattern (with an eighth note robbed from the second beat) will be clear and most comfortable. This, alternated with the two pattern, will best meet the musical demands of the passage.

Figure 71 illustrates the alternation of 4/4, 3/4, 6/8, and 7/8, where the alternation is not indicated by a time signature. In this instance, the composer did not indicate a time signature even at the beginning of the work. This type of alternation is not unusual in twentieth century repertoire even when a time signature is given.

This passage should be conducted in four, three, two, and a modified three. The composer has indicated his preference of 3/4 in the second measure by using a quarter tied to a dotted quarter, followed by the eighth note. Had he intended the measure (even though two and one-half beats of it are taken up with a held note) to be interpreted in 6/8 he would have notated it by using a dotted quarter tied to a quarter before the eighth note. This grouping would denote a division of the six eighth notes into two groups rather than into three. The tempo (composer's suggestion, quarter=96) will not allow a conductor to beat six beats in the third measure, or seven beats in the fourth measure. A conductor should use a two pattern in measure three and a modified three pattern in measure four. The second beat of the three pattern must be extended to incorporate the extra eighth note. The rebound will go higher and further to the right than usual for a three pattern.

Another Halsey Stevens piece, *The Way of Jehovah* is an excellent example of changing meters and shifting pulses (see fig. 72).

The composer has indicated by the time signature that 6/8 and 3/4 will alternate. This does not mean that they will alternate every measure, however. Each measure will have the same number of eighth notes but the pulse and the beat patterns will change. The following beat patterns are suggested for this passage.

Hodie Christus Natus Est

Gordon Lamb

Copyright 1971, Standard Music Publishing, Inc. and Concerto Press, used with permission.

Figure 70

Psalm 8: O Lord Our Governor

Dedicated to the Lutheran Collegiate Music Association

Book of Common Prayer   Halsey Stevens

Figure 71

The Way of Jehovah

Isaiah 40: 3-5

Figure 72

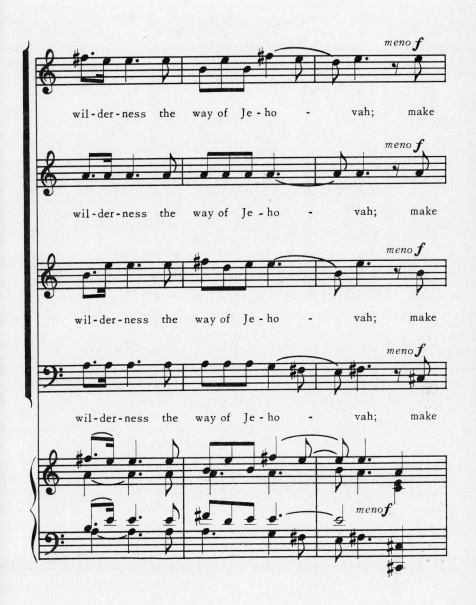

Figure 72—Continued

Figure 72—Continued

Figure 72—Continued

Measure	1	2	3	4	5	6	7	8	9	10
Pattern	2	2	2	3	2	3	3	2	2	2

One must look inside the score to determine the correct pulsation and beat pattern. A measure by measure look at the music to explain the patterns chosen above may be helpful to the conductor in examining future scores with similar problems.

Measure 1   The eighth note rest followed by two eighth notes clearly denotes 6/8 (two beats).

Measure 2   The ordering of the beats in the accompaniment suggests 6/8. Also, the rests in the choral parts are notated in the manner one expects in 6/8.

Measure 3   The text stress indicates 6/8. The words -*pate* and *ye* are to be equally stressed; 3/4 would not get this desired effect.

Measure 4   The notation and stress indicate 3/4.

Measure 5   Clearly a 6/8 measure.

Measure 6   This measure must be conducted in three. The key to the decision is the accompaniment rather than the choral parts. The accompanist would have extreme difficulty placing the third beat of the measure if the measure was conducted in two.

Measure 7   The text stress suggests that three beats will be best. The unstressed second syllable of *level* would receive an accent in 6/8. The accompaniment also indicates 3/4.

Measure 8   For the same reason this measure is in 6/8. The word *desert* should receive two pulses rather than a syncopation in 3/4.

Measures 9, 10   Both measures use 6/8. Indications in both the choral parts and accompaniment are clear.

Works that include dispaced accents or changing meters:

1. *Festival Te Deum,* Britten, Boosey and Hawkes
2. *Rejoice in the Lamb,* Britten, Boosey and Hawkes
3. *The Way of Jehovah,* Halsey Stevens, Helios, (Mark Foster)
4. *O Lord Our Governor,* Stevens, Helios, (Mark Foster)
5. *Sing unto God,* Fetler, Augsburg Publishing House, #1244
6. *Make a Joyful Noise,* Fetler, Augsburg Publishing House, #1476
7. *Anthem of Faith,* Diemer, Standard Music Publishing Co., #A25MX4

The Fermata

A fermata indicates a moment when the rhythmic motion of a composition ceases. There are basically two types of fermatas:

1. A fermata that contains two or more beats in the rhythm of the preceding passage
2. A fermata of undetermined length

There are instances when the fermata signifies the end of a previous tempo and the next note begins a new tempo. Fermatas are also often preceded by a slowing of the tempo into the fermata itself.

In moderate or slow tempos, or when a ritard is indicated, the conductor can show the coming of the fermata by a broadening of his conducting gestures. Except for sudden fermatas, this will be the guiding rule. In instances where the preceding note(s) is indicated with a ritard, the broadening will be coupled with a slowing of the tempo at that point, into the fermata.

If the tempo of the piece resumes, the cutoff of the fermata can often be used as the preparation of the next entrance. The conductor must be careful to have the hands in a position at the end of the fermata that will allow him to continue with ease.

If the fermata is to be followed by a pause (as in fig. 73) either indicated by a rest or by a stylistic implication in the score, the cutoff will be a complete gesture in itself. The conductor will then need to indicate the next entrance as he would any new entrance.

Figure 73

If the fermata is followed by a change of tempo, the preparation must be in the new tempo. One example of this type of fermata is seen in figure 74.

Figure 74

The question is often raised as to whether or not the conductor should continue to beat time during a fermata. In most instances a conductor should not conduct a part of a beat pattern during a fermata. Instead, the right hand might continue to move slowly, giving the ensemble an indication to keep the tone vibrant during the fermata. This is not the case with all fermatas, however. Some fermatas contain no internal rhythm (at least none that will warrant conducting motion). These fermatas can be held with the arms raised and extended. Avoid holding the arms with the palms up in these instances. One has no control over the ensemble with the hands in this position. The conductor will maintain a better conducting gesture if the palms face inward and the hands remain slightly cupped (if a baton is not being used).

Works that contain examples of fermatas:

1. *Break Forth, O Beauteous Heavenly Light,* Bach, Lawson-Gould
2. *Psalm 150,* Schutz, Robert King Music Co. #601
3. *A Boy Was Born,* Britten, Oxford University Press, #84.092
4. *Twenty-one Chorales,* Bach, Schmitt, Hall, and McCreary
5. *Why Are Roses So Pale?,* Carr, Standard Music Publishing Co., #B319 MX1

The Left Hand

When the left hand is not in use, it should be held in front of the body, across the waist. This is a position of both rest and readiness. It is also out of sight of the audience. When the left hand is simply dropped at the side of the body, it is viewed from the audience as a limp, lifeless piece of extraneous material. When held in front of the body, it also aids in assuming a posture of alertness.

Since the left hand is basically free from time-beating chores, it can be used for cueing, to indicate dynamics and style, to assist in starting and stopping the ensemble, to aid in changing tempo, to control the balance, and occasionally to assist with the beat patterns. The use of the left hand in starting and stopping the ensemble has already been discussed.

Assist with Beat Patterns

Many conductors, both choral and instrumental, let the left hand mirror the motions of the right hand most of the time. This is usually of no value to the ensemble, and is mostly a result of the conductor not knowing what to do with the left hand.

The left hand can assist in the beat pattern when the conductor wishes to help in making the beat clear to the left side of the ensemble (at a most crucial point), when the music is broadening and the conductor wishes to stress this fact to the ensemble, when the music begins to climax, when the conductor needs to reaffirm the beat (particularly for a large ensemble), and when there is a tempo change and the conductor wishes to use the left hand to help define the change for the ensemble. Finally, the left hand can be used any time the conductor feels that its use will help clarify the beat for the ensemble. Its use is likely to be greater when conducting a large festival chorus than it is when one is conducting a smaller ensemble.

If the left hand assumes a major role in the conducting of beat patterns, however, the conductor will present a confusing, often windmill appearance, both to the ensemble and to the audience. If the left hand is to be used to conduct a beat pattern, its use should be limited and only for good reason. To conduct the pianist with only the left hand because the piano is on the left side, for example, is not a good reason. Either place the piano on the right side or turn toward the pianist and conduct with the right hand.

Cueing

Although the left hand is used for much of the cueing, it must not be considered as the only means of cueing. Cueing refers to the numerous times a conductor needs to indicate important entrances (while the music is in progress) or important parts that need to be emphasized. Cues can be given with either hand, a nod of the head, or a glance by the conductor. There are often so many cues in rapid succession that even the use of both hands cannot meet the demand.

The left hand is the logical hand for cueing since it does not have the responsibility for beating the pattern. The cue is similar to other entrances. It needs to have a preparation and must be in the character of the music to come. This is important since there are occasions when the cue signals a different mood in the music. The preparation for the cue is best given one beat before the entrance and the gesture is made directly at the section or performer involved. Cues that are not specifically defined are of no value to an ensemble. The members must know for whom the cue is given. The best cue occurs when the conductor can make the cue with the hand and reinforce it with eye contact as well. Whenever possible and particularly for the most important cues, this should be done. There is not always adequate time to do this, however.

One must practice giving cues so that the two arms operate independently of each other. The beat pattern must continue unhindered as the left hand executes an entirely different type of function.

Most conductors of amateur ensembles overdramatize their cues, because of the likelihood that the amateur will not respond in kind and needs to be reminded in a dramatic way. It is best to be safe and overcue amateur ensembles and avoid the disastrous results of missed entrances. A missed entrance by an entire section will do more to destroy a piece than almost any other kind of error. Confident, well-defined cues can prevent these mistakes.

Dynamics

The left hand can indicate dynamic changes to the ensemble. Normally an upward motion means an increase in volume and an opposite motion indicates a decrease in volume. Either gesture must be made in a gradual manner; otherwise the response of the ensemble will be too sudden and the crescendo or decrescendo will be ineffective. A conductor must be particularly careful about the decrescendo gesture since most ensembles go too quickly to a soft level leaving not enough room for a further decrease in volume.

The indication to crescendo should be given with the palm up as the left arm rises. The gesture to get softer should be given with the palm down. A gesture with the palm toward the ensemble can remind them to remain soft or to wait to begin a crescendo. Subito dynamic changes can also be given with the left hand, although the entire conducting posture (right hand, eyes, head, and body) will help with this indication.

Change in Tempo

A most critical moment in a composition is a moment of tempo change. The conductor must use every means at hand to make the change as precise as possible. The left hand is a resource the conductor can use to make his intentions clear to the ensemble. The left hand would only be used for a short period of time, until the new tempo is established.

Controlling Balance

The balance between the parts of an ensemble is also controlled by the left hand. A gesture to control the balance will be similar to those that indicate dynamics, except that it will be specific to one part or, on occasion, to one voice. Most of this will take place in rehearsal and by the time of performance the conductor will usually have few balance problems. However, new concert hall acoustics, performance excitement, or the illness of one or two key people can create balance problems.

In performance these gestures must be cautious ones so the performers do not misinterpret them and overreact. It must be remembered that they have most likely rehearsed at a certain volume level, and any change from that will seem new to them.

Tempo

The tempo of a musical composition will be governed by a number of factors that are a part of the music. These factors may be labeled as external markings and internal markings. In addition to these, there are other factors that contribute to the selection of the proper tempo. These are not indicated on the score and refer to the acoustics of the performing hall and other such considerations. It should be stated at the outset that there is no *one* tempo for every piece. There *is* a tempo that is best for every group at that time. A conductor must determine what tempo will best suit his ensemble and his performance situation.

External Markings

The term *external markings* refers to the indications placed in the score by the composer, or in the case of older music, by the editor. Figure 75 can be used to indicate how a conductor can use these markings as a first guide to an understanding of the tempo.

Since this piece was written in 1969, we know that the M. M. marking is the composer's indication and not that of an arranger or editor. We know that the composer "heard" the piece at this tempo as he conceived it. If the composer has an excellent understanding of choral ensembles, his tempo indications will be usable for most groups.

A conductor should take this tempo indication and the stylistic indication (when given) as the basis on which to establish a tempo. Some deviation from the marking is permissible, but if one strays too far, the integrity of the piece will be destroyed. In the case of this piece, one can go somewhat faster, perhaps to quarter=118 without any problems; but if the piece is slowed to even quarter=108, the rhythmic life is lost. The external markings are the first step in determining the tempo.

Internal Markings

There are other factors that help a conductor choose the right tempo for his ensemble that are contained within the music itself. These include:

Text. If there are many words that come upon each other rapidly, the tempo cannot be too fast. The same type of piece with fewer words might be taken at a faster tempo. The character of the text should also be taken into consideration. Texts that are languid in mood, for example, should not be sung at fast tempos.

Musical Style of the Period. Determining the approximate date of the composition will aid in the selection of an appropriate tempo. For instance, tempos of the nineteenth century tended toward the extremes more than those of the Classic period. (See chapter eleven.)

Harmonic Complexity. A work that is quite simple and direct harmonically will lend itself well to faster tempos. Works that are quite chromatic, for example, are most difficult to perform at fast tempos. Usually the more complexity a work contains harmonically, the less chance there is that it should be taken at a very fast tempo.

Let All the World in Every Corner Sing
For Four-Part Chorus of Mixed Voices
a cappella

George Herbert (1593-1632)   Sven Lekberg

Figure 75

Rhythmic Complexity. The same standards that apply to harmonic complexity apply here.

The Smallest Rhythmic Unit. A musical composition can go no faster than the smallest rhythmic unit can be successfully and musically negotiated. If sixteenth-notes abound in the work, they will limit the speed at which the piece may be performed. A conductor needs to subdivide rhythm mentally in order to establish a tempo that will not rush the fastest units.

The Overall Character. After a conductor has examined the external and internal indications of a score, he should look again at the mood of the entire work, keeping in mind the pieces of information that have been gleaned from the examination. The conductor can then put this information into the perspective necessary to determine the flow of the composition.

Factors Not in the Score

There are several considerations that must be made that affect tempo that are not found in the musical score. They are important to the establishment of a tempo for a given performance. The decisions based on the considerations listed above will help a conductor determine the tempo that he feels is musically proper for the piece. The following considerations will help determine the tempo for a *specific* performance situation.

Size of the Chorus. Large choruses are usually less able to perform at very fast tempos than smaller ones. It is simply more difficult to keep a larger chorus together at fast tempos.

Capability of the Singers. If the singers have developed a good technique they will be able to perform complex works at a faster tempo than those singers not so equipped. This does not mean that all works should go faster with better singers. It means that works whose external and internal markings indicate a fast tempo will be more easily realized with singers with a good technique.

Change of Tempo

One of the most problematic moments of any musical composition is the moment when it changes tempo. There can be a few chaotic measures while the ensemble and the conductor search for the new tempo. This search is sometimes made separately, to the embarassment of the audience as well as the performers. There are a few points that will serve to aid a conductor in changing tempos.

1. Unless the music is marked with a ritard or similar marking that would slow the tempo, do not slow the last one or two beats of the first tempo, when it is followed by a slower tempo. The reverse would also be true. The

tempo change begins with the first beat of the next measure where the indication of the change of tempo is located.

2. The length of time between the final beat of the first tempo and the first beat of the new tempo must remain in the first tempo. Often conductors will reflect the new tempo in the final motion connected with the last beat of the first tempo. Many conductors anticipate the new tempo in this manner, often destroying the musical intention of the composer. The new tempo will be indicated by the distance between the first and second beats of the new tempo. If the tempo is to be faster, for instance, less time and distance between beats will give the ensemble the proper indication of the change.

Figure 76

3. The tempo can change somewhat from one performance to the next due to acoustics of the performance hall. These changes must be judiciously made to insure that the musicality of the work is maintained. Performances in concert halls that have considerable reverberation can be conducted at a slower tempo than in a hall with little reverberation. The "live" hall helps sustain the tone and, in fact, if the tempo is too fast, the chords will become blurred as one sound is carried over into the next.

Performance areas that have little reverberation will prompt a conductor to move the tempos just a little faster. This will help the sound of the ensemble.

Establishing the Mood

The conductor must establish the mood or character of a musical work. He can do this by his facial expression, the size of beat pattern, the level of the gestures (the conducting plane), and the style of the gestures.

If one is to conduct a serious piece that is legato, one must absorb those characteristics into the conducting gestures. The gestures in a legato work can be very fluid, avoiding any sudden or sharp motions. On the other hand, crisp and very exact gestures would be appropriate for a piece that is quite rapid and staccato.

Expressive Conducting

The rigidity of the conventional beat patterns must be modified in order to allow the expressive qualities of a conductor to be injected into his gestures. Expression must be displayed in the gestures and on the face of the conductor in order for the ensemble to be affected by it. Many conductors seem to be able to grasp the expressionistic qualities of music, but are unable to convey that quality to others.

Performance Conducting

The gestures that are acceptable in a rehearsal are not always acceptable in a performance. The conductor is encouraged to inject energy and excitement into the rehearsal and to use almost any means to do so. However, when the conductor approaches the performance he should refine his gestures in the last few rehearsals to those he intends to use in the performance. If he does not make the change gradually, the ensemble will be surprised at the new gestures used in performance.

Performance gestures should remind the ensemble of the techniques learned at rehearsal. Indications of dynamics, for instance, will not need to be so exaggerated. The members of the ensemble are extraordinarily alert for a performance, and fewer but more personal gestures will suffice. The audience must also be taken into consideration. While it may be in vogue to marvel at some professional conductor's exaggerated gestures with a symphony, the same gestures may be ludicrous with a choral ensemble of amateur singers.

The ensemble should be long past the point where only exaggerated gestures will evoke responses. Temper all the conducting gestures for the performance, and be sure that no new ones are added that will be confusing to the ensemble.

Discussion Questions

1. Recall the various conductors, both instrumental and choral, under whom you have performed. What facets of their technique were enviable? What facets were not?
2. When do you feel it is most appropriate to use a baton?

3. Must a conductor of choral groups understand the principles of singing technique?
4. What are the personal attributes of a good conductor?
5. How much effect will the style, tempo, dynamics, and mood of the text have on the basic conducting gestures.
6. In how many different ways can a conductor show the character of the composition?
7. Is it more important to conduct the score as one believes that the composer would have wanted it performed, or should a conductor add his own interpretation to the score? Can conductors ever disagree about the interpretation of a score, and yet the results of both conductors be musical?

SUGGESTED READINGS

Davison, Archibald T. *Choral Conducting,* chap. 1 and 2. Cambridge: Harvard University Press, 1945.

Ehmann, Wilhelm. *Choral Directing.* Minneapolis: Augsburg Publishing House, 1968.

Green, Elizabeth A. H. *The Modern Conductor.* 2d ed., sec. 1. Englewood Cliffs: Prentice-Hall, Inc., 1969.

Marple, Hugo D. *The Beginning Conductor.* New York: McGraw-Hill Book Company, 1972.

McElheran, Brock. *Conducting Techniques: For Beginners and Professionals.* New York: Oxford University Press, 1966.

Thomas, Kurt. *The Choral Conductor,* chap. 2. New York: Associated Music Publishers, 1971.

chapter 10.

score study

The importance of score study cannot be overemphasized. It is in the examination of the score that final questions regarding style are answered. One can know many things about the musical period, the social structure, the composer's life, etc., but the real answers are found in the music. Is the music representative of the period or does it contain characteristics that represent one of the crosscurrents of the period?

The first study of the score should determine the scope and overall impact of the work. What is the thrust of the music? Where does it climax? What techniques does the composer use to achieve the climaxes? For example, climaxes are often results of harmonic and rhythmic intensification. When one has determined the techniques used, one can incorporate their importance into the rehearsal and performance of the music.

A conductor must be able to grasp the musical essence of the score and impart this knowledge to the ensemble. It is true that members of the ensemble will probably not be able to understand the score in the same depth as the conductor. However, in order to achieve artistic performances, the performers must understand their role in the overall scope of the work.

Examine the large dimensions of the work. Compositions can usually be divided into sections. Determine the sections of the work and label them A B etc. Some workers will have a clear form, A B A, for example, while others may seem to establish a form of their own, a hybrid form related to, but distinct from other formal structures. Choral works often have a form that "follows the text" since choral composers are extremely conscious of text. Many composers let the text itself establish the direction of the composition.

This overall but thorough examination will often reveal one aspect of the work that seems to be most important. It may be the overall rhythmic impact of the work, such as occurs in Carl Orff's *Carmina Burana,* or the harmonic beauty of the piece. If one aspect seems to be most important, the conductor must keep this in mind as he continues his analysis. He must recognize every possibility that exists in the score to help him establish and convey that one most important quality of the composition.

Be certain to consider external and internal indications in the score as you study the music. An external indication of tempo, for instance, is a metronome marking or words to indicate the tempo such as *fast* or *allegro*. Internal indications, either in addition to or in lieu of external markings, include the character of the text, harmonic rhythm, and the speed of the smallest rhythmic unit. Additionally, one must also consider the type of performing ensemble, its size, and the performing hall. None of this is revealed in the score however, and is discussed in chapter nine. A conductor must learn to look beyond the external indications for a full understanding of the composer's intent.

Melodic Considerations

Determine the type of melody—major, minor, modal, or synthetic. After this has been determined, examine the melody closely. Use the following questions as a guide to that examination.

1. Does the melody consist of long or short phrases?
2. Is the melody archlike?
3. Can any sequences be found?
4. What are the intervals of the melody? Are there any intervals that will cause problems for the ensemble?
5. Is the melody conjunct or disjunct?
6. Do the intervals outline triads or special interval groupings? What are the harmonic implications of the melody?
7. What is the range of the melody?
8. Is the melody the most important aspect of the composition?
9. Where is the most important part of every phrase? Of the entire melody?
10. What are the characteristics of the melody that can be used to help teach the work to the ensemble? Does it have any unique characteristics that can be used as teaching aids in the rehearsal?

Harmonic Considerations

Conductors must understand the harmonic idiom in which the music is written and be able to grasp its harmonic flow. Although one may do a chord analysis, it is not always necessary. After examining many scores a conductor will be able to name the chords and describe their function without writing this on the score. This is true in traditional works at least. A conductor needs to know the chords and their functions, however, if he is to realize the full harmonic implications. He must be able to recognize nonchordal tones, or doubled notes of chords so each may receive the correct emphasis. One must also be able to identify important notes, such as leading tones, root progressions, etc., so they may receive proper emphasis.

The following questions can serve as a guide to the harmonic study.

1. What period does the harmonic style indicate?
2. If a twentieth century work, what is the harmonic vocabulary—traditional, twelve-tone, modal, etc.?
3. Is the harmonic rhythm fast, medium, or slow?
4. Is the harmony the most important element of the work?
5. What part do nonchordal tones play in the harmonic structure? Will they need to receive special attention?
6. Do the chord movements themselves provide any special problems?
7. Harmonic interest is often derived from harmonic tension, which, in turn, is often achieved through dissonance. If this is the case, discover how the dissonance occurs. How can a conductor heighten the points of harmonic tension?
8. Where are the points of dissonance?
9. If the piece modulates, how is the modulation accomplished?

Rhythmic Considerations

A study of the melodic and harmonic structures will have revealed the large rhythmic dimensions of the work. Further study will show the rhythmic force of the composition and the smaller dimensions of rhythm.

The following questions can be used as a guide to this study.

1. Is there one rhythmic pattern on which much of the rhythmic structure is based? If the study establishes this, consider other rhythmic elements in their relation to this one most important factor. How will this knowledge affect the rehearsal and performance of the work?
2. Are there any rhythmic sequences?
3. What is the tempo? Tempo directly relates to rhythm difficulties. Rhythmic complexity at a slow tempo may be easy, but at a fast tempo it may be difficult.
4. Does the meter present any problems? If the piece contains changing meters, problems of rhythmic continuity almost always occur. The conductor will have to teach the ensemble how to manage the changing meters and the consequent fluctuating rhythmic stress.
5. Remembering that choirs usually have their first difficulties with the rhythm, what can one do to instill an understanding of the rhythm of the piece in question?

6. Which places will cause the most difficulty for the singers? What techniques can be used to most effectively teach the rhythm at these trouble spots?

Part Examination

A conductor must be able to sing each part without accompaniment, and know each part thoroughly. He must also know the relationship of each part to the other parts. The following questions should be answered regarding each voice part.

1. What is its melodic importance? How can this best be brought out?
2. Are there any difficult intervals? Do they coincide with difficult intervals in other parts?
3. What is the range and tessitura of each part?
4. Are there any phrasing considerations that differ from those of the entire ensemble?
5. Are there instances of text repetition or fragmentation that are unique to one or more parts?
6. How does each part relate to the others melodically, harmonically, and rhythmically?
7. Can trouble spots be identified?

Text Considerations

The text has already passed inspection to a degree, or a conductor would not be going into rehearsal with a composition. Another examination is necessary however, to determine how the text will affect rehearsal and performance of the work. Questions, like the following, can help in that analysis.

1. Is the text setting syllabic?
2. Is the text fragmented? How will this affect the transmission of the text?
3. Does the text influence rhythm?
4. How is the text inflected?
5. Are there awkward syllables or words? How can they be handled?
6. Can instances of word painting be found? How can a conductor highlight these instances?
7. Is text most important? There are times when a composer is not as concerned with direct transmission of the text as he is with conveying the sense of the text. Are there occasions when the text is blurred by contrapuntal lines or instruments? If so, are there key words that can be emphasized to project the text and the line itself?
8. If the text is a translation, has the inflection been changed so unimportant

or unstressed syllables are stressed? Can the text be changed to prevent this?

Texture

Through the study of harmony, melody, rhythm, and text, one will become aware of the texture of the work. The following questions should still be asked to prepare the work for rehearsal.

1. What are the demands of the texture? Is it thick? Transparent? Can the choir meet these demands?
2. How often does the texture change?
3. Does the composer utilize texture as a means of achieving variety?
4. Does texture often seem to be the most important aspect of the score?

The following discussion of Paul Fetler's *Praise Ye the Lord* is the result of applying the procedure outlined above. Following that is an overall view of *Now Thank We All Our God* by Johann Pachelbel. The overview is necessary for conductors to be certain they do not become so engrossed in the details of the score that they lose sight of the large dimensions of the work. The chapter ends with a discussion of indeterminate scores and the specific problems they present.

Praise Ye the Lord, Paul Fetler
Published by Standard Music Publishing, Inc.
No. A25MX4

The short choral phrases in this concert anthem are inserted into the unrelenting fabric created by the staccato piano part. The overall dynamic scheme of *pp—fff—pp* presents the choir with the full gamut of dynamic possibilities in this distinctive setting.

Figure 77 shows the opening piano accompaniment and the first choral statement. Both are representative of much of the writing throughout the work.

Melodically, the work is comprised of a number of short phrases quite similar to those in figure 77. Intervals of particular importance are the ascending minor third (as seen in the alto and bass of measures 7 and 8) and the perfect fifth (which occurs later in the composition).

The harmony is conservative twentieth century writing using many chords of open fourths and fifths. Harmonic interest is achieved through frequent major second dissonances that occur as a result of paired fourths and fifths and as melodic occurrences as seen in figure 77, measure 7.

The single most important element of the piece is the rhythmic activity.

Praise Ye the Lord
(Laudate Dominum)

From Psalm 135

Paul Fetler

Figure 77

Figure 77—Continued

Figure 77—Continued

Syncopation creates interest and excitement as it occurs in the choral parts over the constant eighth note in the piano. This rhythmic activity at the fast tempo is one of the outstanding qualities of the work.

Fetler uses brief moments of legato writing as contrast, as seen in figure 78. Except for the one instance of two-part writing, these legato passages occur as unison statements.

One of the first rehearsal, and later performance problems encountered is the fast tempo. Of course, first rehearsals need not be at tempo, but it later becomes an element of concern. Although the accompaniment is not technically difficult, it is hard for a pianist to maintain the desired tempo, and to do so at the various dynamic levels required in the score. Conductors must also resist the urge to allow the music to become slower. Performances often start at tempo but a slowing occurs (usually within the first thirty measures) that dulls the urgency and excitement the composition should have.

Other than the usual problems of correct notes, intonation, tone, etc., the two major problems caused by the rhythmic activity and the fast tempo are (1) lack of clarity and (2) poor diction.

Because of the speed, clarity becomes a particular problem of this piece. The articulation of the notes must be clean. The choir will have to adopt *some* of the staccato quality of the piano accompaniment in order to sing these passages cleanly.

Figure 78

praise___ ye the Lord,___

Figure 78—Continued

Good diction not only allows the audience to understand the text but also contributes substantially to solving the problem of clarity mentioned above. One of the problems of this piece is the fast articulation of "Praise ye." Choirs often sing "Prāshee" instead of the correct "Prāz ye." The *s* in *Praise* is sounded as a *z*. Conductors will find it necessary to emphasize to the choir that the *z* must be carefully sounded and that it should not be too long.

Although *Praise Ye the Lord* is not a difficult work, conductors will find that it must be well paced; that the choir must be cautioned not to reach a *forte* too quickly. Close attention to the careful dynamic markings of the composer will aid the conductor's pacing of the piece. The urgent intensity of the very soft passages explodes in the *fortissimo* center section of the work. The return to *pianissimo* is not easy to achieve but provides a satisfying ending to the composition.

Now Thank We All Our God (overview), Johann Pachelbel (edited by Eggebrecht)
Published by Concordia Press
No. 98-1944

This setting of a chorale tune is only one section of a larger work. The chorale is in the soprano, preceded by alto, tenor, and bass parts derived from the tune. This is often referred to as one type of cantus firmus treatment before Bach. A tempo of a quarter note equaling eighty (eighty quarter notes in a minute) is suggested. The alto, tenor, and bass are important until the entry of the chorale tune, at which time they must become subordinate to the melody. One must keep the three lower parts from becoming too heavy. A light, free texture is necessary.

The rhythmic life of the lower parts, coupled with a clearly defined cantus firmus, is the key to success in this piece. Attention must be given to the eighth note; each must be a full eighth note. A slight broadening of the second and third eighth notes in the groups of three will help obtain the rhythmic security so necessary to this work.

Rehearsal Analysis of Indeterminate Music

Indeterminate music (also referred to as aleatoric or chance music) refers to that which is unpredictable before a performance. Until the performance a conductor will not know exactly how the piece will sound. He will have an understanding of the overall sound of the work but not of its individual sounds. Most works that include indeterminacy are not totally indeterminate. They may contain sections that are completely predictable and carefully notated, and those that are not. They may also contain sections that range anywhere between these extremes.

Indeterminate music requires a new kind of analysis and a different rehearsal approach than traditional repertoire. Conductors are required to use their musical imagination more in the study of these scores because one cannot "play the notes" or visually see the texture, range, harmonic coloring, etc., since the score may consist of only written instructions or nontraditional notation. A conductor will have to read the instructions carefully and, based on his own experimentation and his knowledge of vocal sounds, predict the overall sound.

It is usually impossible to sight-read indeterminate music in the manner of traditional sight-reading. Often, a conductor should prepare a short lecture, including his own demonstration, about the music. Nothing will be accomplished by asking the singers to "read" the score unless they have an understanding of it. It is best to find a section of the work that is the most accessible and rehearse it first. The singers will be able to more clearly accomplish the composer's intentions, and can better appreciate the sound that will be achieved when the work is fully prepared.

For example, a passage like that in figure 79 would be a good one to extract from a work as a beginning to its rehearsal.

The composer has indicated a unison C which is then expanded to a range of approximately two and a half octaves. Singers are allowed to choose

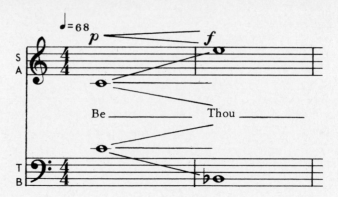

Figure 79

any notes between and including the notated B-flat and E. The conductor will need to assign several voices to the two notated pitches and then ask the other singers to fill in the sounds between those two notes. At first singers will tend to bunch the pitches; that is, not uniformly filling in between the two notes. The conductor may have to select some voices for certain ranges to get a uniform cluster.

Other examples of choices are not as easily rehearsed. Figure 80 contains an often used technique that requires some explanation from the conductor and experimentation from the singers before the section will be comfortable to the choir.

Only after several attempts will singers begin to feel comfortable with the section. After many rehearsals, such a passage will begin to sound the same every time because the singers will forget to be original in their choices and simply sing it the same way each time. If this is the case, the spontaneity of the passage is lost.

It is most important for the conductor to totally understand indeterminate scores before presenting the work to the choir. He will most likely "talk" the ensemble through the work, explaining the intent and type of sound expected. He can also describe how continuity is achieved in the work and how the parts relate to each other.

It should be emphasized that conductors must study the score carefully, anticipating difficulties that may arise for the singers. Every conductor must remember, however, that even with one's own choir, an attempt to determine which characteristics of a piece will need the most attention is a gamble. The conductor's gamble is based on his experience with voices, with people, and with his own choir. There will be times when anticipated problems do not occur and when others, not anticipated, do occur. The conductor must be able to recognize when he has miscalculated and be flexible enough to

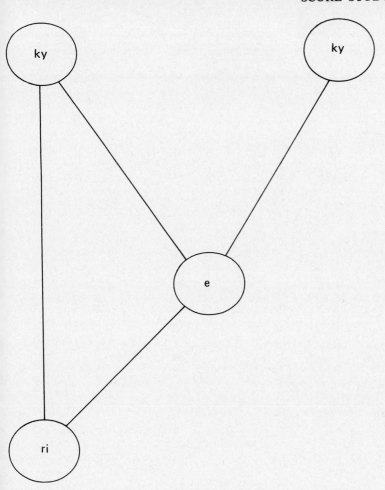

Figure 80

change direction, responding to the immediate needs of the choir rather than
to his rehearsal plan.

Discussion Questions

1. What are internal indications in music?
2. How well must the conductor know the capabilities of the choir in
   order to accurately predict rehearsal and performance problems?
3. Select several choral pieces. Can you apply the principles of score
   study to these works?

4. How much will a conductor be hampered by a poor theory and analysis background?

SUGGESTED READINGS

Lamb, Gordon H. "Indeterminate Music for Chorus," *The Choral Journal* May 1970, pp. 12-15.

La Rue, Jan. *Guidelines for Style Analysis.* New York: W. W. Norton, 1970.

Pooler, Frank and Pierce, Brent. *New Choral Notation (A Handbook).* New York: Walton Music Corporation, 1971.

chapter 11.   interpreting choral music

In the past fifteen to twenty years choral conductors have become increasingly aware of stylistic considerations and performance practices. This chapter is intended to be a guide to an understanding of the styles of the various musical periods. As brief a study as this must be considered as an introduction to style, a door to a continued study that should never stop. One's understanding of style must be constantly reviewed as new information is gained through research.

General compositional characteristics are listed for each period. These represent general elements of style with the understanding that exceptions are found throughout each period. Crosscurrents exist in every style period. While the main stream of composition may be going in one direction, composers may also be found working in another direction. The final test is a thorough examination of the music itself.

Performances of early music require each conductor to decide exactly how *authentic* he intends the performance to be. A totally authentic performance, of course, is not possible since original performance conditions are impossible to duplicate. Conductors must research performance practices as carefully as possible and respond artistically to the musical implications of the score. This may mean that instrumental substitutions must be made. It is the conductor's responsibility to make these substitutions compatible with the musical style of the work.

The Renaissance (1400-1600)

The choral music of the Renaissance is a valuable source for amateur (high school, university, and community choirs). Young voices are particularly suited to this music. The characteristics normally associated with the Renaissance are most aptly applied to the music written between 1400 and 1600, and particularly that written between 1450 and 1550. Some of the qualities of Baroque music are found before 1600, and characteristics of the Renaissance are found much later than 1600. The dates of this period, as with all periods, must be taken as only guidelines since stylistic changes represent an evolvement, not abrupt changes. The Renaissance composers were part of an intellectual community that began to be as concerned with their life on earth as well as their life after death.

Characteristics of Renaissance music include:

1. Polyphonic texture, equal voice lines
2. Use of fewer modes, and a move toward major and minor tonality
3. Melody influenced by plainsong
4. Conjunct melodic movement
5. Controlled dissonance
6. Text important to formal considerations
7. Nonmetered rhythms
8. Overlapping points of imitation

Meter and Tempo

It is in the area of rhythmic flow that many performances of Renaissance music are deficient. Since most of the music was unmetered, the barline that appears in many modern editions can be misleading to conductors. A metrical accent must not be placed on the first beat of the measure. Ideally, the stress is determined by the text; the rhythmic flow is closely tied to the text flow.

Renaissance music is horizontal in nature, and singers must be aware of the importance of the linear qualities of the score. While one part may have textual stresses at one time, another will have an altogether different stress. It is difficult for amateurs, particularly young singers, to achieve the full linear implications of the score. Often each part can be sung separately; the stress determined and then placed with the other parts. Also effective is the technique of rebarring each part to fit the text flow.

The tempo is also influenced by the text. Notational features affect the tempo changes in the music, although these are usually not apparent in modern editions, having been changed to modern notation by the editor. Unless indicated, the tempo does not appreciably vary during a section of a work. Syllabic sections may often be taken at a slightly faster tempo than polyphonic sections. Although the music must not be taken so fast that the inherent beauty of the polyphony is destroyed, conductors should guard against a very slow tempo that impedes the linear flow.

Ritards should generally be avoided. A slowing down of the music was achieved by "building it into the score." This was accomplished by lengthening, often doubling, the note values. The conductor who dwells on a cadence and distorts the tempo at that point is achieving a special effect at the expense of the overall style of the music. The word *restraint* has long been applied to Renaissance music, and its application is well deserved.

Dynamics

The dynamics should be moderate and in keeping with the mood of the text. Since composers of the Renaissance did not use dynamic markings, any markings in modern editions are those of the editor, not the composer.

Although overlaping lines do not lend themselves to a climax at any one given point, the composers were not unaware of the intensity that could be realized. Conductors must be responsive to the suggestions of the music, but must also guard against any tendency toward excessive dynamics.

Texture

Although Renaissance music is horizontal, the composers were becoming aware of the harmonic implications of their music. There was a concern for harmonic beauty resulting from the combination of vocal lines. The clarity of each moving part is of primary importance. In fact, the parts were written down in part books, rather than in full scores as we use today. Clarity is best achieved with a tone that has little vibrato since excessive vibrato will destroy the transparency and forward motion of the line. Younger voices rarely have a problem attaining the desired quality since they are usually naturally light.

The texture is a well-contained body of sound that has constantly moving parts of quite equal importance. A subtle emphasis of dynamics or of the beginning of a line will bring out desired points of importance.

Suspensions are vitally important to the texture of Renaissance music. The suspended note must receive slightly more emphasis than its resolution. A conductor should avoid telling a choir to accent this note. It can be stressed with a slight growth in the tone on the suspended note.

Although long known as a great era of a cappella singing, instruments were used frequently to augment the singers or to double the voice parts. The use of instruments was left to the discretion of the performers. Present conductors must make the same decision except that this decision is hampered by a lack of knowledge of performance practice of the period. As a general rule one can be freer in the use of instruments in secular music that in sacred. The liturgy also prohibited use of instruments at certain times during the church year.

The acoustics of the performing hall will also play a part not only in the tempo of the work, but in the manner in which the polyphonic motet, for instance, should be performed. A very live hall will necessitate a very cautious control of dynamics and of tone. The most subtle shading, already being carefully managed, will be magnified under extremely live circumstances.

Renaissance Composers

John Dunstable (c. 1385-1453)
Gilles Binchois (c. 1400-1460)
Guillaume Dufay (c. 1400-1474)
Johannes Okeghem (c. 1420-1495)
Jacob Obrecht (c. 1453-1505)
Heinrich Isaak (c. 1450-1517)
Josquin Des Prez (c. 1450-1521)
Jean Mouton (c. 1470-1522)
Thomas Tallis (c. 1505-1585)
Jacob Arcadelt (c. 1510-1567)
Andrea Gabrieli (c. 1510-1586)
G. P. Palestrina (c. 1525-1594)
Richard Farrant (c. 1530-1580)
Orlando di Lasso (Roland de Lassus) (c. 1532-1594)
William Byrd (c. 1543-1623)
Tomas Luis de Victoria (c. 1549-1611)
Jacobus Gallus (Jacob Handl) (c. 1550-1611)
Orazio Vecchi (c. 1550-1605)
Luca Merenzio (c. 1553-1599)
Thomas Morley (c. 1557-1603)
Carlo Gesualdo (c. 1560-1613)
John Dowland (c. 1562-1626)
Hans Leo Hassler (c. 1564-1612)
John Wilbye (c. 1574-1638)
Thomas Weelkes (c. 1575-1638)
Orlando Gibbons (c. 1583-1625)

Suggested Works for Study

O Vos Omnes, Esquivel (G. Schirmer 11231)
Domine Exaudi Deus Orationem, di Lasso (G. Schirmer 11422)
Magnificat in Primi Toni, Palestrina (Lawson-Gould)
O Magnum Mysterium, Victoria (G. Schirmer 7626)
O Quam Gloriosum, Victoria (G. Schirmer 13448)
Call to Remembrance, Farrant (Bourne ES 17)
Ave Maria, Mouton (Mercury Music DCS-40)
Jubilate Deo, di Lasso (Boosey and Hawkes 5490)
Tu Pauperum Refugium, Josquin (G. Schirmer 9565)

The Baroque Period (1600-1750)

The Baroque period was anticipated before 1600, although that date remains as a convenient marker for the start of the period. It is a period of dramatic expression, of a vigorous, highly ornamented art. An era of absolute monarchies, each court had its own group of musicians, both vocal and instrumental.

The Doctrine of Affections of the Baroque relates to the portrayal of emotions through music. A recognized musical vocabulary expressed certain emotions. Within this overall context, composers used musical techniques to vividly describe the meaning of the words. Rising passages are found at words such as "resurrection," "heaven," etc. Descending passages were used for such phrases as "to the depths" and "descended into hell."

It was also a period of scientific discovery and reasoning. New findings in the sciences were vitally important to knowledge on the continent. Although we are usually concerned with Baroque music of the continent, it was during this period that the settlement of the New World began.

Rhythmic energy, coupled with a strong melodic thrust, makes performances of Baroque music appealing and satisfying to musicians, both amateur and professional.

Characteristics of Baroque choral music include:

1. Vertical structure rather than linear
2. Major-minor tonality established
3. Figured bass
4. Outer voice polarity—soprano melody over a figured bass
5. New counterpoint—subordinate to the harmony
6. Concertato style important
7. Terraced dynamics
8. Instruments influenced texture
9. Form determined by musical considerations
10. Doctrine of Affections
11. Virtuosity and improvisation are important elements
12. Steady pulsating rhythm—barlines introduced

Although 1600 is generally acknowledged as the beginning of the Baroque period, Renaissance characteristics are found long after that. The two styles, *stile antico* and *stile moderno* existed side by side, particularly in the early Baroque. Composers often wrote in both styles; consequently, a conductor must look beyond the name and dates of a composer to determine the style of the music.

Rhythm and Tempo

Music became metered during the Baroque period and the barline was used with regularity. A certain rhythmic drive is found in repertoire of this period. A crisp, very clean articulation is necessary to bring about a successful performance of much of the music.

There are several rhythmic practices that are generally considered as correct interpretations of Baroque music. One is the technique of extending the duration of dotted notes, shortening the duration of the note that follows. This is more true of the French style. ♩.. ♪ will be performed as ♩. ♪ The double dotting of the note will create the effect of a very short rest between it and the next note. When such a passage occurs at the same time as a triplet figure in another part, the dotted rhythm should be changed to conform to the triplet figure, as follows:

There are, however, occurrences in which the two figures should be played as written. The reader should refer to Dart's *The Interpretation of Music* and to Donington's *The Interpretation of Early Music* (both listed in the bibliography) for detailed information.

As with Renaissance music, tempos of Baroque works should also be moderate. Extremely fast or slow tempos should be avoided. The rhythm is motorlike, constantly pulsing, and very steady. Broad rallentandos are anachronistic. The terms allegro, presto, vivace, etc., were used to indicate the character of the music more than a specific tempo. Occasionally the term largo is found at the last phrase of a work. This should generally be interpreted as being twice as slow as the previous tempo. Its use in this case is a means of emphasis at the final cadence. Composers also "built in" such changes of tempo by using notes of greater duration. The conductor does not need to apply a ritard to these passages since its effect already exists in the notation. An added ritard will increase the tempo change and distort the composer's intention.

The underlying constant pulsation, a vital part of Baroque music, must be maintained, keeping in mind that the melodic line should not be punched, but performed with lyric ease. The Pergolesi *Magnificat,* published by Walton Music Corporation, is an example of this type of writing. The melodic line is lyric and rides on top of the motorlike eighth notes in the accompaniment. Accompanying instruments should be played in a slightly detached manner, which in addition to contributing to the style, prevents the performers from rushing the tempo.

Texture

The independent line of polyphony gave way to the concept of a single melodic line supported by chords. This change coincided with an evolvement of the major and minor system rather than the modal system of the Renaissance. The modes continued to be used for some time but the major and minor harmonic structure became more and more important. Although polyphony was rejected by many composers in the early Baroque, it emerged as a new counterpoint, more dependent on the harmonic movement.

Accompanied and unaccompanied singing were both acceptable in the Baroque. Instruments were used when desired or where practical, but a cappella performances were equally acceptable. There are instances of composers writing a choral work with a figured bass, and also copying the work for a choral collection with only the choral parts given, leaving out an indication for accompaniment. When instrumental parts do not exist for a given work, one should not automatically assume that instruments were not used. Instruments may have doubled the voice parts, a part may have been improvised, or the parts may have simply been lost. For instance, a cappella performances of Bach's motets are now questioned.

Modern instruments are constructed differently than those of the Baroque period; consequently, the tone of our present instruments is considerably different. In addition to the quality of sound, the balance of instruments and voices must be adjusted. A Baroque composer may have indicated a desire for sixteen voices and an equal number of instruments and would have been assured of an appropriate balance between the two groups. A conductor today that substitutes modern instruments and maintains the same number indicated above may find he has an inadequate number of voices. Even the most basic continuo part on a modern harpsichord and cello is noticeably different from that of an authentic harpsichord and gamba.

The soprano-bass polarity is important to the texture of music of this period. The soprano melody is supported by a strong bass line with many root movements. This can be demonstrated to a choir by having only these two parts sing. The strength of these parts will be apparent to the entire choir.

Variety was achieved by terraced dynamics, alternating instruments and voices, or by different combinations of voices and instruments. Dynamics changed at new sections and were usually constant during each section. Dynamic levels were moderate, staying between *piano* and *forte*. Excessive dynamics should generally be avoided.

Tone Quality

Although a wider range of emotions is possible, and a warmer tone quality employed in Baroque music, singers must again be cautioned against a wide vibrato. A wide vibrato will impede the rhythmic drive and directness of the music.

Tone painting, passages that depict the meaning of the text, can be emphasized without removing them from the musical flow. One may color the voice to match the desired quality of the music which in turn was written to depict the meaning of the words.

Composers of the Baroque Period

Giovanni Gabrieli (c. 1557-1612)
Jacopo Peri (1561-1633)
Claudio Monteverdi (1567-1643)
Michael Praetorius (c. 1571-1621)
Heinrich Schutz (1585-1672)
Johann Schein (1586-1630)
Samuel Scheidt (1587-1684)
Giacomo Carissimi (1605-1674)
Jean-Baptiste Lully (1632-1687)
Dietrich Buxtehude (c. 1637-1705)
Johann Pachelbel (1653-1707)
Giuseppe Pitoni (1657-1743)
Henry Purcell (1659-1695)
Alessandro Scarlatti (1659-1725)
Antonio Lotti (1667-1740)
Antonio Vivaldi (c. 1678-1741)
Johann Sebastian Bach (1685-1750)
Domenico Scarlatti (1685-1757)
George Friedrich Handel (1685-1759)
Giovanni Pergolesi (1710-1736)

Suggested Works for Study

Magnificat, Pergolesi (Walton)
Cantata, no. 142 (*For Us a Child Is Born*), Bach (Galaxy)
Magnificat, Charpentier (Concordia, #97-6343)
Nun Danket Alle Gott, Pachelbel (Robert King Music Co. #604)

The Classic Period (1750-1820)

Music in the Classic period existed under the patronage of the aristocracy. Some composers, Haydn for example, flourished under this arrangement while others, such as Mozart, did not. The development of the orchestra, sonata-allegro form, and the symphony meant increased importance for instrumental music. The symphony, piano sonata, and the opera took precedence over choral music during this period. Some of the most important choral music were the masses written for the Catholic church.

When we speak of the music of this period, we refer mainly to that of the Viennese school—Haydn, Mozart, Beethoven, and their contemporaries. Elements of the stile galant, Empfindsamer stil, Enlightenment, and Sturm und Drang are synthesized in their music. The music was formal, objective, and exquisitely balanced. The sacred music of the Viennese school was influenced by the opera and symphony.

Characteristics of Classic music include:

1. Importance of formal structure
2. Instrumental forces enlarged
3. Dynamic levels increased
4. Ornamentation restricted
5. Universal tonal language
6. Clarity and balance typify the music
7. Vertical structure—little counterpoint

Rhythm and Tempo

Although the music of the Classic period is refined, there are certainly moments of real power. Conductors must be careful not to allow heavy metrical accents that will destroy the style. At the same time conductors must be cautioned against performances that lack virility. The crisp rhythm should prompt the performers to respond with a crisp, clear articulation. A light beat and restrained gestures are appropriate when conducting much of the music.

In this period composers marked their scores with more specific tempo indications than preceding composers. The terms allegro, adagio, etc., referred to tempo and not just to the character of the music. Tempos are moderate and extremes are to be avoided.

Classic composers employed tempo rubato, but with greater restraint than it is later used. Basically, a strict tempo should be followed with tempo rubato carefully applied where the text seems to demand its use. Accelerando and rallentando are also used in music of the period, particularly in the last part of the period. Again, reserve and restraint must be applied to their use.

Texture

The Classic period was one of clarity and stability. Where the Baroque texture had been weighty, the Classic is lighter. Although contrapuntalism is found occasionally (especially in the Masses), most of the music is vertical in structure with the inner parts receiving more attention than in the Baroque. Melody is important, and is supported by the entire harmonic structure, rather than by a strong bass line.

Formal structure became a primary concern, and ornamentation, while still prominent, is more restrictive. Composers are reluctant to rely on the performers for accurate interpretations, and more instructions to the performer are included in the music.

Dynamics

Terraced dynamics gave way to crescendos and decrescendos. Contrast in dynamics is vital to the music but the dynamic range does not reach the extremes of the Romantic period. The crescendos and decrescendos generally mean to increase or decrease the dynamic level one point (*Mp* to *Mf* or *Mf* to *Mp*). More extreme crescendos and decrescendos are the exception rather than the rule. Greater contrasts are indicated by dynamic level markings rather than through crescendos or decrescendos. These dynamic shadings were enlarged as a transition was made into the Romantic period.

Special attention must be called to the practice of contrasting successive identical phrases. When the first is *forte,* the repetition is usually *piano.* The reverse is also true.

Composers of the Classic Period

Christoph Willibald Gluck (1714-1787)
Franz Joseph Haydn (1732-1809)
Michael Haydn (1737-1806)
William Billings (1746-1800)
Wolfgang Amadeus Mozart (1756-1791)
Luigi Cherubini (1760-1842)
Ludwig van Beethoven (1770-1827)

Suggested Works for Study

Missa Brevis in F, Mozart (G. Schirmer)
Lord Nelson Mass, Haydn (C. F. Peters)
David's Lamentation, Billings (Walton Music Corp.)
Mount of Olives, Beethoven (G. Schirmer)

The Romantic Period (1820-1900)

Heralded by the French Revolution, the Romantic period was one of subjectivity. The artist, no longer supported by the aristocracy, enjoyed the role of a castoff, meagerly existing in a garret as a rebel against society. The music is intensely emotional, deriving its strength from massive forces and vivid orchestration.

Choral music takes a back seat to the symphony and opera. However, a number of composers contributed great choral works to the repertoire, and works for large chorus and orchestras rank among the finest works of the century. A cappella repertoire is found in small amounts but several composers, including Brahms and Bruckner, wrote beautiful and moving unaccompanied settings.

Characteristics of Romantic music include:

1. Less emphasis on form
2. More emphasis on texture and color (orchestration)
3. Subjectivity is important to both composers and performers
4. Chromaticism
5. Wide contrasts in dynamics and tempos
6. Composers explored the limits of the major-minor harmonic system
7. Program music became important
8. Almost completely vertical structure

Rhythm and Tempo

One does not find the technique of changing meters used as it is used in the twentieth century, but the effect of changing the meter without changing the meter signature was achieved by displaced accents. Other methods of syncopation and intricate rhythm problems were a part of the subjectivity of the music.

Tempos range from extremely slow to extremely fast, and are related to the mood of the music. Where tempos had been moderate before, they were excessive in the Romantic period. Fast tempos were very fast and slow tempos were taken very slow. Abrupt changes of tempo are also found often.

Tempo rubato was employed often and to the fullest possible extent. Every opportunity to exploit the mood of the music was taken. Accelerando and rallentando were also employed frequently, and with greater abandon than in previous periods.

Texture

The harmonic possibilities of tonality were explored by the Romantic composers. As a result, more chromaticism and dissonance are found in the music. Late in the century cadences were obscured or avoided entirely. The texture was a rich full one that employed every instrumental and vocal possibility. The music is vertical and opportunities to color the vocal sound should be taken to achieve the rich sonority demanded. Full, mature voices are needed for the best performances of this repertoire. Without a contrapuntal element, much of the choral music is static, relying on beauty of tone for its success.

Dynamics

The dynamic scheme is the broadest yet, from *pppp* to *ffff*. Excessive dynamics are employed in many instances. Sharp contrasts of dynamics are also found often. The short, but far-reaching crescendo is commonplace (*p* to *f* in a measure or less). The dynamic scheme of Romantic music allows greater freedom for the conductor to achieve the greatest possible contrast with an ensemble. The difficulty of such a freedom is that the proportion of the dynamics is often lost. When does *ff* become *fff?* A judicious balance must always be maintained dynamically, so the full impact of each level can be felt and heard.

Romantic music is very expressive. Where the Classic composer's goal was formal objectivity, the Romantic's was personal freedom of expression. Tone color was most important to their compositional style, and is always an important consideration to conductors.

Composers of the Romantic Period

Karl Maria von Weber (1786-1826)
Gioacchino Rossini (1792-1868)
Franz Schubert (1797-1828)
Hector Berlioz (1803-1869)
M. I. Glinka (1804-1857)
Felix Mendelssohn (1809-1847)
Robert Schumann (1810-1856)
Franz Lizst (1811-1886)
Richard Wagner (1813-1883)
Giuseppe Verdi (1813-1901)
Robert Franz (1815-1892)
Charles F. Gounod (1818-1893)
Cesar Franck (1822-1890)
Anton Bruckner (1824-1896)
Johannes Brahms (1833-1897)
Camille Saint-Saens (1835-1921)
Theodore Dubois (1837-1924)
John Stainer (1840-1901)
Antonin Dvorak (1841-1904)
Gabriel Faure (1845-1924)
Leos Janacek (1854-1928)
Edward Elgar (1857-1934)
Mikhail Ippolitox-Ivanov (1859-1935)
Hugo Wolf (1860-1903)
Sergei Rachmaninoff (1873-1943)
Paul Tschesnokov (1877-1944)

Suggested Works for Study

Create in Me, op. 29 no. 2, Brahms (G. Schirmer #7504)
Liebeslieder Walzer, op. 65, Brahms (Lawson-Gould)
Salvation Is Created, Tschesnokov (J. Fischer #4129)

He Watching over Israel, Mendelssohn (G. Schirmer)
Mass in E Minor, Bruckner (C. F. Peters)
Requiem, Faure (G. Schirmer)
German Requiem, Brahms (C. F. Peters)
Mass in G, Schubert (G. Schirmer)

The Twentieth Century

The divergent musical styles of the Twentieth Century include impressionism, neo-classicism, post-romanticism, pan-diatonicism, twelve-tone, electronic, and aleatory (indeterminacy). Composers at the end of the nineteenth century realized that Romanticism had reached its peak and that new directions were necessary if music was to continue to grow. The reader is referred to discussions of these various styles in several books listed at the end of this chapter. This discussion is directed toward the general performance considerations of twentieth century music.

Characteristics of twentieth century music include:

1. Numerous meter changes
2. Exploration beyond limits of tonality
3. Pointillism
4. Nonsinging vocal sounds
5. Acceptance of any sound source as valid
6. Composers renew interest in small ensembles
7. Complex scores
8. A new music notation
9. Aleatoric composition (performance is dependent on chance)
10. Increasing demands on the vocalist
11. Increased dissonance (the term dissonance becomes obsolete in the discussion of new music after the middle of the century)
12. Growing number of choral works demanding limited staging, lighting or similar effects

Rhythm and Tempo

Use of rhythm in Twentieth Century music is varied. Composers strive to achieve a variety of rhythmic accents and groupings. Intricate rhythm patterns are usual. Twentieth Century composers use rhythm as a means of achieving tension. Many composers utilize changing meters to achieve rhythmic variety and excitement. Choral composers often use this technique in an attempt to create a musical inflection of the text. Constant meter changes are not unusual. Each use must be examined individually; no one solution can be applied to all occurrences. The conductor must determine the simplest and most direct method of realizing the intention of the composer.

Tempo is related to the musical style and mood of the text. Extremes in tempo are frequently found. Tempo changes are often abrupt and require skillful handling by the conductor. Composers mark their scores carefully and use metronome markings to indicate the tempo they prefer. A conductor should respect these markings, and consider them as guidelines to their performance tempos. Of course, he must also consider the performance hall acoustics, ensemble size, and performers.

Texture

Many and varied textures are demanded in Twentieth Century choral music. There has been an interest in chamber choirs by composers. This is both a reaction against the gigantic forces used by the later nineteenth century composers, and a practical consideration utilizing smaller groups to perform complex scores. Each score must be examined carefully regarding texture. Impressionistic and post-romantic music usually involve a vertical structure whose harmonic movement is fluid, with an emphasis on harmony and beauty of tone. Twelve-tone scores are more horizontal and less emphasis is placed on individual chords. Its dissonance demands a tone quality with a minimal vibrato. Additionally, the singers must be thoroughly skilled in the singing of intervals in order to learn and perform this repertoire.

Twentieth Century composers often utilize a number of textures and moods within one work, changing both texture and mood often. Wide variations in tone quality will be necessary to make these changes effective. Although most of the choral music performed is only mildly dissonant, more avant-garde music is finding its way into performance halls. Electronic music is not really new, but music for prepared tape and chorus has only recently been accepted by most choral conductors (and performed by only a modest percentage of those). Aleatoric (indeterminate or chance) pieces are performed by the more adventurous conductor. Works that are considered avant-garde are likely to require anything from a normal singing tone to whistling, whispering, and other assorted vocal sounds.

More textural possibilities exist today than ever before. The choral conductor may find music for chorus and many instrumental combinations which substantially expand the texture. It is the conductor's responsibility to understand the tonal and textural requirements of each work, and to determine whether or not his ensemble can meet these requirements. Not every choir or conductor will be able to successfully meet the performance requirements of each work.

Dynamics

The dynamic range is even wider than that of the Romantic period since it now includes whispering, singing as loud as one can, and even yelling.

Sudden changes in dynamics are also more numerous than ever before. Many works even require a dynamic scheme that changes on every count of the measure for several measures. It is quite usual to find different dynamic indications in different parts on the same passage. For example, the composer may wish the tenors and sopranos to be prominent and will mark them *forte* while the bass is marked *mezzo-forte* and the alto, *piano*. Although this type of dynamic scheme is not new, it is used more frequently by Twentieth Century composers.

Tone Quality

Twentieth Century choral music requires many different tone qualities. Less than other periods, no one choral tone will suffice. It can be said that a tone with a minimal vibrato is usually best because of the numerous occurrence of small intervals and the overall dissonance of the music.

Specific types of tone quality are occasionally requested by composers. Conductors will find such requests as "with a full, rich tone," "sing with a thin, white tone," or simply "senza vibrato" in scores. This is a result of a composer wishing to to achieve a certain sonority usually prompted by the text.

Special Requirements of New Music

Since the 1950s, composers have incorporated aleatoric aspects into their compositions. Many works are published that combine traditional and non-traditional notation. The problems that face the conductor of much new music are:

1. Determining the meaning of the notation (when nontraditional)
2. Convincing the choir that the new sounds are valid musical choices
3. Achieving a thread of continuity through a work that utilizes several twentieth century techniques

Each new work must be thoroughly examined to understand the composer's intent. This is true of all music, of course. Every new work may have its own particular notation unlike any other piece, even another by the same composer. New notation follows only such rules as the composer may apply to a specific work. There is no standard, although a few notational features are being used consistently by a number of composers to mean the same thing. This use is approaching a standard and one will eventually be set. Usually composers place an explanation of their notation in a foreword to the score. Performance suggestions may also be included.

It is most important that the conductor have the complete confidence of his choir in order to successfully perform aleatoric music. The conductor must also accept the music as being valid and be willing to work as hard on that music as he would on any traditional piece. The rehearsal planning will be different but nonetheless important. (See chapter ten for a discussion of score analysis of aleatoric music.)

Music for prepared tape and choir has become plentiful recently and has received a number of performances. As with all music, the quality of these works vary and conductors must judge each work on its own merits. Several works will no doubt become "standard" pieces in the choral repertoire while others will be discarded.

Conductors should be cautioned about use of tape and voices together. Unless a certain quality is specified by the composer, a full singing tone should be employed. The tone should be vibrant, containing a minimal amount of vibrato, and not be an attempt to mimic the electronic sounds. The composer is aware of the natural qualities of the human voice and wishes to capitalize on the difference between the voice and the taped sounds. He does not expect one to sound like the other, except where carefully specified.

Another important consideration is the quality of playback equipment. Conductors should use only high quality tape and speaker systems. The full dimensions of tape music cannot otherwise be realized.

Choral Composers of the Twentieth Century

Claude Debussy (1862-1918)
Frederick Delius (1862-1934)
Ralph Vaughan Williams (1872-1958)
Gustav von Holst (1874-1934)
Charles Ives (1874-1954)
Martin Shaw (1875-1958)
Ernest Bloch (1880-1959)
Healey Willan (1880-1969)
Bela Bartok (1881-1945)
Zoltan Kodaly (1882-1967)
Igor Stravinsky (1882-1971)
Heitor Villa-Lobos (1887-1959)
Ernst Toch (1887-1964)
Arthur Honegger (1892-1955)
Darius Milhaud (1892-   )
Paul Hindemith (1895-1963)
Leo Sowerby (1895-1968)
Carl Orff (1895-   )
Howard Hanson (1896-   )
Virgil Thomson (1896-   )
Roy Harris (1898-   )
Francis Poulenc (1899-1963)
Carlos Chavez (1899-   )
Randall Thompson (1899-   )

Sven Lekberg (1899-   )
Aaron Copland (1900-   )
Jean Berger (1901-   )
William Walton (1902-   )
Paul Creston (1906-   )
Normand Lockwood (1906-   )
Hugo Distler (1908-1942)
Samuel Barber (1910-   )
William Schuman (1910-   )
Benjamin Britten (1913-   )
Norman Dello Joio (1913-   )
Irving Fine (1914-1962)
Gail Kubik (1914-   )
Vincent Persichetti (1915-   )
Paul Fetler (1920-   )
William Bergsma (1921-   )
Lukas Foss (1922-   )
Daniel Pinkham (1923-   )
Leslie Bassett (1923-   )

Suggested Works for Study

Collect (with electronic tape), Bassett (World Library of Sacred Music)
Nine Choral Fragments (aleatory), Childs (Keynote Music Co.)
All the Ways of a Man, Nystedt (Augsburg Pub. Hse.)
Carols of Death, Schuman (G. Schirmer)
Rejoice in the Lamb, Britten (Boosey and Hawkes)
Christmas Cantata, Pinkham (Robert King Music Co.)
Aleatory Psalm, Lamb (World Library of Sacred Music)
Household Magic, Kubik (MCA Music Corp.)

Discussion Questions

1. What musical style is the most difficult for amateur singers to perform?
2. Is it stylistically incorrect to perform Renaissance motets with a fifty or or sixty voice choir? Can performances of Renaissance music by a large ensemble be musically rewarding?
3. How far can one go toward authenticity in the performance of early music?
4. How would performance practice differ between music of the Renaissance and the Baroque; the Baroque and Classic; the Classic and Romantic?
5. What are the difficulties encountered by a conductor who wishes to perform Baroque music as it was originally performed?
6. To what degree should a performance represent the composer's wishes? To what degree should it represent the conductor's wishes?

SUGGESTED READINGS

Apel, Willi. *Harvard Dictionary of Music.* 2d ed., rev. Cambridge, Mass.: Harvard University Press, 1969.

Bukofzer, Manfred F. *Music in the Baroque Era: From Monteverdi to Bach.* New York: W. W. Norton & Company, Inc., 1947.

Cope, David. *New Directions in Music.* Dubuque, Iowa: Wm. C. Brown Company, Publishers, 1971.

Crocker, Richard L. *A History of Musical Style.* New York: McGraw-Hill Book Company, 1966.

Dart, Thurston. *The Interpretation of Music.* Rev. ed. London: Hutchinson University Library, 1960.

Dolmetsch, Arnold. *The Interpretation of the Music of the Seventeenth and Eighteenth Centuries.* London: Oxford University Press, 1946.

Donington, Robert. *The Interpretation of Music.* London: Faber and Faber Limited, 1963.

Grout, Donald Jay. *A History of Western Music.* New York: W. W. Norton & Company, Inc., 1960.

Hansen, Peter S. *An Introduction to Twentieth Century Music.* 2d ed. Boston: Allyn and Bacon, Inc., 1967.

Lang, Paul Henry. *Music in Western Civilization.* New York: W. W. Norton & Company, Inc., 1941.

Machlis, Joseph. *The Enjoyment of Music.* 3d ed. New York: W. W. Norton & Company, Inc., 1970.

Pooler, Frank, and Pierce, Brent. *New Choral Notation (A Handbook).* New York: Walton Music Corporation, 1971.

Reese, Gustave. *Music in the Renaissance.* New York: W. W. Norton & Company, Inc., 1954.

Strunk, Oliver, Ed. *Source Readings in Music History.* New York: W. W. Norton & Company, Inc., 1950.

Ulrich, Homer, and Pisk, Paul A. *A History of Music and Musical Style.* New York: Harcourt, Brace & World, Inc., 1963.

III

**ORGANIZATION
AND
MANAGEMENT**

chapter 12.

organizing small ensembles

There are several types of small ensembles that can be formed from the membership of the concert choir, including the madrigal, chamber choir, mixed quartets, swing choir, etc. Each will vary in its makeup and in the repertoire it will perform. Two of these possibilities will be discussed in this chapter—the madrigal group and the chamber choir.

First, one must ask, "Do I need or want a smaller, more select ensemble?" The answer will ultimately depend on the situation and the people involved. Most directors and schools find these ensembles to be desirable. They give the most talented students an opportunity to be involved with repertoire that they would not otherwise be able to sing. It also gives the finest choral students a chance to become more musically involved than the large choir experience will allow. The choral director also has a chance to work with the most gifted students in a unique situation and with a repertoire he would otherwise miss.

The administration can usually see the advantage for the fewer highly gifted and motivated music students. They will also probably view the group as a good public relations vehicle for the school. This attitude is normal and although it may not be culturally idealistic, it does provide an opportunity for this type of ensemble to flourish.

The concert choir can perform a wide variety of repertoire but there are some works that lend themselves to performance by a smaller number of singers. It is also easier to meet short notice performances with a smaller ensemble. Fifteen to twenty singers can be more easily excused from classes for a performance than sixty or seventy.

The Madrigal

A most popular ensemble and one with a ready-made repertoire is the madrigal. Although the madrigal does not have to be limited to the music of

195

the Renaissance, it should include these pieces as a stable part of its repertoire. A madrigal may also perform chamber vocal music from any period and some choral music. One must be extremely careful regarding the choice of choral music, however, to be sure that it is adaptable to a small number of voices.

Number of Students

How many voices should there be in a madrigal ensemble? This is a question most often heard and discussed regarding madrigals. The answer to this depends on the talent and on the types of voices that are available.

There are a number of so-called madrigals performing in the United States with sixteen to twenty singers and occasionally more. Ensembles of this size, though they may be well trained, often sound more like a choir than a madrigal group.

Madrigals and other repertoire of a similar nature are best performed with two and, no more than, three to a part. Some of the finest madrigal ensembles number between nine and fourteen. This size is large enough to develop a full tone and small enough to be adaptable, and somewhat soloistic when necessary. In this ensemble, one may have two to a part for up to seven parts.

This size of ensemble (and many other groups) should contain several *floating* voices; that is, voices that are capable of singing two parts. A first alto that can sing lower soprano parts or a baritone that can sing some of the tenor parts will be valuable in a madrigal. The repertoire for madrigal ensembles contains many different scorings. If a director has several voices that can switch parts at almost any time he will find it much easier to properly balance the ensemble.

Flexibility

A most important requirement for voices in a madrigal group is that they should be flexible. One often hears that light voices are best for madrigal singing. This is not as important as flexibility. Madrigal voices need to be able to sing a ringing *forte* as well as an intense *piano*. A small ensemble that does not have a wide dynamic range can be at least as boring as a choir with the same deficiency. An entire ensemble of light voices will not have dramatic capabilities.

Large voices tend to be less flexible and, for this reason, are often undesirable for madrigal singing. That a voice is large is, in itself, insufficient reason to eliminate it. It is difficult to gain a unity of qualities, however, if one voice is of much greater size or more mature than the rest. If the larger voices are flexible, though, they will be an asset to the ensemble.

Intonation

Another important consideration is intonation. This is always important to a choral ensemble, but its importance is magnified in a small ensemble. This is one of the most crucial points in the selection of members. If the person has a poor ear or lacks the vocal technique to sing in tune, it is best to leave them out of a madrigal. It may be difficult to omit what may seem to be an outstanding voice quality, but if the person cannot sing in tune, he or she will be a constant problem in rehearsals and performances. Make intonation one of the most important parts of the selection process.

Blend

This characteristic of good choral singing is also important, but in a different way, for a madrigal ensemble than for a choir. Originally, much of the repertoire was performed with one person on a part, singing or perhaps even playing the part on an instrument. If your definition of blend means a "complete merging of all voices," you will probably develop a boring madrigal and may not even like to hear smaller ensembles. The blend of a madrigal is one of matching qualities rather than the "complete merging of the voices." In a small ensemble it will be possible to hear individual voices. There is nothing wrong with this. An individual flair is important to the success of the ensemble. Yet, there will be moments when all of the voices will merge as one. Do not be afraid to allow individuality in a madrigal. Be sure that "blend" does not become "bland."

Reading Ability

Every director would like to have only good music readers in his ensembles. Unfortunately, this is rarely the case at the amateur level. A director can be only as strict in this regard as the level of his students allows. It would be useless to require that all students in the madrigal be able to read all of the music at sight if, by doing so, one eliminates all students from consideration. The ability to learn the music will determine the complexity and amount of repertoire the ensemble will be able to perform. The ability to learn is of more importance than the ability to sight-read. If the student is so motivated that he takes the music home and learns his part quickly, he is equally as valuable as the person who can accomplish the same thing within your rehearsal. Often, the former will be a more valuable member because of his eagerness to contribute to the ensemble. In any event, be as strict as the situation will allow. If there is a choice between two otherwise equal candidates, choose the one that will learn the music the quickest.

Nonsinging Considerations

Members of a madrigal ensemble need to be able to project the music to an audience. They should be personable students who are able to reflect the drama of the music in their faces and with their gestures.

It is also desirable to have students who can move gracefully. You may not wish to have them dance but the members will occasionally need to move about in front of an audience. They must be able to do this with confidence.

Each member must be willing to make some sacrifice for the ensemble. Students must want to be chosen for the madrigal. The infectious enthusiasm of a few students, selected for a group that has prestige, is a major factor, not only to the success of that group, but to the success of the choral department. People that are selected for the madrigal should be secure academically because the rehearsal and performance demands can become rigorous at times.

Use of Instruments

Instruments can lend variety to a concert of vocal chamber music. Several instruments are particularly suited to the madrigal ensemble.

The recorder, forerunner of the modern flute, is enjoying a return to popularity. It has a pleasant tone that is complimentary to voices, particularly to high school voices. It is relatively easy to learn to play; a good student should be able to learn to play most madrigal part lines within a week. If some members have had training on other instruments, it would be advantageous to use them on recorders. They will probably learn to play the instrument quicker than noninstrumentalists. It is easiest to begin using soprano and alto recorders and add the tenor and bass as desired. Several recorder dealers are listed in Appendix B.

Experiment with recorders and voices. Use the recorders on the voice parts doubling the voices; use them instead of voices on one or two parts; use them alone for a section or verse of a piece. Recorders can add an enjoyable dimension to the madrigal ensemble.

Other instruments can also be used. The harpsichord is not as easy to acquire as the recorder but, when available, it is a worthy addition. A modern flute can often be used. There is usually a flutist of adequate ability available from the instrumental department.

Several percussion instruments can easily be used—finger cymbals, tabor, tambourine, etc. Be sure to keep the use of percussion to small instruments and their playing time at a minimum. They can be effective if used tastefully, but are ruinous when used without discretion.

Above all, be imaginative regarding the use of instruments. The *a cappella* madrigal is a myth. When the madrigal was at its peak of popularity there was no hesitancy to use instruments with the voices or in place of part, or all of the voices.

The Chamber Choir (an all-purpose ensemble)

Another ensemble that is often desirable is a group of singers also chosen from the concert choir that is not limited to the performance of vocal chamber music. These ensembles more often range in size from fourteen to fifteen to as many as thirty singers. The term chamber choir is used here for lack of another term which adequately describes the ensemble. It is really an all-purpose group.

This group may perform a variety of repertoire, including folk music, popular music, sacred, and serious secular music. It is a valuable ensemble because its repertoire can be tapered to meet specific performance needs. If a performance at a local service club is scheduled, music can be chosen from the ensemble's repertoire that will be enjoyable and interesting to that particular audience. Some of the music the group may perform can be chosen from the concert choir's repertoire.

The size of this group may also vary but it is usually better to have more students than in a madrigal. It will be easier to perform a varied repertoire with a few more singers. Actually, eighteen to twenty-four singers is a good size, offering *divisi* capabilities, but still small enough for limited movement. The membership of this ensemble may include the madrigal singers, who are then available to perform several pieces as part of the program.

It is important to stress that this group should perform many different kinds of music. There is a need for high school students to sing light music. This should be balanced by a similar amount of serious music for the same ensemble. This author is convinced that high school singers can and will enjoy both kinds of music. It is not necessary to form a group that sings only the popular music of the day. The ensemble should not be limited only to the "throw away" music whose popularity is based more on an emotional or fad appeal than on musical value.

Choose from the popular types of music just as you would from the serious. Apply the selection criteria guide in chapter seven. If the text is in poor taste, don't perform it; if the parts are poorly written, don't perform it; if unstressed syllables are stressed unmusically, don't perform it; in short, if it can't measure up to the criteria by which you measure serious repertoire, one should not perform it.

Concert Dress

The concert dress of this ensemble can be appropriate to the fashions of the year and to the school or community. Some groups tie their attire in with the traditions of the school, for example, the Vikings, the Indians, the Irish, etc. When this seems undesirable, a concert dress that relates to the particular area of the state or country is often worthwhile. When either is not wanted, a costume can be designed that is specific only to the group. Students can be quite imaginative in the designing of their costumes and, with a little guidance, often create outstanding ones.

Naming the Group

The name of the group can also be suggested by the students. Again, it can be an outgrowth of the school traditions, reflect the area, or be entirely original with the group. When a group of this type is formed, it is best to invite the students to participate in the selection of apparel, names, and later in decisions that affect the group, such as trips, number of performances per semester, etc. All musical matters, of course, are clearly the responsibility of only one person, the director. In other areas students can be found to be resourceful, imaginative, level-headed, and capable of much self-management. One must guide them, allow them to err inconspicuously, and encourage them as they recover from their mistakes.

If a group is quite active, officers can be helpful, not only from the student's standpoint of developing leadership capabilities, but from the director's standpoint as well, relieving him of some management problems. For every group that is successful with officers however, there is another that is equally as successful, and happy, without. Let such things happen as natural succession of events. They will be more meaningful and more successful.

Student Exploitation

A word of caution must be made regarding the number and type of performances that an ensemble of this nature should give. Students may learn as much about music, and the stimulation of performance from fifteen performances as they can from forty-five performances. A limit of some type should be placed on the number of performances the group will present in one year; the number of times the students will be released from school for performances; the number of weekend performances; and the number of out-of-town trips. When an invitation to perform occurs that is in excess of the established performing guidelines, the school administration and students should be consulted before any decision is made.

Students can be exploited for the benefit of the school's public image or to increase the popularity or the reputation of the conductor. Trips that will not contribute to the students' musical and educational growth should not be taken. If the group is successful, there will undoubtedly be performance opportunities that are beyond the usual performance goals of the ensemble. Each opportunity must be weighed carefully to determine if it really is an opportunity, and for whom the opportunity really exists, the director or the students.

Discussion Questions

1. Will students today be enthused about performing music of several centuries ago and with some of the appropriate instruments?
2. How can a director know the difference between music that can be successfully performed by a madrigal and that which cannot?
3. How many performances should a special ensemble give during one school year?
4. Must a director lower the selection standards in order to accommodate the inclusion of popular music? Can popular music meet the criteria as given in chapter seven?
5. Under what conditions is it justified to project a tour for high school students that will last several days?
6. If a director cannot meet with either of the ensembles discussed in this chapter during the regular school day, should he postpone organizing them until they can be incorporated in the school schedule?

SUGGESTED READINGS

Dart, Thurston. *The Interpretation of Music,* pp. 140-49. New York: Harper and Row, 1963.

Grentzer, Rose Marie. "The Chamber Ensemble." *Choral Director's Guide,* pp. 55-76. Edited by Neidig and Jennings. West Nyack, N. Y.: Parker Publishing, 1967.

Wilson, Harry R. *Music in the High School,* pp. 148-52. New York: Silver Burdette Co., 1946.

Young, Percy. *The Choral Tradition,* pp. 51-54. New York: W. W. Norton and Co., 1962.

chapter 13.

clinics, festivals, and contests

Clinics, festivals, and contests are held in every state and can be valuable aids to a choral department. None of these events by themselves can provide a complete choral program, but any or all of them can supplement a well-rounded program. Each of these activities can be valuable parts of a choral program if used carefully and effectively, but no one activity should become the peak of the department's goals. Rather than having one point toward which the efforts of the students and the director are pressed, the choral year should have several peaks of activity, all important, all enjoyed to the fullest. No one activity is more important than any other, but is a direct complement to the others, contributing to the growth of the choral department and receiving strength from the rest of the activities. When this is the case, every student in the department will have at least one activity that he will find the most enjoyable. Since every student will not enjoy the same things, several activities will best meet the interests of all students.

The terms clinics, festivals, and contests are used interchangeably throughout the country. Each term will be defined before its discussion in this chapter.

Clinics

A clinic involves a critique of an ensemble or ensembles, as well as a rehearsal with a clinician. Clinics do not usually culminate in a performance, at least, not a public performance.

Clinics can be very advantageous to a director who knows how to use them. The best clinic is the one that you can have in your own school for your own students. This type of a clinic allows you to make maximum use of the funds spent for a clinician.

There are several ways a clinic can be arranged to provide a valuable experience for your students. The most attractive schedule would be one that allowed you to have the clinic on a school day and have the students released from classes, when necessary, to attend the clinic sessions. Obviously, this is not possible in every school. It can only be possible through the cooperation of the administration. The expense is probably no greater than any other type of clinic but the scheduling problems are more complex. However, this can be dealt with by arranging a schedule as closely as possible to the normal school schedule. In this manner you can show an administrator that the students will actually miss a small amount of non-music class time.

The illustration given in figure 81 is an example of a schedule that expands the normal school schedule.

Clinic Schedule		Normal Schedule	
8:30	Mixed Chorus	8:30	Homeroom
		8:50	Mixed Chorus
9:50	Girls' Chorus	9:50	Girls' Chorus
		10:50	Director's Free Period
11:15	Lunch	11:50	Lunch
	(clinician, local director, principal, choir president, etc.)		
1:00	Concert Choir	1:00	Concert Choir
3:00	Boys' Chorus	2:00	Boys' Chorus
4:00	End of clinic	3:00	Small Ensembles

Figure 81

The schedule does not require choral students to miss much class time. The clinic times overlap the normal rehearsal hours whenever possible. The first group would only miss the homeroom period, while the second ensemble would need to be excused from the first twenty-five minutes of the 10:50 class. The only other conflict occurs with the concert choir (the best mixed ensemble). It is best if the clinician can spend two hours with these students. Anything less than two hours with the top students will not allow the clinician to be effective. The boys' chorus that would ordinarily meet would have to be delayed one hour.

Although this schedule may appear to be a heavy extension of choral time, it really only asks a principal to release choral students from one hour and twenty-five minutes of classes. When compared to the number of hours of school missed by student athletes during the year, one hour and twenty-five minutes will really be a very small request. In fact, the periodic (but constant) interruptions from the administrative office will take more of the student's time in less than one semester than the clinic time requested.

Several other scheduling possibilities exist, including a half day clinic,

or a clinic on Saturday (that would not require any release of class time).
An interesting possibility is a clinic that begins when classes are dismissed for
the day. This clinic could involve a one and one-half hour rehearsal, an
evening meal (choir members and clinician), and a one and one-half to two
hour rehearsal in the evening. This type of clinic is best limited to only one
ensemble and should be utilized for the best performing choir.

This type of clinic has the advantage of not using any school time and
provides three or more hours of concentrated clinic work with one choir. It
is most desirable in large schools where choral students are not involved in
after school athletic programs. It will be more difficult to arrange in smaller
schools where students participate in several activities.

A Saturday clinic could involve one choir or several choirs from the same
school. A clinic on Saturday is often not as desirable because of the number
of students that work on Saturdays or become involved in many nonschool
activities. A clinic held during the regular school day also has the psychological advantage of seeming more important to the students. Students tend
to associate an importance with events that they are released from class to
attend.

The schedule on a Saturday could be as flexible as the local director would
like to have it. If it involves only one choir, a full day's efforts will be a little
too long. In this case, a three to four hour session, with a long break is most
advantageous. When more than one ensemble is included, it is best to spend
at least two and a half hours with the best ensemble. These are the students
most likely to respond to the clinician's directions and to understand his comments about the music. More than an hour with the younger ensembles, or
less talented groups will prove to be too long. They are less able to grasp the
meaning of the clinician's comments and it is more difficult for a clinician to
demonstrate with these ensembles. When possible, they should definitely be
involved in rehearsal with the clinician, however.

The timing of a clinic is quite important. There is no point in bringing a
clinician to a school before the students know the notes. It would be ridiculous
to utilize a clinician's talents for note-chasing. On the other hand, it is not
good to hold the clinic too close to the date of a concert. A clinician will feel
that his hands are tied, that it is too close to the concert for him to change
phrasing or make major suggestions. Plan to bring in a clinician at a point in
your rehearsal schedule when the notes are learned and the students are free
to respond to his musical suggestions. This time will vary with every choir,
but a point approximately two weeks before a concert will probably work well
for most ensembles.

While the clinician is rehearsing the ensemble, the director should be
constantly observing and taking notes of all items of interest. He should also
write down any questions that he will later be able to ask the clinician. Do not

ask questions of the clinician while his work is in progress. This will only slow him down and interrupt the flow of the rehearsal, a rehearsal that is limited already by the schedule.

After the clinician has rehearsed the choir, or choirs, plan to have thirty to sixty minutes during which you can discuss performance practice of the works in question, ask him any questions you may have jotted down, and get his suggestions for continued progress with the choir. This discussion can be held over a cup of coffee, but it is important that you have the opportunity to spend some time alone with the clinician and discuss the day's events.

The selection of a clinician is crucial to the success of the clinic. He should be a person who has had some experience with high school age students. He should also be able to offer something musically that will expand the musical understanding of the choir. He has to have the ability to step in front of a new choir, analyze their performance, identify the problems, know the cause, and have several ideas on how to solve the problem. His choral philosophy should not be radically different than your own. While it is valuable to get new ideas, it is detrimental to have a clinician whose choral ideals are completely opposite to your own.

Not every choral conductor makes a good clinician. Some conductor's personalities do not lend themselves to the openness and warmth that must be present in a clinician. Other conductors are effective with their own students, whom they have in a specific rehearsal situation daily, but are not able to communicate with other choirs in a short period of time.

In the final analysis, much of the success of a clinic will depend on the local director. If he fails to plan properly for the clinic, it may be only fifty percent (or less) as effective as it otherwise would be. In the days leading up to the clinic, the students must be prepared to respond to a new director and his suggestions. It is a good idea to obtain some information from the clinician about himself so the students will have some idea of his background. If possible, have his picture on a bulletin board in the choral room and some information about the clinician with it. Since students will not know as much about the clinician as you will, it is up to the local director to heighten their enthusiasm for the clinic, and discussing the clinician with them will help to do this.

The students must be ready to accept new tempos and possible new interpretations without viewing them as strange and somehow wrong. Young students often assume the tempos or interpretations of their director are the only possible ones for a given piece of music. The director that promotes his own image with his students will find it difficult to free his students from this idolatry and help them to accept the ideas of another conductor. There is no reason that the local director should attempt to sterilize a piece of music and avoid trying to interpret it in order to keep it free for the clinician. Simply go ahead and teach as you would normally teach and try to achieve the best musical result you can achieve. If the clinician finds your interpretation radically different from his, he can quickly comment that he would like to try another interpretation and the students will probably respond very quickly for him. If he finds the interpretation much different on one selection, he may not wish to rehearse it but will wait and discuss it in detail with the director. The local director should not be too concerned about the number of things a clinician may find wrong with the choir. He will often be surprised at the number of points the clincian will make that will reinforce his own teaching. These are often as valuable as new points because they confirm his teaching and increase the students' confidence in him. It is always good for the students to hear from an "expert" some of the same things a director has said. They tend to listen more carefully to the statements made by a clinician, particularly from somebody that is new to them.

In the days that follow the clinic, the local director can pursue the points established by the clinician. After the session between the director and clinician, the director should spend several hours carefully examining all the music and the comments made by the clinician. A clinician often will demonstrate a phrase several different ways with a choir to illustrate to the choir and to the director that there are several possible and valid interpretations. If it is possible to tape record the clinic sessions, a director will find study of these tapes quite valuable. He may then study the different interpretations a clinician may use and determine the one that seems to get the most musical sound from the choir.

In some instances it may be desirable to sponsor a choral clinic and invite neighboring schools to participate. This can stimulate more choral activity in the area and improve the quality of all the groups.

It is apparent that the value from a clinic is only obtained by solid groundwork laid by the director, stimulating sessions between the students and clinician, and careful follow-up to the clinic itself. It must also be remembered that a clinic is not a cure-all for poor teaching. Although the choir may temporarily respond to a good clinician, they will soon revert to their previous level of performance. A clinic should *not* be used as a device to prepare the choir for a choral contest. Most directors that attempt to do this, bring a clinician in far too late and expect him to make it possible for the ensemble to receive a superior rating. In short, a clinic should not be used except as an integral part of the complete year's activities. It is one of several means of supplementing the choral program and adding another dimension to the choral education of the students.

Festivals

The term, choral festival, as used here, refers to a situation in which groups of musicians meet together and rehearse for a day or two with a guest conductor. The festival usually climaxes in a public performance. Festivals are held at every level, from those that are statewide to those that bring students from just one county or city.

Young people can have some excellent musical experiences in festivals if they are well prepared for the day's events. The preparation must be more than simply being able to sing the right notes at the right time. In order to get the most from a festival, the students must be primed to take advantage of the opportunity to rehearse and perform under a new conductor. They need to be musically alert to a possible new interpretation of each specific piece of music. When the students are properly motivated by their own director, the festivals can be a stimulating and exciting experience.

There are several basic types of festivals, all of which can be valid activities of any choral department. Some festivals involve the entire choir from each of several schools in rehearsal and performance. These are usually held at a local level, often citywide or countywide in nature. These can be good experiences for most of the students provided that:

1. The level of abilities of the participating choirs is not too varied.
2. All the choirs are well prepared.
3. Meaningful repertoire can be performed with all ensembles.

This type of festival is usually most meaningful to the more average singer in the ensembles, the singer that would not usually be chosen to participate in a select festival.

Another festival that is rewarding is the type that is reserved for the best singers from a number of choirs. This festival can be successful at virtually every level, from a local festival to one that is statewide. The All-State Festivals that are held in most of our states are an example of this festival. The selection for this festival varies from area to area. In some situations each local director recommends his best students, and a panel of his associates selects the festival chorus on the basis of these recommendations. Each school is usually guaranteed representation under this method. Several excellent musical festivals are successful following this method. It is obvious that much weight is given to the director's recommendations. He then must have the professional integrity to recommend only qualified students or the quality of the festival will deteriorate.

Probably the most widely used method of selection is the audition method. Students are given the music to rehearse and on an appointed day attend area auditions at a central location. They may be auditioned as mixed quartets or on an individual basis. Auditions seem to be the best method of guaranteeing that the best singers will be chosen for the festival chorus. The students audition using the festival music for the tryout, assuring that this music will be learned before the day of the festival.

If a festival is to be successful, it is necessary that the music be learned before the festival. It is for this reason that the audition method works so well. It is possible, however, to have a successful festival of selected students without auditioning. Some directors feel that the auditioning for the All-State Choirs is enough and that an area or regional level festival could be held without strenuous contestlike auditioning procedures. Assuming that a number of schools are involved, a procedure like the one that follows could be, and has been, successfully used.

Students may be chosen in mixed quartets by the local directors. Each school may be similarly represented, assuring that all schools will be represented. When warranted, the participating schools may agree that very large schools may send an extra quartet. The music is chosen by a small group of directors elected to perform that task and by the festival conductor. One observation is necessary at this point. It is a fallacy to believe that, because only the top students will be singing, music of greater complexity than usual can be chosen. While only the top students are involved, it must be remembered that the students have never sung together and that they will have only a limited amount of rehearsal time.

The greatest problem is to see that the festival music is learned. This can be done by having rehearsals for schools located in adjacent areas. One director in each area can be appointed as chairman of the area. It is his responsibility to notify all participating schools of the rehearsal dates and locations. If at least two rehearsals are held, all festival students can be required to attend at least one prefestival rehearsal. Those schools whose students do not attend should be eliminated from participation in the festival.

Such a festival can be self-supporting and can be started on little or no budget. In areas where adequate choral interest has not been achieved, the area festival can serve as an excellent stimulus to the choral departments.

A festival of selected students offers the better musicians in each choir an opportunity to perform excellent music with other performers of similar proficiency. The selection will be an honor for the choir members and a goal toward which each can aim.

Contests

Contests refer to situations where either large choral ensembles, small vocal ensembles, or soloists compete against each other, or against a *standard of excellence* for a rating. Usually a written critique is given and occasionally a verbal critique as well. Most often the judges are rating the ensembles or soloists against an unwritten standard, which means that more than one ensemble may receive a superior rating. There are some contests, usually private contests, that also give an outstanding choir award, runner-up award, etc.

Music contests vary from state to state. Some states have area or district contests, then a regional contest, and finally a state contest. Some states have only regional and state contests while still others have only a state contest. One set of guidelines will not fit all of the various programs in our country. The discussion concerning preparation that follows is directed at a polished performance in the final contest. This should be a director's goal even when participating in a district contest, or series of contests.

Contest Pros and Cons

Music contests and their value have been a subject of discussion for some years in music education. This is a highly explosive subject and those on both sides of the coin are equally sure they are right. If one intends to remain in music education, one will certainly become involved in a discussion on contest at one time or another, perhaps with an administration or a board of education. It is best to be familiar with both sides of the coin, whatever one's personal views are or become. Listed below are some of the arguments most often made for and against contest.

For Contest

1. Contests motivate the singers to perform at a higher level than at concerts.
2. Contests give the students an opportunity to be constructively criticized by an expert.
3. Contests allow students to hear other ensembles composed of students their own age.
4. Contests provide an *espirit de corps*—a winning tradition that builds good departments.
5. Competition is part of the free enterprise of America. Music contests help prepare students for competition in life.
6. Contest results provide an administrator and school community a visible barometer of the success of the program.
7. Directors can learn how their department compares with other similar ones, and students will learn how they rank among other similar age students.

Against Contest

1. Teachers, not contests, are motivators. Good teaching will provide the necessary motivation.
2. A clinic will serve that purpose better than a contest.
3. Most contests are so scheduled that the students do not have time to hear one another.
4. A tradition of excellence will provide the same spirit and one of more lasting quality.
5. Competition in the fine arts is undesirable and stifling. It should be left to sports where distinct winners and losers can be determined.
6. Contests are poor barometers of teaching. The musical level may be considerably raised and still not receive a superior rating.
7. Contests pit directors against directors. Superior ratings at contest accomplish little, other than feeding the director's ego.

All of the above statements have been made in the music education world for a number of years. These facts remain.

1. We have music contests.
2. They are sponsored by the leading music and educational associations in each state who, by their sponsorship, evidently agree that contests are both educationally and musically sound.

Contest Preparation

The rest of this chapter is devoted to ways of presenting your groups so they may receive a superior rating. The director must assume the position that a music contest is just that—*a contest*. Contests could be further boiled down to:

1. You and your students are entered in a contest against other high school students.
2. Contests involve winners and losers.
3. If you are going to compete in contests, compete to win.

One cannot return from a music contest and tell the parents, the community, and the administration that the day was ". . . musically stimulating," or that ". . . the students gave a good performance which was well received." Instead, you will be asked, "How many superior ratings did you receive?" This question cannot be answered in any way except by numbers of ratings.

The following guidelines for developing contest groups, although concerned with the best possible presentation of your ensembles, should not be interpreted to mean that any means of winning is justified. It should be clearly understood that a choral director has a responsibility to his students and to the other directors and competitors. But it is necessary to be completely honest, at this point, about music contests and call them what they are, contests.

Large Ensembles

Before you select your music and begin serious rehearsals for contest, examine the rules governing the contest and be sure that you understand them fully. If you question the wording or interpretation of a rule don't hesitate to seek the guidance of a director in your area who may be more familiar with the contest procedures than you. If such people are not available, write to the body governing the contest and ask for a clarification. These rules vary from state to state, and no attempt will be made here to list them. They are also subject to constant review and change. Consequently, any such list might be out of date by the time it would be printed.

After you have determined the rules of the contest, you will need to select the repertoire that your ensemble will perform. It is necessary to understand that there is some difference between selecting music for contest and selecting music for your concerts. When you select the music for your concerts you will be selecting music for more than performance. Sometimes you will want to teach specific vocal techniques, general musicianship, or study of a specific period of choral literature. As a result, you may do music that is a "gamble" during performance, but that is important in the study of choral music.

When selecting literature, the director is interested in presenting the best impression of his group that he can. This is not the occasion for "gambling." It is true that one ought to be able to choose music from the spring program and perform it successfully at music contest. However, this is only true if one is careful about which pieces are chosen. If your choir has just begun a performance study of Baroque repertoire, it would be foolish to place these works on the contest program. The students probably will not be secure enough in the style to stand the type of scrutiny that contest judges will give to the performance practice of the music. Usually a director will choose several works for the spring concert with a contest performance in mind. This will allow a public performance of the contest pieces before the contest itself.

Several suggestions regarding repertoire follow. Most of these are compatible with the requirements you would make for any piece of music you would program for a concert. All of the criteria in chapter three apply here but several suggestions pertain especially to contest repertoire.

1. Be careful not to *over challenge* the ensembles for the contest performance. Do not select a piece that you think your group *should* be able to do or that you would *like* to do that particular year. Avoid music that is experimental as far as you and your groups are concerned. A contest performance is a time when your students are under a great deal of pressure; this is not a time for experimentation. It is best to stay fairly close to the type of music your groups have performed during the course of the year. For example, if you have not performed contemporary music during the year, your students will probably not have the understanding necessary to adequately present one at contest. Adjudicators have often made the statement that, ". . . the ensemble probably could have received a superior rating if they had not attempted more than they could do well." Of course, "they" refers directly to the conductor of the ensemble since he chooses the music.
2. Select music that will command the respect of the judge as being worthy of performance. Avoid popular tunes or Broadway musical show tunes.

There is a fantastic amount of beautiful choral repertoire that the students will enjoy singing and a judge will enjoy hearing. Some states require at least one selection from an approved list and allow other works of the director's choosing. At the same time do not choose music solely on the basis that it will impress a judge, especially a particular judge. Often directors know who the judge will be and attempt to choose repertoire that is directed toward his known likes. This often backfires because the judge is so exacting regarding this repertoire that his standards unconsciously become higher and he is therefore more difficult to please.

3. Choose music that will demonstrate the best qualities of the ensemble and minimize the weaker points. If your tenors are a weak section, try to choose music with tenor parts that are not demanding. If the soprano section is strident in the upper range, try to avoid pieces that have a high soprano tessitura. Avoid music that requires your weakest voices to sing any exposed passages.

4. The range of the parts is always an important consideration, but it is especially important in the selection of contest music. Each part must be carefully examined to be sure that it presents no problems for any of the sections of the specific choir under consideration. As a director you may feel more inclined to ignore a few range problems in order to perform some literature in concert that you feel to be of educational value. In contest literature, however, one cannot ignore any range problems. If the piece you are considering contains any problems in the area of range, it is better to look elsewhere rather than hazard the success of the ensemble.

A word regarding the transposition of music may be in order at this point. Directors should not be afraid to transpose a piece to a more suitable key for a specific ensemble. Usually transposition is considered particularly about music written before the twentieth century. It should be remembered that many editions have already been transposed and that further transposition will not defile an early composer's name. One must be cautious, however, when transposing to cure the range of one part, that the transposition doesn't create problems in another part. When transposing, it is generally best to include a note on the music to that effect for the judge's benefit.

5. With groups of limited experience it is best to avoid pieces that divide parts to a large extent. In fact, a conservative approach is best with an experienced ensemble also. There are many fine choral works that require only four parts, or divide only occasionally. One should not assume that because a piece has divided parts it is necessarily better or will impress a judge. The judge will be impressed only by the quality of the performance.

6. The length of the work should be another consideration in the selection of contest repertoire. Usually a time limit is included in the contest rules.

Do not assume that all of the time must be used. Most contest rules allow large ensembles to perform more than one piece. In fact some state rules require it. It is better to use two selections of a contrasting nature than to use one longer work. Longer works require a continuity that is difficult to achieve with young performers who are performing under an unusually large amount of pressure. Two shorter works give the ensemble an opportunity to achieve musical clarity and demonstrate the musical style in a short space of time.

It is also easier to achieve a contrast musically when using two works. You can select works that contrast, such as:

A. One sacred and one secular piece
B. One Renaissance and one twentieth century piece
C. Two works in contrasting tempos
D. One work in a foreign language and one in English

7. Foreign language departments exist in almost every high school. Many students participating in choral groups will have taken one to three years of a foreign language. If a director would like to do one or more works in a foreign language, it would be easiest to choose one that is presently being taught in the school. This is particularly true in cases where students have not previously performed works in other languages. The students will be familiar with the foreign language before it is presented to the ensemble. The director also has the foreign language teacher available as a consultant if he has not studied that language. If a director decides to perform a piece in a foreign language at contest, he should be doubly sure that he knows *exactly* how the text is pronounced. Judges seem to have less patience with ensembles that pronounce a foreign language badly than they do with poor English diction. Usually a judge assumes that if the group can't do the foreign language properly, the work could have been done in English.

Latin pronunciation is improving with choral groups, but some flagrant violations still appear in concert and contest groups. There is no reason for the poor singing of Latin that does occur. The fault can obviously be placed directly on the individual conductor, whose responsibility is to determine the correct pronunciation.

8. The final rehearsals for contest are similar to those for a concert, except that the ensemble will probably be performing far less repertoire for the contest performance. This can be an advantage if handled properly. One can polish several pieces in the last few rehearsals and not have to be concerned with the pacing of an entire program. It does have the disadvantage of offering so much repetition to the young singer that he tires of rehearsing the music. It can become difficult to achieve the spontaneity that is desirable in a live performance. Often contest ensembles can sound

mechanical if the conductor has not allowed the music to rise above the rather mechanical functions of tuning, precision, etc. The information in chapter four should be applied to the final rehearsals before contest.

Some of the following information that specifically applies to small ensembles is also applicable to larger ensembles. Some of the previous suggestions for choirs also applies to the small ensemble. When this is the case, it will not be discussed again in this chapter.

Small Ensembles

The selection of small ensembles is somewhat different than the original audition procedure used to establish the concert choir. Usually the students in the small groups are chosen from the concert choir. In fact, it is a good rule to establish—that no one can be in any small ensemble unless he is also a member of one of the larger choral ensembles. Many state contest rules also require this.

A director may not need to audition as many voices to select small ensembles. He should know the voices well at this point and can screen them without extensive auditioning. It is good to mention at this point that all students in the choir should understand that they may audition for any of the small ensembles. The director can also invite students individually that he knows he wants to hear. Allowing all students to audition often takes more time than a director will want to spend, but it is good for morale. Occasionally a student will improve considerably, for one reason or another, from the first audition without the director being aware of the extent of the improvement. This student would otherwise not be noticed.

Whenever possible, have the final auditions for each ensemble at a time when all those you would like to hear can come together. If you are selecting students for a mixed octet from eleven or twelve finalists, you can alternate voices until you find the combination that gets the best blend and tone quality. You may be able to use one of the works that the students know from the choir's repertoire for an audition piece.

Some voices will work very well in a large ensemble but have some quality (heaviness, a wide vibrato that is not controllable in a small group, an edge that shows up in a small ensemble) that may not lend those voices to good madrigal singing, for instance. This should be carefully explained to the students who will otherwise become discouraged. When possible, it is a good idea to have many people from the choir involved in small ensembles. Use as many different voices as you can without allowing the quality to drop. It is important that these ensembles be of consistently high quality though. If this means that one must use the same voices in every ensemble for the first year or two, this is better than having poor ensembles represent the department publicly and in contest. An image of excellence cannot be built by poor ensembles.

As is the case with the contest rules themselves, states vary regarding the number of small ensembles that can be entered as well as the type of ensembles. Regardless of the number of groups allowed, it is best to enter a fewer number of groups and have them well prepared. This is the best way to begin a winning tradition for a department. Enter only those groups you can personally rehearse. It is admirable to encourage student leadership but at this point you will not have sufficiently mature students to provide such leadership. You have been trained for the position you hold, your students have not. It doesn't follow logically that one would leave the supervision of ensembles that will represent the director, the music department and the school, to untrained high school students.

It is advisable to form ensembles of the largest nature possible. For instance:

1. Mixed octet
2. Boys' octet
3. Madrigal
4. Girls' sextet

Your students will have more confidence when there are two to a part. You will have a better chance of obtaining a better tone quality with groups of this size than with smaller groups, particularly when you are working with inexperienced students. Enter the following groups only when sufficient talent is available to form ensembles of high quality.

1. Mixed quartet
2. Girls' trio
3. Girls' quartet
4. Boys' quartet

Music of excellent quality is also more readily available for the first list of groups than the last.

Selection of Music for Small Ensembles

In addition to the points made earlier in this chapter, there are some factors that one needs to take into consideration when choosing pieces specifically for small ensembles.

1. You should choose the music your groups will perform. This is mentioned again in this discussion because students in small ensembles will often

want to suggest pieces that they have heard or know. What they don't know is whether or not their particular group has the right voices to perform that piece. This does not mean that you would not consider any compositions that the students might suggest. The final decision, however, must rest with the director, not with the students. The director should be qualified to judge whether or not the music is suited to the ensemble.

2. It must be remembered that music that is usable with a large choir may not necessarily be suited to a group of eight voices. This includes four-part compositions that one might assume to be easy for eight voices. Many times one or two characteristics will preclude the use of such a piece for a small ensemble. For instance, a piece that is very dramatic in nature and demanding vocally, would not be a good choice for a small ensemble entry in contest.

This does not mean that some music that is successful with a large group cannot also be successful with a small group. An example of this is *Suddenly There Came a Voice from Heaven* by G. Aichinger and edited by Payson (published by Frank Music Corp.), or *Three Choral Vignettes* by Gordon H. Lamb (published by E. B. Marks Music Corp.). If the students do not read well and a great deal of time is necessary to prepare a piece for performance, it may be advantageous to program a work on the choir program and then use the piece with the mixed double quartet in contest. This is also a helpful suggestion if small ensemble rehearsal time is at a premium.

3. Do not overchallenge a small ensemble for contest. This is so important it needs to be repeated here. The results of overchallenging—poor tone quality, lack of precision, poor intonation, poor blend and balance—will be even more apparent with a small ensemble than with a large one.

4. Be careful of choosing divisi repertoire with small groups. Smaller ensembles such as mixed octets and boys' octets, have more clarity and tonal security when performing four-part music.

5. Always be more conservative in the selection of contest music, but even more in the selection of contest music for small ensembles. Don't make the mistake of rationalizing that these are the best students, consequently they will be able to do even more difficult repertoire than the concert choir. Remember, they will be under considerably more pressure in a small group and quite conscious of the fact that much of the ensemble's success hinges directly upon their contribution.

Contest Rehearsal Schedule

The following comments regarding a rehearsal schedule for contest ensembles pertain particularly to the small ensemble. These guidelines are most valuable in situations where these rehearsals must be held outside the normal class day, or sandwiched into an already busy schedule.

When one is attempting to build a successful contest (and ultimately a choral) program, more rehearsal time is usually necessary than later when the entire choral program is well established. At the beginning, the students probably won't read very well and won't have had the experience of singing in a polished ensemble. Many directors continue the following plan even when the program is established because the plan worked to build a successful department and it will work to maintain it.

Contest rehearsals should start at least five weeks prior to the contest. Sometimes it may be necessary to start six weeks before the contests, although the six week schedule can become very tiresome for all before the day of the contest itself. If at all possible, schedule each ensemble for at least two, one-half hour rehearsals each week. (This does not include the last week of rehearsals.) When selecting students for the ensembles, one may find two quite equal voices under consideration. When this is the case, select the student that is the easiest to schedule. This may seem a bit hardheaded, but that decision will contribute to the success of the ensemble. A fine singer won't do the ensemble any good if he can't attend rehearsals.

Some directors allow students to be in only one or two ensembles and a solo. This may be acceptable in large schools, but it is unrealistic in smaller schools. In small and average size schools it is understood that many of the good students will also be involved in one or more instrumental ensembles. Generally speaking, one should tend to disregard that and in all cases place the best talent available in the contest groups. There is no point in leaving your best students out of the contest. The schools with whom you will be competing will be bringing their best students, and you will want to bring your best. Your second best students may not be quite good enough. It is commendable to want to include more students, but it is easy to go beyond the real talented students that are available. If a student is involved in several instrumental ensembles and several vocal ensembles, and the question of overparticipation arises, ask the instrumental director if he will be willing to substitute another person for this student. Generally, you will find that he also wants to enter only his best; so should you.

If you cannot schedule the group for two, one-half hour rehearsals a week, you must seriously consider the following alternatives:

1. Have the group perform one number that a large group has previously performed, leaving only one piece to learn.
2. Have the ensemble perform only one number in contest. (There are some states that require that an ensemble sing *only one* piece in contest.)
3. Drop the group. There is no point in believing that the group will "work

itself out." The group won't develop into excellent readers overnight nor achieve a nice blend when they haven't sung together before.

When you organize your contest rehearsal schedule, meet with the instrumental director(s) if he is also involved in rehearsals for contest about the same time. If the entire music department is entered in contest, there will likely be some duplication of personnel in the ensembles. (Again, contest procedures vary state to state. Some states hold all music contests, vocal and instrumental, on the same days, while others have separate days for each department. Usually the latter situation still involves much overlapping of rehearsal time since the two contests are normally quite close together.)

The rehearsal conflicts, because of overlapping personnel, can be worked out between the respective directors before they occur. When the conflicts of student duplication are solved in this manner, misunderstandings and unnecessary hard feelings will not occur. Be careful that no student is caught in the position of having a rehearsal for an instrumental ensemble and a choral ensemble at the same time. If a student has two rehearsals scheduled at the same time and is required to make a choice, he will be wrong no matter what his decision. Most rehearsal conflicts can be resolved as the schedule is being set. All rehearsal conflicts should be handled by the directors. This lets the students understand:

1. That there is cooperation between the departments
2. That both departments are important
3. That all he has to do is to concentrate on learning the music

Once a director agrees on a schedule with the other director(s), he must vary from it only when it does not interfere with the other director's schedule.

Last Week of Contest Rehearsals

The last week of the contest rehearsal schedule is a very important time. As a director you must culminate all of the previous rehearsals into a musical performance. The detailed work that has been done should now show a meaningful contribution to the total piece of music. The memorization should be complete or very nearly so. How then, can the maximum musical capacity of the ensemble be reached?

At this point the most rewarding rehearsals will be more rehearsals for a shorter length of time, rather than longer rehearsals. Fifteen minute rehearsals are quite effective at this stage and, if possible, should be held every day. These rehearsals can be most beneficial if the groups are really ready to polish their selections. These fifteen minute times can be arranged within your total schedule with the instrumental director. He should also be at this stage of his contest preparation. Since you have been rehearsing in modules of thirty minutes it is very easy to work out a compatible schedule using fifteen minute modules. In a situation where the choral and instrumental departments have no schedule conflicts, this schedule is simple to arrange. It then becomes a matter of condensing the existing schedule.

In each brief rehearsal you should be able to spend your time polishing phrasing, intonation, blend, dynamics, and musical style. You will want to sing through sections of the work or the entire work without stopping, as much as possible. Make your comments to the ensemble concerning a section of the piece and then concentrate on realizing the goals you have discussed. The measure by measure work should be finished by now.

It is very important to instill confidence in the ensemble. This is true even if the ensemble has not lived up to your expectations. If you are dissatisfied with the ensemble, try not to show your dissatisfaction in your attitude during rehearsal. Of course, you should be demanding musically, but exasperation with their inability to learn will generally do more harm than good now. Remember, the ensemble has progressed to its present stage through your direct leadership. If they don't sing well, a good share of the responsibility is yours.

If the group has not lived up to your expectations, you may have thoughts about cancelling its contest appearance. Only under extreme circumstances should you *now* cancel the group's entry. You have committed yourself to an entry and the students have given a great deal of their time in rehearsal with the understanding that they will perform. Instead of cancelling the ensemble now, you should have had the foresight to cancel the group earlier.

During these last rehearsals try to be optimistic and encouraging. There is no point in berating an ensemble at this stage in the contest preparation. It definitely will not help the attitude of the group and will certainly do much to hurt it. Work the students hard, but be sure that they are aware of the progress they are making. Don't be afraid to tell them if they do something good. However, don't allow them to become overconfident.

It is well to keep in mind that contest performance presents pressures to performing groups that are not met in normal concerts. In concerts the students will be singing in physical surroundings familiar to them, where they have had some rehearsal, and for an audience generally composed of parents and friends. These audiences are usually not very critical and are anxious to find something about the performance they can praise. In a contest situation this will probably not be the case. The students may be performing in physical surroundings quite foreign to them; possibly a small classroom with poor acoustics and with an inferior piano; for a judge that will probably be writing criticisms as he listens; and for an audience (where allowed) composed mostly of strangers, some of them other students also participating in the contest.

Consequently, some overpreparation is best for a contest performance.

There will be times when the last few rehearsals may seem unnecessary to you as the group may seem to have reached its potential and improvement is not likely. It is best to assume the attitude that consistent performances at their highest level are necessary since adequate performances five out of ten times is not good enough. There is no guarantee that the contest performance will be one of these five good performances. Most groups will not quite perform at their highest capacity in contest. Overpreparation will pay off, since a performance that doesn't reach the precontest rehearsal standards will still come closer to the group's actual potential than it otherwise might.

Final Preparations

While the director is working feverishly with several groups and soloists, he must also organize many nonmusical aspects of the contest procedure. Among these is a time schedule of the contest day activities for each student. This is particularly important for a solo-small ensemble contest. This schedule should include:

1. Time of appearance.
2. Place of appearance.
3. Where and when to meet you for warm-up.
4. Their behavior during the contest day—(A) caution them not to tire themselves by unnecessary walking, and (B) not to do anything that will jeapordize the performance of their group in any way.
5. What time they leave and how they will travel.
6. What to wear (keep in mind comfort during a long day).

Prior to the day of the contest you should meet with your accompanists and go over the complete contest schedule. Help them arrange all of the music they will need for the day, and clip a note on each selection designating the group or solo, performance time, and place. The accompanists should be responsible for their own music during the day of the contest.

The director should be responsible for the judge's copy of music for each entry. Clip the same type of note to each selection and place the selections in order of appearance. A large clipboard or folder is useful to keep this music together.

Instruct each group or soloist to meet with you a prescribed number of minutes before they appear on the contest program. Each entry needs an adequate warm-up period. The amount of time necessary for each may vary. Groups or soloists appearing early in the day, 8:00 or 9:00 AM, will need to meet with you at least one-half hour before they sing. Those appearing later in the day will not require as much vocal warm-up. These groups will probably need to be settled down. Being involved in three or four groups at various centers tends to get the students excited and puts them on edge. They will not perform well in this state of mind. Your warm-up time will be spent putting them in the correct attitude toward their performance. Twenty minutes prior to their scheduled performance is usually enough time with these groups.

The director should meet with all groups and soloists prior to their performance time. Do not turn the students loose and expect them to determine for themselves when they are ready to perform. You have been trained to understand when a student is ready, both physically and psychologically, to sing. Consequently, only you should make that decision. Don't add to the pressure on a young student by making him responsible for decisions that he doesn't have the background to make.

If the schedule is tight and one or more students have some distance to travel between contest centers, try to make arrangements for a car to be available to take them to their next performing center. The student will be of little value to an ensemble (or to himself) if he is out of breath.

When the entire music department competes in a contest on the same day there will undoubtedly be some schedule conflicts. One student may be scheduled to perform in an instrumental group at or very close to the time he is to perform in a choral group. Again, the choral and instrumental directors should examine the schedule and resolve any conflicts *prior to the contest day*. Then both directors can instruct their students as to the corrected schedule. Sometimes it will be necessary to have an ensemble or soloist appear out of order on the schedule. The rules of the contest generally prescribe the manner in which this may be done. In cases where there is a conflict between a solo and an ensemble, it is usually best to have the soloist appear out of order. This will be the least disruptive to your schedule and involve changing the least possible number of students. With the full schedule duplicated before the day of contest, including all comments regarding out of order appearances, the students will know in advance exactly when the performances will occur and how conflicts will be handled.

Contest Solos

The procedure of handling soloists will vary from school to school. In some high schools the choral director also teaches voice classes or individual voice lessons as part of his regular schedule within the school day. Other schools schedule this person with a full load of choirs and allow him to use school facilities to teach private voice after school and on Saturdays. In still other situations, the director handles the choral groups and does not teach any private voice, during school or after school. In most larger cities, the students that are interested in studying voice may study with a private teacher. The above situations are basically those that exist in our schools today. There are some variations on these but the fundamental approach is the same.

If the choral director teaches all of the voice students that he will be entering in contest, he won't have any of the problems discussed below. But, if the soloists study privately with someone else, certain problems can arise. How will you determine which students will be allowed to compete in contest? In some states each school may enter as many students as it chooses while others have limitations of some nature. Even if there is no limitation, a director will not want to throw the gates open and allow any interested students to enter in contest. The students will represent the director and the school music department in contest. Usually the people at the contest will not know that the soloist has been trained by another teacher. Therefore, each director should make the final decision regarding which students shall participate. All the soloists must be of the highest possible quality.

Music contest is not a dumping ground for the voice students of a private teacher so he doesn't have to present them in recital. If there are several voice teachers and many of the students are studying privately, a local competition can be held to determine which students will represent the school. You may have several competent teachers from nearby schools judge the local competition. However, since it is your department the students represent and your reputation and position that go on the line with each singer, you are the logical person to determine which students shall sing at contest.

Unfortunately, the teaching of private voice is an erratic one. Within the same city there may be several excellent voice teachers and several persons purporting to teach voice who have no real qualifications and should not be teaching. It is for this reason that you should protect yourself and decide what students will participate in contest.

Don't feel compelled to enter as many students as the rules allow. Contest is not the place to send students to gain experience. Instead of being encouraged by this experience there is a better chance that the mediocre or poorer student will be discouraged. These students can find opportunities for experience within their community. A good rule of thumb is to send only those students who have a fifty-fifty chance of receiving a superior rating. The other students will be better off not participating.

If you teach your own voice students, most of the above problems disappear. You will have worked with them all year and will know each voice very well. You should be able to choose the music that the student will perform and you can coach the student on the performance of that piece.

The selection of the solo is an important decision. Don't make any decision without some real thought regarding the suitability of the piece for the student's voice. It is often possible to give the student several pieces for a time and then select the contest piece(s) from these.

The Accompanist

The selection of the accompanist for a soloist is also very important.

When you do not have a student who is a capable accompanist, try to find a fine pianist among the adults of the community. If possible, pay this accompanist from the choral budget. In instances where this is not possible, the students sometimes pay a share of the cost.

In cases where student accompanists are used, one has to be cautious regarding the complexity of the accompaniment. A nervous high school student can be totally upset at contest by an accompanist who cannot satisfactorily play the accompaniment.

Some teachers ask the soloist to find their own accompanist. This is generally not a good idea. Many times the soloist will want a certain person to play for him in contest but the decision is not made for musical reasons. The person is a friend and, as far as the student knows, plays the piano. The soloist may not be aware of the technical demands of the accompaniment or the actual capabilities of the pianist. A pianist that sounds great chording in a living room sing-along may not do so well with a difficult accompaniment. Before you approve of any accompanist, you should hear him play the accompaniment in question.

The above suggestions would seem to take a great deal of the director's time, particularly if there are a number of entries. This is true. If you are not willing to take that amount of time, enter fewer students in contest. Do not make concessions in quality of teaching and concern for the student's welfare because there isn't enough time. Only enter the number of students you can effectively work with individually.

Discussion Questions

1. Recall your own high school festival, clinic, and contest experiences. Which ones seemed the most important to you at the time? In retrospect, which do you feel was of the most value?
2. What other points can you name in favor of or against contests?
3. Can choirs, small ensembles, or soloists be objectively and fairly evaluated?
4. In which of these activities would you prefer to have your students participate?
5. Which activity do you feel you could most adequately justify to the administration in terms of student benefit, and time and money spent?
6. Can a high school ensemble be overrehearsed?

SUGGESTED READINGS

NIMAC Manual, the Organization and Management of Interscholastic Music Activities. Music Educators National Conference, 1963.
Selective Music Lists—1968, Vocal Solos and Ensembles. Music Educators National Conference, no. 321-10364.

chapter 14.

management of a choral department

The ability to organize and implement the various activities of a choral program is extremely important to the success of the department. Choral conductors who are unable to properly organize a choral program will be constantly hampered in their attempt to establish a full choral department. Administrators who do not feel qualified to judge the conductor's musical achievements do feel competent to judge his organizational abilities. Administrators also deal with the organizational qualities of a director on a regular basis while they view the musical achievements only sporadically. They may consequently evaluate the choral director on the basis of his management capabilities as much, if not more than his musical capabilities.

Careful planning will also free the choral director from last minute flurries that often get in the way of musical preparations. The necessity of efficient planning cannot be overemphasized.

Scheduling

The types of scheduling throughout the country vary from a modular scheduling, which is quite flexible, to a six-, seven-, or eight-period day. Choral departments have flourished under all systems. It is not so much the type of schedule that affects the choral department as the attitudes of the people who control it—the administrators. Whatever the schedule, there are a few principles of scheduling that should be stressed.

Experience has shown that no matter what schedule is proposed, the choral department will flourish or perish on the basis of the strength of the department at the time of the change. If the department is strong when the changes are made, it will probably occupy a solid place in the new schedule.

The spokesman for the choral department must be knowledgeable of the rest of the schedule, and be willing to discuss all possibilities with administrators. He must also be a strong negotiator, able to compromise at the right time and ready to stand firm when necessary.

A favorable schedule is crucial to the growth and success of a department. It indicates administration approval and a good climate for choral music. If the administration will provide the choral ensembles good scheduling times during the school day, they can probably be induced later to provide more money with which to operate. When, in the early development of a program, there is a choice of more money or an excellent schedule, it is suggested that the director choose the better schedule. No matter how much money is available for materials or how many students want to join the choirs, the program will never be successful until a director is allowed sufficient rehearsal time when qualified students can participate.

In order to develop excellent choral ensembles, it is best to meet each group one period each day. The continuity necessary for good rehearsals can best be maintained by this regular schedule. There are many schools that do not offer this type of scheduling to their students. Some schools alternate choral music with physical education classes or other classes that do not meet daily. These schedules should only be considered as stop-gap measures and one should work toward complete absorption of the choral program into the schedule on a daily basis.

Excellent High School Schedule

8:30 Free Period
9:30 Girls Chorus II
10:30 Concert Choir
11:30 Boys Chorus
12:30 Lunch
 1:00 Mixed Chorus
 2:00 Girls Chorus I
 3:00 (after school) Solos, Madrigal, All-State
        and contest rehearsals.

Note: All classes meet daily.

Figure 82   High School Choral Schedule

The best advice when accepting a new position is to determine the scheduling used at present and if inadequate, begin attempts to improve it then before accepting the position. This is always a good time to bargain. Many situations or salaries are improved at a change of directors. Once the position has been accepted, changes can be expected only as the department becomes more successful. Once again the bargaining position will be strong. Similarly as the successful department receives more budget, it will also receive a more favorable scheduling position.

Constantly work toward curricular acceptance of the choral program. Where choral music is out of the schedule, work to have it placed in the schedule. If it is a part of the schedule, strive to have it fully credited and meet regularly as every other class. Always try to stimulate and promote a curricular, rather than extracurricular, image.

Choral Offerings

A well-rounded department should offer a choral experience for every qualified student. A good feeder program has always been described as a necessary part of a good music department. While this is true, the philosophy of the department should be one of offering the right choral experience for the student. Not every student will have the capabilities to sing in the concert choir (the term used here to represent the most select of the large ensembles). A student may have sufficient talent and interest to be a member of the mixed chorus (this term is used to represent the ensemble that is less select and the one that students will usually perform in before being admitted to the concert choir). If the student remains in this ensemble for three years because that is the level of his ability, the experience should be a satisfying one for him.

Structure of a Senior High School
Choral Department

Chamber Choir   Madrigal   Girl's Sextet

Concert Choir

Boy's Chorus   Mixed Chorus   Girl's Chorus

Figure 83   A Senior High Choral Department

Some departments, where size, type of school, and administrative climate allow, will have as many as six or seven choirs. Others will have two or three choirs that still meet the musical needs of the students. Every school situation does not dictate that two or more choirs should be maintained. Concentration should be aimed at providing the type of department that meets the musical and educational needs of each individual school.

Budget

There are almost as many methods of budgeting as there are schools in the United States. Very large systems may have an overall budget for the many schools with a music supervisor responsible for the disbursement of funds. Small school systems may designate a certain amount of money for the choral department and allow the choral director to spend it as he sees fit. In between these two extremes are many different types of budgeting procedures. Whatever the procedure, there are certain important considerations every choral director should remember.

1. Education costs have risen steadily and there is every indication that this trend will continue.
2. Each department in the school wants and may need more money.
3. The choral department must operate as efficiently as possible and in a businesslike manner in order to get administration approval.
4. It is better to get small increases in budget year by year than to wait and try to make large gains in one year.
5. The director must plan far in advance, anticipating the needs of the department.
6. The director must be able to show how each new item requested will directly benefit the students.

Remember, administrators respond most quickly and most generously to the successful departments in a school. They also respond to those requests that they can see will be most beneficial to students.

When asked to submit budget requests, do so on the budget forms that the administration provides. Where these are inadequate, supplement them with additional information as is necessary to support the inclusion of each item. Many budget requests will have more than one part; perhaps a section for those items necessary to continue present operations of the department, and a section for items necessary to support the department in its anticipated growth.

There is still another type of budget that asks personnel to develop a "hold the line" budget, allowing no increases in expenditures. This type of request will usually require that some priorities be shifted since, although the budget may "hold the line," costs probably will not. Consequently, for the same money the director will be expected to operate the department just as successfully as he has in the past, and occasionally be expected to provide a steady growth and development. When this is the case, a director must be able to adjust his program to allow for what will be an actual decrease in buying power. Often, plans to use budget for new performance apparel, or to provide for instrumental accompaniment that cannot be otherwise provided, can be delayed until another year. This will allow the budget to cover necessary expenses such as music, folders, etc.

When the administration does not provide a budget request form, the form given in figure 84 or a variation of it, may be useful.

Music	Amount
Concert Choir	_____
Boys Chorus	_____
Girls Chorus	_____
Mixed Chorus	_____
Contest (including solos)	_____
Recordings	
Disc	_____
Tape	_____
Clinic Expenses	_____
(includes clinician's fee	
and all administrative costs)	
Apparel Maintenance	_____
Music Folders	_____
New Folder Cabinet	_____
New Rehearsal Piano	_____
(bids attached)	
Total	_____

(Piano tuning and equipment repair is included
on building and equipment maintenance budget)

Figure 84   Choral Department Budget

This example is the most brief and concise portion of the budget. In any budget submitted, include on one page the total budget request and a small breakdown as shown. Administrators prefer this information for their use as they develop the total budget. Further pages should then detail the requests made and include estimated costs when known. These pages should also contain the reasons for the expenditures and all supporting evidence for them.

When any new item is included in a budget, support the request with evidence that:

1. Demonstrates the need for the item
2. Demonstrates how it will be of value, educationally, to the students
3. Shows how similar uses in other schools have been successful (if known)

Whatever the requests that are made, whether for new items or for budget increases, the priorities will be somewhat different with each choral director. However, every director should be careful to keep the education of the student as the primary consideration in all budget requests. This does not mean that a request for office help will not ultimately benefit the students, because it may free the director to spend more time with the students or in his preparation for teaching. Luxury items that benefit only the director cannot be justified.

There are certain expenses that can be placed on other budgets, allowing better use of the choral budget. Items such as chalk, overhead transparencies, ditto masters, student workbooks, sight-reading manuals (that do not contain performance music) and the like can often be placed on instructional materials budgets. This will take some pressure off the choral budget. All office items can usually be placed on a schoolwide budget.

In many situations, maintenance items such as piano tuning and repair, and wardrobe maintenance, can be placed on school maintenance budgets, again providing relief for the choral budget.

It is usually best to separate the budget into those items that are recurring ones, such as the cost of music, and those items that can be called one-time purchase items, including stereo systems, tape recorders, etc. At least do this on the department level if not at the administrative level. In this way a choral director will be able to easily know his operating costs. When costs rise, it will be simple to determine how much more money will be necessary to support the department.

It is most important that the choral director be knowledgeable about all areas of his budget. When he is called on by the administration to discuss or to defend items in his budget request, he must be able to substantiate his requests and explain the need for each item. He should also have a very good idea of the approximate cost of items. This can be done by checking with commercial firms in advance regarding costs. A director should do his homework well before meeting with the administration. They will be impressed by this and it will reinforce the requests.

School Purchases

Again, each school has its own procedures which faculty are to observe when they buy materials. If a choral director is new, he should determine what these procedures are *before* making his first purchases. If these procedures are found to be binding and prevent efficient use of the director's time, he should then discuss it with the administration in an effort to establish a procedure that will be mutually agreeable to both parties.

Some situations allow directors to purchase items under a certain limit without administration approval. This allows him to buy music freely, making orders at conventions and reading clinics possible. This is a most desirable situation for a director.

Purchase of Large Items

The purchase of large items such as stereo sound systems, risers, concert attire, etc., normally require administration approval. Again, there will be different methods of purchase in each school. In any case, one should follow the procedure listed below.

1. Determine that there is a need for the item.
2. Decide what type of product will best meet your specific needs.
3. Investigate commercial products to select several that adequately meet the needs. Establish standards which each competing product must meet in order to be considered.
4. In situations where bidding is required, be sure that each bidding firm is bidding according to the same standards. Be especially careful of manufacturers that claim an "equivalent" product. Be sure that it is indeed equivalent and meets the same specifications as other products.
5. Don't buy the cheapest product unless it is also the best product. Be aware, however, that the expensive product is not always that much better than a cheaper one. Purchase quality rather than price. When possible, find out how the product has performed in similar circumstances.
6. Definitely make recommendations to administrators if they do the actual purchasing. Do not involve yourself in the active bidding process where this is the procedure. Do not let yourself become involved in any dealings with the company that will place you in a comprising situation, such as accepting a kickback on the sale, or other consideration from the firm in question.

Buying Music

The purchase of choral music is the one that choral directors will make the most. If a choral director visited a music dealer or publishing firm, he would be amazed at the vague orders for music that pour in to these firms. Orders are most often delayed because the person doing the ordering failed to provide correct information; or when correct, enough information. The following guide should be followed when ordering music.

1. Follow the ordering procedure of your school. If the business office must approve each expenditure, be sure that every order goes through their office. Cooperate with these people and they will be more inclined to help you with a rush order when the need arises.
2. State clearly the title, composer (if an edition or arrangement, the name of the composer and editor or arranger), the publisher, publisher's octavo number, voicing (satb, ttbb, ssa, etc.), number of copies desired, and how you want the copies sent—parcel post, 1st class mail, etc. Unless you specify, the firm filling the order will probably mail the music by fourth class mail. If you want quick delivery, it is best to specify first class and under-

stand that you will usually be charged the cost of mailing in addition to the cost of the music. On normal orders it is best to order five percent more than your immediate needs to allow for growth and music loss.

Where should you place your order? This will depend on the type of city in which you are teaching. If you are in a metropolitan area, there is probably a large music dealer close by who can handle any type of order that you place. If, on the other hand, you are in a smaller city or in a rural area, the music dealer closest to you may not be equipped to properly place your order. The dealer must know how to order the music from the many publishers and must order enough music on a regular basis in order to give you a good price. Most small dealers do not stock choral music in quantity. If a choral director orders from this type of a dealer, he should expect a long wait for the music and the prospect that part of the order will probably never be completed.

There are a handful of music dealers across the country that are large enough to stock many standard and new choral works in quantity. Most of these dealers will send choral music on thirty-day approval. If this large dealer does not have a particular choral work in stock, he can get it quickly directly from the publisher. Some of these dealers are listed in Appendix B. Schools and churches may receive a small discount from some music dealers.

Some choral music may be ordered directly from the publisher. There are publishers that seek the direct business and others who refuse to sell to anyone but music dealers. Either method is legitimate. It is then a matter of knowing which publishers will accept direct orders and which will not. Experience has shown that orders are not necessarily filled faster by music publishers than by dealers. This simply depends upon the publisher and the dealer. Experience with the firms is the only way to determine which method is best for each director.

Copying Music

Copying of Copyrighted Music Is Illegal!

Since the 1960s almost every school in the country has been equipped with a copying machine. This has made copying music no longer the laborious process it once was. Copies can be made in seconds on good machines that rival the original in quality. There are also machines that produce a ditto master which can then be used to duplicate pages of scores in quantity. These copies are very poor and most difficult to read.

The copying of copyrighted material cannot be condoned, and published music is almost sure to be copyrighted. The music publisher has heavy printing and advertising costs, including royalties that are paid to composers and arrangers. These people are responsible for providing the music that is available to choral directors. Without the publishers and composers, there would not be music available to perform. Yet, when copies are illegally made, only the manufacturers of the machine and those that sell the paper the machine uses, benefit. The persons who provided the music, the composer and the publisher, lose substantially.

Additionally, the copying of copyrighted music is clearly illegal. People who would not think of stealing in other circumstances, do not hesitate to steal from people in their own music profession. In instances where administrators suggest copying music, its illegality should be pointed out. Any teacher would be within his rights to refuse to perform an illegal act.

The ideas expressed in the flyer in figure 85 from one music publisher are appropriate.

The Choral Library

The choral library is the heart of the choral department. If it is operated efficiently and smoothly, many hours and many copies of music will be saved. If it is a haphazard arrangement, the efficiency of the department can suffer.

There are several aspects of the choral library—the card index, storage, repair, and distribution. In each of these areas, there are further delineations. Each of these will be discussed below.

Card Index File

A card index file is a necessity for a choral library. A good file system can save many hours searching for pieces that were thought to be in one place, only to find that they were filed in another. A card file should contain all the pertinent information that a director would want to know before he wanted to see the music itself—voicing, number of copies on file, accompanied, and library number.

One can make file cards by determining the information one wishes to include and dittoing this on three- by five-inch cards. There are cards available commercially that are convenient and usable. The card in figure 86 is available from Southern Music Company in San Antonio, Texas. The card in figure 86 is the composer's card, which is blue. Available in other colors are title cards and classification cards.

This system of cataloging each piece under the three areas indicated is one that provides a method of finding music quickly and easily. As each piece is purchased and entered into the library it is stamped to indicate ownership and given a folder number (if music is assigned by number to each student). The necessary information is then entered on the three cards—the title card, the classification card, and the composer's card. Each card is then filed sepa-

Shawnee Press inc.

DELAWARE WATER GAP, PA. 18327 / TEL. (717) 476-0550

MORE about COPYRIGHT LAW

(This message is being enclosed with all of our current ship-
ments as part of the Music Publishers' Association's continuing
program of consumer education in the field of copyright observ-
ance. MPA is a voluntary trade association of music publishers
whose members publish most of the music played and sung in
American churches, schools and concert halls.)

HOW CAN YOU OWN THE PAPER

WITHOUT OWNING WHAT'S ON IT?

(or, When Was the Last Time You Photocopied a Dollar Bill?)

This is one of many fascinating aspects of United States Copyright Law:
it gives ownership and control of intellectual property to the original creator
and his agents.

This concept has been part of our social and economic fabric since its
unanimous adoption at the Philadelphia Constitutional Convention in 1787. In
the absence of royal patrons of the arts, it has given composers and authors direct
compensation for the use of their work.

In the case of music, it means that the composer or his publisher have the
exclusive right to sell, trade or give away that particular piece of intellectual
property in all its manifestations: printed copies, manuscript copies, arrangements,
recordings, performances, etc.

So, when you buy a piece of printed music, you own the paper, and you
can sell, trade or give away that paper. But if the music is copyrighted, you do
not own the music! That's why it is illegal to make unauthorized copies: it is,
quite literally, infringing on someone's intellectual property rights.

It's something like the dollar bill in your wallet. You own the paper,
and there are many ways you can use it. But you do not have the right to make
copies! Think of music the same way, and you'll be on the right track.

HAROLD FLAMMER INC.

DELAWARE WATER GAP, PA. 18327

Figure 85

FORM 5

COMPOSER'S CARD

NAME OF COMPOSITION _____

COMPOSER _____

☐ SACRED ☐ SECULAR

CLASSIFICATION

In. Lib.	Voice Arr.	Arranger	Pub.	Text & Eng.	A Cap.	With Acc.	With Solo	With Band	With Orch.	Grade	Per Time	No. Copies	Lib. No.
UNISON													
SA													
SSA													
SSAA													
SAB													
SATB													
TB													
TTB													
TBB													
TTBB													
BOYS													

REMARKS

COPYRIGHT 1941

SOUTHERN MUSIC CO.

Copyright 1941, Southern Music Co., used with permission. Copyright renewed 1969.

Figure 86   Composer's Card

rately. Only one composer card and one title card will be completed, but as many classification cards can be used as the director sees fit. *O Clap Your Hands,* by Ralph Vaughan Williams (Galaxy Music Corporation, #CCL 222) could be classified under *Sacred* (Praise), *Festival,* and *Works with Instrumental Accompaniment,* for example. Each new piece is given a library number and all music is numbered consecutively (without regard to alphabetical order). The music is then placed in a filing envelope or folder and placed in the storage library.

The information on the file cards should be kept up to date. As each piece is withdrawn from the chorus folders, the number of copies should be determined and, if different than the original notation, a change should be made on each file card. It is extremely aggravating to assume that there are enough copies of a work available in the library for the entire choir, only to find at the last minute that fifteen copies have been lost.

It is also good to keep an accurate record of any music loaned to other schools, churches, or to students. This can be done by making notations on one of the above mentioned cards or by using a separate card.

The Storage File

There are several ways of filing the music itself. The copies can be placed in an envelope and filed in a metal filing cabinet; filed in a box that is made for that purpose and placed on shelves; or placed in filing envelopes and stored on shelves.

The first method is probably the least desirable but has the advantage of taking up little space. In situations where space is a problem, it may be the only usable method.

Where room is available, music storage on shelves is preferred. If possible, store the music in boxes that, by their rigidity, protect the music. The music should be stored vertically rather than stacking one piece on top of other pieces. The filing boxes pictured in figure 87 are available commercially.

Music Repair

Choral music is handled more than instrumental music. The singers hold it instead of using music racks and often two singers share copies, causing greater wear on the music. As each piece of music in need of repair is withdrawn from the folders it should be placed on a shelf reserved for music to be repaired. There are several products available to repair torn music. The music should be repaired before it is returned to the file box and shelved.

Distribution of Music

Choral music is distributed in many different ways. Some directors distribute each piece at the beginning of each rehearsal and have the students

Used with the permission of J. W. Pepper and Son, Valley Forge, Pa.

Figure 87   File-finder Music Library Box

return the music at the end of the rehearsal. Other directors find that precious rehearsal time can be saved by having the music placed in folders and each folder assigned to one or sometimes two singers. Avoid distributing the music during rehearsal time. Rehearsal time should not be wasted for such a perfunctory task, particularly when it is completely unnecessary. This added handling of the music also destroys the music quicker. Less handling and the protection of a folder will save money on music replacement.

Most directors use some sort of folder system in which a folder is assigned by number to each student and they are responsible for the music that is placed in that folder. A folder cabinet can be built or purchased commercially and located in a convenient place in the rehearsal room. An example of a folder cabinet that is available commercially is pictured in figure 88.

When a particular piece is to be withdrawn from the folders, the singers can be asked to place that piece on top of the folders after rehearsal. The choral librarian (usually a student appointed or elected to that position) can then easily collect the music in numerical order.

Photo provided by and used with the permission of Wenger Corporation, Owatonna, Minnesota.

Figure 88

Concert Wearing Apparel

The concert attire of choral ensembles undergoes changes just as the fashions of a society do. The change may not be quite as abrupt but definite changes have occured over the past fifteen to twenty years. Where it was once the norm to have all choirs perform in choir robes, the robe is now only one of several different concert attires. The robe came to the school situation from the church and the church related college choirs. Since much of the repertoire that choirs perform also stems from the church, the relationship seemed quite natural.

The choir at the university and high school level is less likely to be wearing robes than it once was. A number of other costumes have become popular, including tuxedos, formals, blazers (for both girls and boys), and specially designed costumes. Many ensembles that perform often have an informal attire and a formal concert attire so they may dress according to the type of situation in which they are performing.

Advantages and Disadvantages of Various Wearing Apparels

Each type of wearing apparel has certain advantages and disadvantages for the choral director. These are presented here not to discourage anyone from a particular concert attire but rather to apprise people of the possibilities.

Robes. Advantages—robes give a choir a uniform appearance more than any other attire because the flowing capabilities of the robe eliminate personal features that would be apparent in other attire, particularly that of over-weight persons. Robes are adaptable to the use of several ensembles with very little trouble. Robes also eliminate the necessity of purchasing accessories such as shirts, ties (if stoles are worn that cover the collar), or matching slacks.

Disadvantages—the robe may seem out of place for concerts that are primarily secular. Robes are not as adaptable to community type perform-ances as other attires. When robes are purchased there will usually not be a change in concert attire for as many as ten years, eliminating any variety in the ensemble's appearance.

Tuxedos and Formals. Advantages—tuxedos and formals create an at-mosphere that can be sacred or secular. Variety can be achieved by the use of accessories or by a change of color of both the tux and the gown. The formal may be made from patterns by the girls and this aspect of the group's appearance can be changed every other year or so. An ensemble can have a very distinctive look by the use of this attire.

Disadvantages—tuxedos and formals are not easily interchangeable. Poor fits will be easily noticed and after two personnel changes the group can become rather ragged looking. They are also not easily suitable to informal type of appearances. Accessories are important with this attire and often necessitate additional purchases by the members. Patterns for women's gowns are discontinued after the pattern has been on the market a relatively short period of time. Extra patterns of various sizes should be purchased to avoid problems later. The material and color for the dresses will probably be impossible to match exactly a year later.

Blazers. Advantages—the blazer offers a distinctive appearance and a refreshing one, particularly for young singers. They are also most adaptable for groups that perform a high percentage of secular or even light repertoire.

Disadvantages—again, the blazers are not easily interchangeable. They are also not as appropriate for formal or sacred concerts as other attire. As with tuxedos and formals, individual size and weight differences are most noticeable. Accessories are also important when blazers are worn.

Designed Costume. Advantages—no other ensemble will have a concert attire exactly like yours. The students may participate in the designing of the costumes. Since the costume is being designed by the people involved, it may reflect the type of music that the group most often performs.

Disadvantages—the disadvantages of a specially designed costume are similar to those for the tuxedos and formals as regards to their interchangeability. While the girls' dresses may often be easily made, boy's costumes are not as easy to make.

It is apparent that there are several different types of concert attire that are quite acceptable. Usually the type and number of performances of an ensemble will make a wearing apparel choice easier. A few general comments should be considered.

1. Don't use the extremes of the present fashions for a concert attire. Temper the current fashions with some conservatism.
2. It is best not to limit membership in any ensemble to only those that can afford to purchase the concert attire. If it is necessary to make such purchases, try to make it possible for students to earn their share of the cost if they do not have the money. If a director is resourceful it is never necessary to eliminate a person from consideration because of financial concerns.
3. As a general rule, don't overdress young singers. Allow the freshness of youth to be highlighted in the wearing apparel.
4. Most costumes are now available in synthetic materials that resist wrinkling, making them particularly good for travel. Be sure to choose good quality material.

Student Officers

The election of student officers for musical ensembles seems to meet with universal approval. Officers of an ensemble seem to be accepted whereas officers for History 201 would not. The choir, however, will perform beyond the classroom, making community appearances, staging performances, and possibly undertaking fund raising promotions. Where activities such as these occur, student officers can make valuable contributions and receive leadership training. Officers can relieve the director of time-consuming duties that students can easily perform. Many directors let students handle, under his close supervision, most nonmusical functions such as wearing apparel, librarian duties, fund raising, and decorating for concerts.

Student officers should be kept informed and consulted regarding yearly plans for the choral department. They can participate in many decisions and, when possible, should be allowed to do so.

The following offices will usually fulfill the demands of the ensemble: president, vice-president, secretary, treasurer, wardrobe chairmen, (both boys and girls) and librarian. Each office should have specific duties that are clearly assigned. There is no point in having officers if the positions are empty ones.

Public Relations

Effective public relations will mean increased public support for the choral music program. Public relations involves the director's relationship with colleagues, with the administration, and with the community. The public image that the choral department has can be an effective tool in requesting more funds, etc.

In order to have a totally successful choral program one will need the support of the school community. A director should start building a public image of the choral department from the very beginning. The following suggestions will aid a choral director in creating a desirable public image for his department. Public relations can be equated to advertising in the business field. Advertising is only a means of getting customers. If the product is not of high quality, the customers will not return. The choral program must be built on sound musical ground or the best possible public relations program won't keep it growing. Surface or shallow programs are found out very quickly and the community wastes no time in labeling them for what they are.

Public Relations with Colleagues

It has already been mentioned that music should be conveyed as a curricular image. This should be reemphasized at this point. A director must convince colleagues that he wants music to progress just as history, mathematics, and other classes do. Other teachers must understand that the choral director is also interested in the progress of each student. One must want one's department to grow, but not at the expense of others.

It should be remembered that the history or mathematics teacher is rarely in the limelight as the choral director is. Be especially careful to show that you are not trying to exploit students for your own personal advancement. This will not be done by what you say as much as by what you do. Try to show how performance is a natural culmination of musical studies. Then make every attempt to show that your performances are of value to the students.

Show a genuine interest in other departments. Make it a point to know what is going on in the school. It won't be hard to find out what the football team is doing, but it might take some investigating to discover that the home economics department is in the midst of a special project that warrants your interest as a fellow faculty member. An interest in the work of others will, in turn, generate an interest in your department.

During one of your free hours, visit another class, and find out what the other teachers are doing. Of course, it is always best to ask permission to visit another teacher's class. This is best done when, in the course of a conversation, you can show an interest in a topic that is going to be the basis for his class in the near future. You may also find a valuable teaching technique by observing another teacher. It is also interesting to watch students whom you have in a choir situation as they participate in another class.

One of the most important qualities of good public relations is that of sharing the honors. If other faculty members contribute to the success of a concert or appearance, be sure to have this fact made public. Often they can be thanked publicly at the beginning or end of the performance. See that the names of persons who have contributed in some way are acknowledged on the program when one is printed. Don't be afraid to back out of the way and let others receive credit. One method is to send a newspaper release before the event that advertises the performance but also credits people contributing in other than musical ways. One example would be to publicize the works of the art department that is contributing backdrops for a concert. Have a picture taken of the art teacher at work with students on the backdrops. This not only credits people who help you but spurs them on to even greater achievements.

When possible, cooperate with other departments and offer assistance when you can be of help. Musicians too often are labeled as temperamental and unwilling to cooperate with others. This does not have to be the case. Contribute to the total success of the school, and the choral music department will benefit, just as will everyone else.

Public Relations with the Community

Become acquainted with the people who are program directors of local radio and television stations, editors of newspapers, officers of music clubs, officers of service clubs and people with other similar positions. If you are new in a community, you will want the opportunity to talk about the choral department you are trying to build. Write a short, concise statement of what you are trying to do and don't pass up any opportunity to "tell your story."

Buy some thank you notes and keep them in your desk. When someone does something for your department, thank him in writing as well as in person. People enjoy being thanked for their efforts. They will be more willing to help the next time if their remembrance of the first experience is good.

The news release is the logical means by which the choral director can present information about the department to the local news media. Each newspaper and radio or television station will not be able to send reporters to solicit information about your program. They won't always know the right time to expect a news story from your department.

When you write a news release put all of the pertinent information into the first paragraph so a reader can determine the nature of the entire article from the first paragraph. Not everybody will have time to read all of every article in the newspaper but they will be able to grasp the gist of your story from the first few sentences.

Use good English with a minimum of words. When student's names are involved be sure that they are spelled correctly and that they are the proper names (don't use nicknames). Avoid musical terms that the layman will not understand.

Release the story early so there will be an adequate amount of time for the editor to determine its usability, check to see if he wants more information, and rewrite the story where necessary. Most news stories will be rewritten. This is done mostly so the articles in the newspaper are consistent regarding style. After you have sent several releases to editors, it is good to call them or visit them to see if your releases meet their requirements. Modify them to fit the particular needs of the editors.

Figure 89 is an example of the form for a typical news release.

FROM:

John Jones
Choral Director
Central High School
Telephone, 393-4785

FOR IMMEDIATE RELEASE

Four students of the Central High School Concert Choir were selected as members of the All-State Chorus, according to choral director, John Jones. This marks the seventh consecutive year that Central High School has been represented in the Chorus.

Mary Jones, soprano, Jane Smith, Alto, George Miles, tenor, and Marvin Brown, bass were among forty students chosen from over two hundred students auditioning in Lakewood on March 10. Jane Smith is returning to the chorus for the third year.

According to director Jones, the competition was especially strong this year. Jones, in his eighth year as choral director at Central High, said, "The overall quality of students auditioning this year was higher than ever. The All-State Chorus will be one of the finest ever."

Figure 89

News releases should be sent only when there are bona fide news stories. If releases are sent to editors when there is no real news, he will begin to doubt the value of all of the releases he receives from the department. A release should be sent before every concert and to announce anything that is unusual about the department. For example, the fact that another soprano has joined the choir in October is not worthy material for a news release. If that soprano happens to be an exchange student from Sweden who joins the choir after having sung in one of Sweden's community choruses, it has news value. It will have even more value if the girl is living with the family of another member of the choir and the tie of choral music can be shown both at school and at home.

Other possible news releases include: auditions held, officers elected, honors chorus students selected, officers plan fund raising, concert backdrops being painted, Christmas concert, chorus invited to perform at annual service club dinner, fine arts festival, contest, and any awards received. These are only some of the possibilities. Every school has some unique qualities that are newsworthy. Don't underestimate their news value.

Other Methods of Publicity

The following methods of publicity are also good, depending upon the situation. Probably the best publicity is word of mouth. People who have attended concerts in the past will, by their positive comments, influence the attendance of other people at future concerts. The best publicity then is a fine performance. Use the following means of publicity as they are best adapted to each specific situation.

Posters. Student-made posters are acceptable and even desirable if they are neat, original, and convey the message. Twenty posters placed in the areas of the most traffic will produce better than fifty poorly placed ones. Excellent locations to place them are banks, shopping centers, utility companies, grocery stores, and stores immediately adjacent to the several busiest intersections in any community.

Handbills. These are only valuable if they are brief and are delivered to houses.

Public Service, Radio, and Television Programs. Most stations allow short announcements for nonprofit organizations. Contact these stations well in advance. They often have early deadlines and strict rules regarding the announcements they will broadcast.

Selected Mailers to Program Chairman (or Presidents) of All Local Service Clubs. Ask to have the date and time of the concert announced at a meeting prior to the concert.

Personal Written Invitations. Either the president of the choir or the director can send these invitations to a VIP list that includes administration, board of education, officers of local music clubs, fine arts association officers, and similar people.

Personal Invitations. Members of the choir can personally invite faculty members. Have each member of the choir be responsible for inviting a certain number of faculty members and their family to the concerts.

Photographs

As soon as possible in the school year arrange to have a photo taken of the choir. If a school photographer is not available, have a professional photographer take the pictures. He needs to know that you want the pictures for newspaper and other publicity use so he can provide you with suitable prints. Eight- by ten-inch glossy prints are most suitable for publicity purposes. Make these prints available to the newspaper office with your first story or as soon as they are available. Once copies have been sent, attention can be called to the fact that the office already has a photo of the choir for use with later stories.

Publicity is only the means by which you call the public's attention to your department. A director must be careful not to overpublicize himself, but he must also see that the department receives the publicity it deserves. Build a program and not yourself and you will be rewarded as the program is rewarded.

Activities

The department, in the beginning, may have all the activities it can successfully sustain. As the department grows, however, it will be desirable to add activities that merit inclusion in the program. When the point arrives that new activities can be introduced, try to plan activities that are stimulating to the ensemble. The activities listed below have been successful in a number of schools throughout the country.

Bring in a Clinician. Invite a choral director from a nearby college or high school as a clinician for your choir for a day. The money spent in this endeavor is usually very well spent. This type of clinic is discussed thoroughly in chapter thirteen.

Attend Concerts as a Group. Organize a group of the choir members to attend a professional or college concert. The members will enjoy the opportunity to attend the concert as a member of their special group. Many of the members will attend in this manner but would not have the initiative to attend the same concert on their own. Others would find it impossible to attend concerts because of lack of transportation or lack of funds or both. These opportunities can introduce many students to the finest music in stimulating circumstances.

Exchange Concerts. Plan an exchange concert with a nearby school. If it is not possible to sing for the entire student body of the school, perform only for the choir and have their choir later perform for yours. It is also good to perform a concert for the junior high school that sends students to your high school. This can be a good recruiting device for registration.

Participate in Area Festivals. In almost every area of the United States there are small festivals sponsored by universities or professional organizations. It should not be difficult to become a part of a worthwhile festival that will add to the dimension of your ensemble.

Informal Choir Day. Where several rural schools are close to each other but there are not enough schools of sufficient size to support a festival, an informal choir day can be quite stimulating. The format is wide open—it can be whatever the participating directors want it to be. Use a Saturday to let the members of the choirs get together and enjoy some fellowship as well as an opportunity to hear each other sing. It is usually rewarding to let the singers join together to sing one or two pieces. The day can be divided so that part of the time is spent socially and the rest enjoying choral music.

Madrigal Festival. This can be an informal or formal affair. The more madrigals that participate, the more organization that will be required. This activity can range from two or three madrigals getting together for dinner and some informal singing, to a large scale event with a clinician and performances by several ensembles. The format is again wide open. It is most desirable to allow the format to change, depending upon the schools involved and the interest of the directors and the students.

Commission a Choral Work. This is a project that can be immensely stimulating to a well-established choir in a program of sound musical values. Let the students participate in the selection of a composer by having them choose on the basis of some of the music they have sung. Perhaps there is a composer nearby whose music the choir has performed. If so, he would probably be willing to write a piece for the choir for a smaller fee than usual. This project does not have to be undertaken each year. Let it be something special to mark an anniversary of the school or a convention appearance by the choir.

Discussion Questions

1. How can a director learn to pace himself if he is to conduct four or even five choral ensembles every day? Does teaching choral music require more stamina than that of the average or even good history teacher?
2. What time of the day is best to rehearse the top-performing group?

3. There are certain immovable objects in every school schedule. What are they, and how can one use them to an advantage?
4. Obtain a budget request form from a local school. Prepare what would be a yearly budget for a choral department.
5. If possible, find out the amount of money a nearby school is allowed for a choral budget. Determine how you would best spend that money.
6. Beyond the essential needs of a choral department, such as music, folders, etc., determine the order in which you would wish to buy desirable items, such as tape recorders and the like.
7. What type of wearing apparel do you prefer to see high school choirs wearing?
8. Do high school students enjoy wearing period costumes for madrigal ensembles?
9. Are choir officers always necessary? How can a director avoid letting the election of officers become a popularity contest?
10. What other methods of publicizing concerts can you think of? What, in your experience, has been the best means of publicizing concerts?
11. What type of people usually attend the choral concerts? How can you interest others?
12. What other activities do you think would be worthwhile to a choral department?
13. How important are extensive tours to the development of a good choral department? Is a four-day tour twice as good as a two-day tour?

SUGGESTED READINGS

Hertz, Wayne S. "Physical Facilities and Equipment." *Choral Director's Guide.* Edited by Neidig and Jennings. West Nyack, N.Y.: Parkers Publishing Co., Inc., 1967.

Hoffer, Charles R. *Teaching Music in the Secondary Schools,* chap. 6. Belmont, California: Wadsworth Publishing Co., Inc., 1964.

———. *How to Promote Your Band (A Manual of Public Relations).* Elkhart, Indiana: H. and A. Selmer, Inc., 1957.

Klotman, Robert H. *Scheduling Music Classes.* Washington, D. C.: Music Educators National Conference, 1968.

The School Music Administrator and Supervisor: Catalysts for Change in Music Education, chap. 8-10. Englewood Cliffs, N. J.: Prentice-Hall, Inc., 1973.

Snyder, Keith D. *School Music Administration and Supervision.* 2d ed., chap. 7-9. Boston: Allyn and Bacon, Inc., 1965.

Sunderman, Lloyd F. *Choral Organization and Administration.* Rockville Centre, L.I.: Belwin, Inc., 1954.

———. *School Music Teaching: Its Theory and Practice,* chap. 7-8. New York: The Scarecrow Press, Inc., 1965.

Weyland, Rudolph H. *Guide to Effective Music Supervision,* 2d ed., part 3. Dubuque: Wm. C. Brown Company, Publishers 1968.

Winning Public Support for the School Choral Group. Chicago: E. R. Moore Co.

professional ethics and teacher relationships

Professional Ethics

Professional ethics is a term we attach to certain standards of conduct within the teaching profession. In order for any profession to be respected and to have self-respect, its members must have and live up to these standards. A profession can only grow when its members have respect for themselves and for their contribution as a profession to their society.

The professional standards of conduct given in figure 90 can be used as a guide for people entering the teaching profession.

Teacher–Teacher Relationships

It is most important to be respected by one's fellow teachers. These relationships are ones that will be important to the choral director and to the choral music department.

Be careful about the remarks you make about other teachers and their teaching. Unless you have visited their classrooms you can't know first-hand what type of teaching other people do. You should be particularly cautious about the comments that are made to students about other teachers. Don't undermine another teacher's effectiveness by saying things about him or his teaching that will make students think less of him. Such statements will not make them think any more of you. Teachers are often misquoted by students, and any statements regarding other teachers must be cautiously made. Students tend to hear what they want to hear and will look for meanings in your words that you may not intend.

Confine the discussion of faculty decisions or school policy to faculty or department meetings. Anything but casual or general comments in the faculty lounge, for example, will cause hard feelings and will contribute to the division of a faculty. Do not sit quietly through a faculty discussion and later voice

code of ethics and standard practices for texas educators

The Texas educator should strive to create an atmosphere that will nurture to fulfillment the potential of each student.

The educator is responsible for standard practices and ethical conduct toward students, professional colleagues, parents, and the community.

The Code is intended to govern the profession, and interpretations of the Code shall be determined by the Professional Practices Commission.

The educator who conducts his affairs with conscientious concern will exemplify the highest standards of professional commitment.

principle i
PROFESSIONAL ETHICAL CONDUCT
The Texas educator should endeavor to maintain the dignity of the profession by respecting and obeying the law, demonstrating personal integrity, and exemplifying honesty.

1. The educator shall not intentionally misrepresent official policies of his school district or educational organization and shall clearly distinguish those views from his personal attitudes and opinions.
2. The educator shall honestly account for all funds committed to his charge and shall conduct his financial business with integrity.
3. The educator shall not use institutional or professional privileges for personal or partisan advantage.

principle ii
PROFESSIONAL PRACTICES AND PERFORMANCE
The Texas educator, after qualifying in a manner established by law or regulation, shall assume responsibilities for professional teaching practices and professional performance and shall continually strive to demonstrate competence.

1. The educator shall apply for, accept, offer, or assign a position or a responsibility on the basis of professional qualifications and shall adhere to the terms of a contract or appointment.
2. The educator shall possess mental health, physical stamina, and social prudence necessary to perform the duties of his professional assignment.
3. The educator shall organize instruction that seeks to accomplish objectives related to learning.
4. The educator shall continue professional growth.
5. The educator shall comply with written local school board policies, Texas Education Agency regulations, and applicable state laws.

principle iii
ETHICAL CONDUCT TOWARD PROFESSIONAL COLLEAGUES
The Texas educator, in exemplifying ethical relations with colleagues, shall accord just and equitable treatment to all members of the profession.

1. The educator shall not reveal confidential information concerning colleagues unless disclosure serves professional purposes or is required by law.
2. The educator shall not willfully make false statements about a colleague or the school system.
3. The educator shall adhere to written local school board policies and legal statutes regarding dismissal.

principle iv
ETHICAL CONDUCT TOWARD STUDENTS
The Texas educator, in accepting a position of public trust, should measure success by the progress of each student toward realization of his potential as an effective citizen.

1. The educator shall deal considerately and justly with each student and shall seek to resolve problems including discipline according to law and school board policy.
2. The educator shall not intentionally expose the student to disparagement.
3. The educator shall not reveal confidential information concerning students unless disclosure serves professional purposes or is required by law.
4. The educator shall make reasonable effort to protect the student from conditions detrimental to learning, or health, or safety.
5. The educator shall endeavor to present facts without distortion.

principle v
ETHICAL CONDUCT TOWARD PARENTS AND COMMUNITY
The Texas educator, in fulfilling citizenship responsibilities in the community, should cooperate with parents and others to improve the public schools of the community.

1. The educator shall not interfere with a colleague's exercise of political and citizenship rights and responsibilities.
2. The educator shall make reasonable effort to communicate to parents information which should be revealed in the interest of the student.
3. The educator shall endeavor to understand community cultures and relate the home environment of students to the school.
4. The educator shall manifest a positive role in school public relations.

Adopted by the Teachers' Professional Practices Commission April 5, 1971

Used with the permission of the Teachers' Professional Practices Commission of Texas.

Figure 90   Code of Ethics from the Texas Education Agency

loud opinions in the lounge. If you have something to say, it should be said in the faculty meetings where it can be weighed by all faculty members during a formal discussion.

Teacher–Student Relationships

It is most important for the students to respect you as an educator and as a professional person capable in your field. Each teacher demonstrates this professionalism each day of the school year not just at in-service meetings and teacher's conventions.

A beginning teacher will often have difficulty establishing himself as a leader in the classroom and in maintaining relationships that are clearly teacher–student. This teacher is not far removed from the age of the high school student. The problems that result from too close a relationship will, at the very least, undermine one's teaching. The respect of the other students will be lost as well as the respect of the other teachers.

A teacher will not like all of his students and it is unrealistic to believe that all of the students will like every teacher. Although it is not necessary that all of the students like a teacher in order for him to be effective, it is necessary for the students to respect him. Remember, students are not looking for a friend in the teacher; they have their own friends. Instead, they are looking for a teacher whom they can respect and to whom they can look for leadership. Students do not respect teachers who allow relationships to become mixed. They are too young and immature to know when a relationship as a friend ends and a teacher–student relationship begins again.

Discipline

It can be said that good teachers are always effective disciplinarians, but that good disciplinarians are not always good teachers. Discipline for its own sake is of no value. Discipline for the sake of allowing the students to learn should always be maintained. The best possible method of discipline is to be such a good teacher that the students will be so busy learning that they won't be interested in anything but the subject. Some suggestions are made in the interests of maintaining a classroom attitude that is most conducive to good teaching.

1. Be consistent in the treatment of the students. Demand the same behavior from all the students.
2. Handle each discipline problem as it arises. Do not allow small problems to continue until they become so large that they cannot be handled by the classroom teacher.
3. Do not make threats, and particularly, do not make threats in anger that you will be unwilling or unable to back up later.

4. If it is necessary to punish students for their misbehavior, make the punishment fit the infraction. Do not demand punishments that are contrary to the policies of the school. Check with the administration regarding the holding of students after school hours and other such detentions.

5. Make only those rules that are necessary to your effective teaching. Have a reason for the rules in your classroom and explain those reasons to the students.

6. Recognize incorrigible students and have them removed from the classroom. Not every student can be a part of a classroom learning situation and not every student can be effectively disciplined by a classroom teacher. These people should be removed from the classroom until they are able to function in a learning situation. The learning rights of the other students should not be infringed upon by one or two persons who have no desire to learn and wish only to disturb the class. These people are most likely emotionally disturbed and need professional help beyond that which the classroom teacher is able to give.

7. Administer whatever rules the administration has made. Do not administer only those rules with which you are in agreement. When rules exist that you believe are poor, work to have those rules changed or eliminated. However, until the rule is altered it is your responsibility to administer it. In order for a school system to function effectively, each teacher cannot make personal decisions as to which rules they will enforce and which ones they will ignore.

Counseling Students

Almost every school has a part-time or full-time counselor. Refer students to these people who are trained to handle their problems. Whenever students have special problems, the counselors usually notify the teachers so they can be of benefit to them in the classroom. Whenever teachers begin to detect abnormal behavioral patterns in students, a counselor should be notified so the student can receive expert help if it is needed.

Be especially careful about trying to solve student problems that relate to the home. As a teacher you will hear one side of the story from the student. The side you hear may be honestly but emotionally told and represent part, but not all of the truth. There are occasions when the teacher can be of significant help to parents who recognize a problem in their child and wish to correct it. Students can be helped immensely when the teacher, counselor, and parents work together. Understand, however, that it takes a great deal of understanding, training, and a certain ability to deal with people, to affect a student's life in a positive manner. Honest, but poorly aimed attempts at counseling may create more problems than previously existed.

Teacher–Administrator Relationships

One of the first things a beginning teacher should learn is to go through channels. Whenever one has requests, they should be taken to the immediate supervisor. If this person cannot help, one should proceed up the line until the correct person is reached. If the immediate supervisor is bypassed, he may become antagonistic towards you and erase any possibility of a good relationship that could be advantageous to the development of the choral department.

Keep the administration informed of all plans. Any changes in the total program should be fully discussed with the administration before they are implemented. They may have far-reaching consequences of which the choral director is unaware.

If you disagree with the administration reaction to a request or proposal, do not hesitate to present your views. You may be able to persuade the administration to reach a decision in your favor. If, however, the final decision is not what you wanted, accept it without further discussion. Under no circumstances should a teacher elaborate to the students regarding such matters, or complain about decisions that are not to their liking. If the matter is important to the future of the department, by all means do not drop the proposal. Study the proposal carefully. Perhaps you can revise it and show enough new material as evidence to bring the matter up again and get a new decision. Read the material in chapter fourteen regarding making budget proposals to the administration and apply the same procedure to other proposals. An administrator is impressed with teachers who are well-prepared and are able to explain their proposal logically.

Finally, administrators are most impressed with teachers who are able to read instructions, complete forms correctly, and return them on time.

Teacher–Community Relationships

The choral director is teaching in an area of the school that is often referred to as, "the showcase of education." The public judges much of the school by the music ensembles, debate teams, athletic teams, and other activities that are easily available to them. Conduct yourself in the community in a manner that earns respect for you and the department as well as the school you represent.

Participate in community life whenever practical and possible. Service club memberships are often available. Such activities can be rewarding to an individual. This membership may also provide a path to a better understanding of the choral department's goals by some of the community leaders. Participate in the community as though you will raise your children there and live there the rest of your life—indeed, you may.

Professional Organizations

There are several professional organizations to which teachers may belong. These groups provide the teacher with current ideas and research that is important to the profession. They allow teachers to contribute to one another in the form of articles in journals and as participants in workshop sessions. The professional organizations vary from those that deal with the entire profession (NEA), to those that deal only with a specific portion of the profession (ACDA). Membership in both types is encouraged and all persons who are interested in the well-being of the future of their profession will want to belong to their professional organizations.

The organizations usually provide a journal which includes articles pertinent to one's teaching as well as leadership on a state, regional, and national level. Organizations are effective lobbies for the profession and their work behind the scenes has contributed to the growth and increased stature of the teaching profession. The interest of these professional groups goes beyond the welfare of the teacher however. They are interested in the future of education and the development of techniques and materials that will improve the quality of education in America. Every new teacher is encouraged to belong to organizations whose purposes are as stated above, but he is also admonished to eliminate from consideration any group whose purposes are selfish and self-serving.

Several organizations are listed that a new teacher will be asked to join and with which he should be familiar. Each teacher is strongly urged to obtain membership in all of the following organizations although it may seem a financial burden to a young teacher. The possibilities of life membership in these associations should be investigated. Substantial savings can result from life memberships if they are purchased at the beginning of a teaching career.

Music Educators National Conference

The Music Educators National Conference (MENC) is the largest association of music teachers. Separate associations for choral directors, band directors, etc., are affiliate group members of MENC. It is a general association for all music teachers. The MENC *Journal* is noted for its many articles on music education and for its variety of offerings.

MENC sponsors state, regional, and national conventions that are of value to the music teacher. New materials of music publishers and manufacturers are on display at these conventions, providing music teachers with an excellent opportunity to review and compare the products of the music industry that relate to music education.

American Choral Directors Association

The American Choral Directors Association (ACDA) was formed to further good choral music in America. It offers state, regional, and national workshops and conventions of outstanding quality. In some states district workshops are available that are of immense practical value to the participating directors. The *Choral Journal* is published nine times a year and contains valuable articles on various elements of choral music. The activities of this organization are of practical use to every choral director.

American Choral Foundation

The American Choral Foundation (ACF) is unique among these organizations in that it does not have state, regional, or national conventions. ACF offers a journal, the *Choral Review,* research memos, and a rental library to its members. The *Choral Review* includes worthy articles for the choral director and scholar. The research memos bring selective repertoire lists and other valuable information to the attention of the members.

National Education Association

The National Education Association (NEA) is the largest professional organization of teachers. It has a general membership of teachers from all areas. The *NEA Journal* offers numerous articles related to the teaching profession at large. There are state and local chapters of the NEA. Membership in NEA is usually encouraged by all school districts.

Discussion Questions

1. How can an individual teacher strengthen his professional organizations?
2. What different methods are there of preventing discipline problems from arising? Can certain discipline problems be anticipated?
3. Do teacher's unions differ from professional associations? If so, how?

SUGGESTED READINGS

Brownell, Samuel M. "If I Were Starting to Teach." *Bulletin.* National Association of Secondary School Principals (NASSP) 52: 2-5.
Chapman, Rebecca. "Teaching Is Also Learning." *Bulletin.* NASSP 52: 6-10.
Morris, Jean. "Diary of a Beginning Teacher." *Bulletin.* NASSP 52: 23-27.
Robbins, Jerry H. "Hot Spots in Student Activities—How to Deal with Them." *Bulletin.* NASSP 55: 34.

chapter 16.

student teaching and securing a position

Student Teaching

The student teaching experience can and should be a vital and stimulating part of one's music education. After spending three years in the classroom studying music theory, history, voice, piano, conducting, educational psychology, and methods of teaching music (to name only a few of the important areas that are studied), student teaching offers practical experience for the teacher-to-be under the guidance of a cooperating teacher and a college supervisor.

The student teacher has the opportunity to apply the theories of the classroom in a normal public school music class at the elementary or secondary level. This experience offers the student teacher a chance to plan and to execute that plan under the most realistic conditions possible. The student teacher will also discover both the good and bad aspects of everyday teaching.

It should be mentioned that the student teaching experience can never be completely realistic. The student teacher can never feel that he has total control because he cannot be sure how much of the classroom leadership is due to the influence of his cooperating teacher. It is also impossible for him to make decisions as though they were really his to make. On the other hand it is a unique opportunity to learn the practical aspects of teaching with an experienced teacher to whom one can turn for advice, criticism, and leadership.

Cooperating Teacher

The procedure of placing student teachers and the length of the student teaching experience varies throughout the United States. Whenever possible student teachers are placed with experienced teachers, those who have demonstrated a high degree of success. The purpose is to provide an opportunity for the student teacher to try out his own ideas, and those he has learned, in a practical situation under the close supervision of an excellent teacher. The cooperating teacher should ideally be a person who commands the respect of his students, is acknowledged as highly competent in his field, is willing to allow the student teacher some latitude in developing his ideas, and is capable of offering criticism that will encourage a student teacher to improve. In short, he should be a master teacher with a thorough understanding of the requirements for a beginning teacher.

College Supervisor

This person is usually one with public school experience and is often the professor of the methods class. The supervisor works closely with the public schools. From his knowledge of the student and his association with the teacher in the public schools he carefully pairs the student teacher and the cooperating teachers. He considers the professional strengths and weaknesses of both persons, their personal characteristics, and the particular teaching situation in the placing of student teachers.

The supervisor should make periodic, unannounced visits to observe the student teacher. It is usually best to allow the student teacher approximately two weeks in the situation before visiting him.

The supervisor wishes to see the student teacher succeed and is ready to offer all the help possible toward that goal. A supervisor will offer evaluations that point out teaching strengths and weaknesses. He should also challenge the student teacher toward a higher degree of excellence in his teaching.

The supervisor will also act as a buffer between the student teacher and the cooperating teacher should this become necessary. Both persons are capable of all the human emotions and occasionally misunderstandings arise that call for an independent arbitrator. The supervisor can do this without destroying the effectiveness of either of the people involved. Student teachers should not let small problems grow into large ones before seeking the guidance of the supervisor. Often, incidents can be averted when they can be dealt with at an early stage.

Student Teaching Procedures

Usually a student teacher is allowed to observe the classes for a short period of time before he begins teaching. This helps him learn about the pace of the school, the type of students he will teach, and to reorient himself to the public school classroom. This period of observation often includes taking the roll as a method of learning the students' names, seating classes, and acting as an extension of the cooperating teacher in laboratory situations with one or two students.

A good way for the student to begin teaching is to assume the role of teacher in a limited way, rather than taking the full responsibility of a class immediately. A student teacher may teach for one-half period for a week before taking the class full time. In many situations the student teacher teaches one-half periods in several classes and never assumes the full teaching load. This can also be a worthwhile experience although he should learn the demands placed on the teacher who teaches successive classes without the help of an assistant.

The cooperating teacher should remain in the classroom part of the time so he can give both verbal and written criticism. Written criticisms are especially valuable because the student teacher can take them home and apply them as he plans for the next day's classes.

The following points regarding student teaching should be reviewed before entering into student teaching.

Preparation. It is important to be fully prepared for each class. This cannot be overemphasized. Prepare for every contingency. Prepare more material than you will be able to cover. Always plan for an area which can be listed as *if time*. One may not always teach all that one prepares but one can never be overprepared.

Classroom Goals. Set realistic goals for each rehearsal. Don't try to accomplish too many things at once. Decide what you want the students to learn, then decide what teaching devices can be used most effectively to accomplish that purpose.

Appearance. The student teacher should be pleasantly attired in fashions that are proper for the occasion. It is best to dress conservatively, avoiding the extremes of the present fashions.

Men should wear dress shirts, ties, and sport coats or suits. Since classrooms are more often too warm than too cold it is suggested that light weight coats be worn. Additionally, the physical activity of conducting will prompt one to wear lighter clothing.

Women should wear dresses or matching skirt and blouse combinations. Pantsuits or other attire may be worn after the student teacher is knowledgeable of the dress customs of the school.

Role as a Student and as a Teacher. The student teacher usually finds himself in the position of being a student part of the day and a teacher the other part. Sometimes it is difficult to make the transition from student to teacher. As teachers we must accept responsibility for all activities in the classroom and provide leadership for all the students. The student, on the other hand, has none of these concerns. Since the student teacher is usually only four or five years older than the students with whom he will be working, he must do everything possible to establish himself as a teacher and remove himself from the student peer level. This is particularly true if the student teacher appears to be younger than he really is. Small persons (particularly women) tend to blend into the secondary age group easily. The choice of attire and manner of dress will aid in the separation of student from teacher. (Also see chapter fifteen regarding student-teacher relationships.)

Personal Health. Students are often unaware of the tremendous amount of stamina required of teachers. Student teachers should get plenty of rest so their strength and resistance to disease will be high. Student teachers must understand at the outset that there are no cuts in student teaching (as there are *none* in the teaching profession). One must plan to be on the job and be able to teach effectively every day. If you are up late writing a term paper, you are still expected to be on the job the next day, fully prepared. There are no excuses. Certainly, student teachers should not be teaching if they are ill. However, one cannot expect to complete student teaching satisfactorily if one fails to complete what is considered to be the minimum number of teaching days.

Accept Criticism. No one enjoys being criticized but a student teacher must be able to accept constructive criticism and make changes in his teaching procedure. He must review his teaching and evaluate his own efforts when possible. The evaluations of the cooperating teacher and the supervisor should be reviewed carefully.

Verbal Expression. The student teacher should be careful to use acceptable English as he speaks to classes. Refrain from using slang in the classroom.

Nonteaching Duties. Every teacher must perform certain nonteaching duties such as completing forms for the principal's office, taking roll, ordering music, mimeographing teaching aids, returning materials, etc. The student teacher should expect to be asked to perform some of these tasks. He should not spend an inordinate amount of his time in such activities however. A good rule to follow is to expect to spend about the same percentage of time at such tasks as the cooperating teacher usually spends. The percentage may be the same but the clock hours may differ.

Legal Complications. The cooperating teacher is responsible to the administration for the activities in his classroom. A student teacher should determine exactly who is legally responsible when the cooperating teacher is out of the room. It must be remembered that the student teacher is not an employee of the school system. Some administrations ask the student teacher to teach the classes if the cooperating teacher must be gone for half or all of the school day. When this request is made, the student teacher should discuss the matter with his college supervisor. Generally, the student teacher should not serve as a substitute teacher. In most situations he cannot be paid for this day. He is also placed in a precarious situation legally. Unless the school system accepts the legal responsibility in writing, the student teacher can be in a very weak position legally. It is best if the school system will hire a substitute who can be in the classroom even though the sutdent teacher does the actual teaching.

Selecting and Securing a Position

As one completes his undergraduate training it is imperative that he sum up these few years. They should have given one the foundation on which to build a career as a teacher. These few years must not be viewed as the total preparation for a choral director. The student is reaching the point, however, when he may apply his knowledge in a professional teaching capacity.

Self-evaluation

There are two times when it seems most appropriate to do a self-evaluation—when one finishes something and when one starts something. The graduating senior is in both positions.

Evaluate yourself in terms of your musical strengths and weaknesses and your personal strengths and weaknesses. Make a list of those characteristics that you possess that you think will make you an effective teacher. List also those characteristics that you have that you will want to minimize, those that might detract from your teaching effectiveness. Be frank in your self-evaluation. If possible, talk these strengths and weaknesses over with someone.

If a physical characteristic is one of the weaknesses and nothing can be done to correct it, do everything possible to minimize it. Try to develop other strengths that will overshadow this handicap.

Professional Credentials

During the second semester of the senior year one should begin to develop a set of professional credentials. These credentials should contain a personal history, a photograph, letters of recommendation, and a transcript of college credits. It takes several weeks to accomplish the above even when one has completed student teaching and most of the course work. Plan ahead so the file will be complete when you wish to have it sent to a possible employer.

There are several agencies with whom an applicant may file his credentials. Each of these will have forms available which will include all of the information listed above.

College Placement Office

This is the office that most college graduates use when seeking a teaching position. It has several advantages.

1. It is close and easily accessible to the applicant. He can check quickly to determine that all of the recommendations have been received or that a set of credentials has been mailed. He can also find out quickly about any new positions that are listed with the agency.
2. There is no fee charged to the applicant for positions acquired through this office (except for a nominal file maintenance fee sometimes charged).
3. Occasionally, particularly in smaller colleges, the applicant is personally known to the personnel in the placement office. This can be an advantage to both the applicant and employer. The director may be more able to direct candidates toward positions for which he knows they are best suited.
4. Colleges want to place their graduates in good teaching positions. Consequently, they will often work very hard for the applicant to help him secure the best position available.

The only disadvantage to the college placement office is that most of the positions that are listed are local (within the state or within a certain region of the state). This may not be a disadvantage to new teachers, most of whom, statistics show, take teaching positions within the state in which they receive their degree.

Professional Placement Bureaus

Professional placement bureaus perform basically the same function as the college placement office. They differ in that: (A) they charge a fee (usually five percent of the first year's salary) and (B) they often list vacancies in a larger area than the college office. Usually such an office lists positions for at least an entire region of the country. The firm's listings may be concentrated in an area of the country in which you are not interested.

State Teacher Agencies

Many states maintain a placement office in the state teacher association office. This office is usually available only to members and maintains a listing of positions available in that state only. There is usually no fee required by this agency.

In addition to the above, an applicant has other avenues open to him. He may find out about positions through acquaintances, college faculty, professional colleagues (when actively teaching), and advertisements in newspapers (where these are used).

Applicants may also write letters of inquiry to large school systems requesting an application form and asking to be notified in the event a vacancy occurs. It is unethical however, to apply for a specific position when it is known to be held by another person.

When you are informed of an opening in which you are interested the following procedure is recommended:

1. Write a letter of application.
2. Have your credentials sent.
3. Reinforce the letter with a personal recommendation from someone known and respected by the employer or call the employer yourself.
4. Quietly find out as much as you can about the position and the school system from persons other than the one to whom you applied.
5. Personal interview at the invitation of the school.
6. Accept or decline the position, if offered.

Each of these areas is discussed in detail. Taper all suggestions regarding applications to the specific situation. Every position has its own particular characteristics to which an applicant should address himself.

Letter of Application

The applicant's first contact with an employer is the letter of application. It must be the best possible introduction if one wishes to be considered for a position.

A letter of application should be typed on paper of good quality, be free of errors, and neat in appearance. The letter should also be concise and to the point. It must be carefully written to express the interest and the personality of the writer. Be sure that your use of English is correct. If necessary, have someone help you. Make a carbon copy of each letter for your own file. You may want to know later exactly what you said and to whom you said it.

The first paragraph should state the position for which you are applying and indicate how you were advised of the opening.

In the second paragraph indicate your educational background, emphasizing the particular items that are of special interest for this position. Taper your strengths to the position. If, for example, the position includes teaching a music theory class and you excelled in theory or attained honors in that area, mention it in this paragraph. It will tell the employer of your special qualifications for the position.

In the third paragraph indicate that you are interested in discussing the position further, that you would be interested in a personal interview. Include your address and a phone number where you can be reached. A third paragraph may also elaborate on some experience or qualification that is important to this position.

Enclose a wallet size photo. Proofread the letter and be sure to sign it.

Reinforce the Application

After the letter has been received, an applicant may reinforce the application in one of several ways. He might call the person to whom the letter was sent. He could also ask for a written recommendation from a person who is known to the other party. This letter should be sent directly to the school official.

Investigate the Position

Find out what you can about the position, the school system, and the city. This can be done by talking with people who are knowledgeable about the position in question, perhaps a relative in the city or a friend. Find out what you can about the music program throughout the system and about the position of music in the community. Are the choral programs in the churches vigorous ones? Is there a civic music program? Are concerts well attended? What does the adult in the community know or think about the present choral program? These are some of the questions that can be asked.

The Interview

When you are invited to interview for a position, be sure you understand when and where the interview will take place. Be at the interview on time and be alone. Married persons should not bring a spouse to the interview unless requested to do so. When you meet the school representative (personnel director, music supervisor, principal, or in some instances, the superintendent), shake hands with a firm grip.

Let the other party set the tone of the interview. He has far more experience in conducting interviews than you do. You may expect several questions about your background. Answer these and all questions directly but do not elaborate unless it is of primary importance.

You are at somewhat of a disadvantage at the interview because the school official has much more information about you than you have about him and the school system. He has a complete transcript of your college grades, letters from faculty attesting to your capabilities as a student and their prognosis of your teaching potential. On the other hand you must rely on the previous personal investigation of the position and on the interview itself for your information. One must be a good listener and be able to remember clearly what one hears. It is also important to be able to discern the conviction of the speaker. If one asks whether or not tape cassettes can be purchased, for instance, one must be able to discern from the answer, even if affirmative, just how strongly the official feels about this area and whether or not he will back his statements with budget allocations.

Know how many hours you have in your major and in your minor area. Be prepared to briefly state your philosophy of education.

The other party will have some questions that usually consume the first part of the interview. As areas of interest to you come up in the discussion, you may ask pertinent questions. There will be a point, though, at which you will be given an opportunity to ask questions. Prepare your questions in advance. If areas regarding schedule, budget, salary, choral materials, performing philosophy of the administration, or other areas that you are concerned about are not mentioned in the first part of the interview, you should ask about them at this point. It should be remembered that the interview is a preliminary discussion and that one should not consume too much time with questions. A few questions, well placed, will give an applicant an opportunity to judge the administrator's interest in music and his intent to properly back a strong music program.

A casual, tolerant attitude on the part of the administration is almost impossible to overcome. A strong choral program is dependent on their help. One way to determine the administrator's attitude is to notice if he is enthusiastic about the present music program and its place in the education of the youth of the community. He may indicate a dissatisfaction with the present program and say that he desires a better choral department. He may be direct and emphatic about what he expects from his teachers. If he is, he will usually assure you of his support also. If you don't see a spark of enthusiasm for the school and some pride of his role as an administrator, you may suspect that it will be difficult to develop an outstanding program in this school.

When the interview is over, tell the official that you enjoyed the opportunity to meet with him, thank him for talking with you, and leave. After the interview there is very little that you can do to help your cause. Again, if you know someone that is known in the school system it may be of value for them to speak for you. Otherwise, you can only talk with the school official again if you have something new to tell him that could have a bearing on the position. Resist the temptation to call him and ask about your status. Administrators are just as anxious to have positions filled with the best possible people as are the applicants. They will move with all possible dispatch. If you are not called, it is because there is nothing to tell you. Phone calls at this point initiated by the applicant will endanger his chances rather than improve them.

Accept or Decline Position

When a position has been offered it should be accepted or declined within a reasonable period of time. It is certainly proper to request a few days to consider the offer. Usually one should reply within a week to an offer of employment.

Although a verbal agreement of employment is considered legal and binding upon both parties, one should not close the door to any other possibilities until a written contract has been properly signed by both parties. Once a contract is signed, the teacher should notify the placement agency that he has accepted a position and should not consider any other opportunities for employment. If an applicant has offers from two schools, he must weigh the positions carefully and choose the situation that he feels will be the best for him. He must consider salary, budget, scheduling, the administration's attitude, community support, the elementary music program, the junior high program, the state of the present choral department, the state of the entire music department, and many personal factors such as living conditions and cultural opportunities.

Once employed by a school system, a teacher will find that many states and individual school systems have deadlines after which their personnel will not be released from contracts to accept other positions. In some instances the teacher is required to pay the expense of hiring a replacement after the deadline. Many school systems will not release teachers from contracts after the first of August. Teachers should not seek other positions after these deadlines.

It is a good idea to remain in one position for several years. Job-hopping gives teachers a bad reputation and will decrease the job possibilities after just several years. It must also be understood that a solid choral program cannot be developed in just one or two years. However no one will be concerned about the teacher that makes a true advancement in his profession. There would be no point in remaining in an inferior position when an offer for a much better position has been made.

Discussion Questions

1. In what ways is student teaching an artificial situation? Can it ever be otherwise?
2. Since the cooperating teacher is ultimately responsible for the class, what innovative techniques may a student teacher initiate?
3. What outward signs will be noticed in a school whose music department is of a high quality?
4. How can an applicant find out the many things he needs to know about a school system to which he applies?

SUGGESTED READINGS

Boney, Joan, and Rhea, Lois. *A Guide to Student Teaching in Music*. Englewood Cliffs, N. J.: Prentice-Hall, 1970.

Douglas, Florian N. "Student Teaching," chap. 1. *Guide for the Beginning Choral Director*. American Choral Directors Association, 1972.

Gaarder, Richard. "Choosing and Serving a Choral Teaching Position," chap. 6. *Guide for the Beginning Choral Director*. American Choral Directors Association, 1972.

The following list of choral music is not meant to be a complete listing of all choral music for mixed voices. Such a list would have no value. This is, instead, a selected list of compositions that have been found to be successful when performed by nonprofessional choirs, and particularly high school ensembles. Many pieces listed are also appropriate for college, church, and community choirs.

These pieces may be considered as the core of a choral library, representative of the various compositional styles and periods. It is suggested that students and directors obtain a single copy of works that are unfamiliar to them.

Renaissance

Aichinger, G., Adoramus Te (Walton-6000-4); Suddenly There Came a New Sound from Heaven (Frank Music-F 441).

Anerio, F., Christus Factus Est (McLaughlin and Reilly-2344).

Byrd, W., Alleluia, Ascendit Deus (Stainer and Bell-416); Ave Verum Corpus (Mercury Music); Cantate Domino (Oxford Uiv. Press-27).

Clement, J., Adoramus Te (Mercury Music-MC 126).

Corsi, J. Adoramus Te (Choral Arts-R 181).

Croce, G., Cantate Domino (Walton-2095).

Dering, R., Quem Vidistis (H. W. Gray-1594).

de Wert, G., One Day While Walking By (Theodore Presser-632).

di Lasso, O., Adoramus Te (Arista Pub.); Ave Regina Coelorum (Associated Music-A-406); Ave Verum Corpus (Franco-Columbo-2482); Domine exaudi orationem meam (G. Schirmer-11422); How Long, O Lord (Schmitt, Hall and McCreary-1409); Jubilate Deo (Boosey and Hawkes-5490).

Dressler, G., Let All the People Praise the Lord (Schmitt, Hall and McCreary-1528).

Durante, F., Misericordias Domini (double choir) (G. Schirmer-5403).

Eccard, J., Hosanna to the Living God (Theodore Presser-312-40359); O Day of Greatest Joy (double choir) (Lawson-Gould-971).

Esquivel, J., O Quam Gloriosum (G. Schirmer-11078); O Vos Omnes (Walton-2093).

Farrant, R., Call to Remembrance (Bourne-ES 17).

Gallus, J., Ascendit Deus (G. Schirmer); Dies Sanctificatus (E. B. Marks-4302); Orietur Stella (Schmitt, Hall and McCreary); Regem Natum (Summy-Birchard-5109; This Is the Day (Concordia-98-1702).

Gastoldi, G., Come, Tune Your Voice (J. Fischer and Bros.-8742-4).

Gibbons, O., Almighty and Everlasting God (Oxford Univ. Press-TMC 36).

Hassler, H. L., Angelus ad Pastores ait (Associated Music-A-405); Cantate Domino (Bourne-ES 18); Christ is Arisen (E. B. Marks-26); My Heart With Love is Springing (Bourne-ES 40); Psalm 66 (double choir) (Mark Foster-402).

Josquin, Tu Pauperum Refugium (G. Schirmer-9565).

Morley, T., Agnus Dei (Mercury Music-MC 53).

Marenzio, L., Hodie Christus Natus Est (Concordia-98-1810).

Mouton, J., Ave Maria (Mercury Music-DCS-40).

Palestrina, G. P., Hodie Christus Natus Est (double choir) (G. Schirmer); Super Flumina Babylonis (J. Fischer-7259); These Are My Heartfelt Tears (Lawson-Gould-51029) Magnificat (Lawson-Gould).

Sweelinck, J., Hodie Christus Natus Est (E. B. Marks-4301); Praise Ye the Lord and Sing a New Song (Mark Foster-129).

Tye, C., Praise Ye the Lord (Oxford Univ. Press-TCM 58); Sing to the Lord (Homeyer).

Victoria, T. L., Ave Maria (Witmark-2W2712); Kyrie Eleison (Mark Foster-151); O Magnum Mysterium (G. Schirmer-5573); O Quam Gloriosum (G. Schirmer); Vere Languores (Oliver Ditson-332-13380).

Baroque

Bach, J. C., Songs of Mourning (Broude Bros.).

Bach, J. S., All People That on Earth Do Dwell (G. Schirmer-6810); Alleluia! Sing Praise (Carl Fischer-CM 7140); Break Forth, O Beauteous Heavenly Light (Oliver Ditson-13744); From Heaven on High (Chantry); Gloria in Excelsis Deo (Arista); Honor and Glory (from *Magnificat*) (Plymouth-SC10); Praise We the Name (Lawson-Gould-978); What God Ordains Is Good (Concordia-98-3006).

Buxtehude, D., Command Thine Angel, That He Come (Broude Bros.); In Dulci Jubilo (SAB) (Concordia-98-1500); Magnificat (Edition Peters-66288); Missa Brevis (Mercury Music-DCS 23).

Carissimi, G., Plorate, Filii Israel (Neil Kjos-29).

Crivelli, G. B., O Maria Mater Gratiae (Faber and Faber-11730).

Grandi, A., Exaudi Deus (Faber and Faber-11733).

Graun, K. H., Blessed Are the Faithful (Southern Music Co.-SC 21); Surely He Hath Borne Our Griefs (Concordia-98-1171).

Gabrielli, G., Jubilemus Singuli (G. Schirmer-11810).

Handel, G. F., Hallelujah, Amen (E. C. Schirmer-149); O Lord, in Thee (*Dettingen Te Deum*) (E. B. Marks-4464); Sing unto God (Carl Fischer); Then Round About the Starry Throne (C. C. Birchard-315); Zadok the Priest (H. W. Gray).

Leisring, Let All the Nations (Shawnee Press-A-94).

Liebhold, Commit Thy Way (Concordia-98-1125).

Lotti, A., Crucifixus (E. C. Schirmer-1192); Miserere Mei (Boosey and Hawkes-1938).

Monteverdi, C., Laetatus Sum (Mark Foster-109).

Pachelbel, J., Now Thank We All Our God (with brass) (Robert King-604); On God and Not on Human Trust (Concordia-98-1006).

Pergolesi, G. B., Sanctum et Terribile Nomen Ejus (G. Schirmer-11412).

Perti, G., Ave Regina (Lawson-Gould-515973); Two Motets (Lawson-Gould-51560).

Pitoni, G., Cantate Domino (Bourne-ES 5).

Praetorius, M., In Dulci Jubilo (with brass) (Robert King-606); Hosanna to the Son of David (Schmitt, Hall and McCreary-1516); Lobet den Herrn (G. Schirmer-9817); Psallite (Bourne-ES 21); She Is So Dear (Theodore Presser-332—1455).

Purcell, H., Lord, How Long Wilt Thou Be Angry (Mercury Music-MC 35); O Sing unto the Lord (E. C. Schirmer-1103); Three Short Anthems (Lawson-Gould-624).

Scarlatti, A., Exultate Deo (Carl Fischer-MP 71).

Schein, J., Die Mit Traenen Saen (Mercury Music-DCS-19).

Schutz, H., Ehre Sei Dir Christe (from St. Matthew Passion) (G. Schirmer-10123); Now Let Us All Give Thanks (J. Fischer); O All Ye Nations (Theodore Presser-332-13992).

Topff, J., The Angel to the Shepherd (Associated Music-A-158).

Wagner, G. G., Blessing, Glory, Wisdom (H. W. Gray-661).

Classical

Beethoven, L., Hallelujah (from Mount of Olives) (G. Schirmer).

Billings, W., Bethlehem (Edition Peters-66333); Chester (Edition Peters-66334); David's Lamentations (Edition Peters-66336); Modern Music (Edition Peters-66340); Three Fuguing Tunes (Mercury Music-MP62).

Haydn, F., Gloria (from Heilig Mass) (Walton Music-2031); Kyrie (from Lord Nelson Mass) (M. Witmark-W-3543); Sanctus (Harmonie Mass) (G. Schirmer);The Heavens Are Telling (G. Schirmer-3521).

Haydn, M., Timete Dominum (G. Schirmer-2589).

Mozart, W., Adoramus Te (G. Schirmer-9932); De Profundis (Summy-Birchard-5372); Regina Coeli (Associated Music-5222).

Schubert, F., Christ Is Arisen (Alexander Broude); Kyrie (from Mass in G) (G. Schirmer).

Romantic

Brahms, J., Create in Me, op. 29, no. 2 (G. Schirmer-7504); Four Love Songs, and Four Gypsy Songs (E. C. Schirmer); Let Nothing Ever Grieve Thee (C. F. Peters-1093);Liebeslieder Walzer, op. 52 (Associated Music-ES929A);Liebeslieder Walzer, op. 65 (Lawson-Gould); A Sigh Goes Stirring through the Wood (Associated Music-A-379); Sing Praise to God Who Reigns Above (Augsburg Pub. House-1280); Six Folk Songs (E. B. Marks-9); Zum Schluss (G. Schirmer-10135); Wondrous Cool, Thou Woodland Quiet (G. Schirmer).

Bruckner, A., Locus Iste (C. F. Peters-6314).

Gretchaninoff, A., Our Father (Theodore Presser); Remembrance (Alexander Broude).

Mendelssohn, F., He Watching over Israel (G. Schirmer); In Praise of Spring (Associated Music).

Schumann, G., Yea, Though I Wander (Augsburg Pub. House).

Tschesnokov, P., Salvation Is Created (J. Fischer-4129); Let Thy Holy Presence (Summy-Birchard-B12).

Twentieth Century

Averre, R., Did Mary Know? (Theodore Presser-312-40289).

Barber S., Let Down the Bars, O Death (G. Schirmer-8907); Reincarnation (G. Schirmer-8908-10); Sure on This Shining Night (G. Schirmer-10864); To Be Sung on the Water (G. Schirmer-11644).

Bartok, B., Four Slovak Folk Songs (#1) (Boosey and Hawkes); Three Hungarian Songs (Boosey and Hawkes).

Bassett, L., Collect (tape and chorus) (World Library-CA-2000-8).

Beckhard, R., Six Epitaphs (Rongwen Music Inc.).

Berger, J., Five Canzonets (Alexander Broude); A Rose Touched by the Sun's Warm Rays (Augsburg Pub. House-953); The Eyes of All Wait upon Thee (Augsburg Pub. House); Two Chances (Neil Kjos-5871).

Biggs, J., Auction Cries (Mark Foster-325); Invention for Voices and Tape (Gentry Publications-G-166).

Binkerd, G., The Ebb and Flow (Boosey and Hawkes).

Boyd, J., A Tongue of Wood (G. Schirmer-11511).

Britten, B., Ceremony of Carols (Boosey and Hawkes); Fancie (Boosey and Hawkes-5611); Jubilate Deo (Oxford Univ. Press-42.843); Jesu, As Thou Art Saviour (from A Boy Was Born) (Oxford Univ. Press-46.029).

Butler, E., O Give Thanks (Fine Arts Press-CM 1056).

Carr, A. L., All Under the Willow Tree (Standard Music-B316MX1); Why Are the Roses So Pale (Standard Music-B319MX1).

Christiansen, P., Bread of Tears (Augsburg Pub. House-1058).

Childs, B., Nine Choral Fragments (Keynote Music Co.); Quodlibet (Composers Facsimile); Variations (Chorus, tape and bells) (Composers Facsimile).

Cram, J., A Trio of Tongue Twisters (Carl Fischer-7745).

Copland, A., Ching-a-Ring, Chaw (Boosey and Hawkes-5024); Stomp Your Foot (Boosey and Hawkes-5019).

Creston, P., Three Chorales from Tagore (G. Schirmer-9475).

Dello Joio, N., Hymn to St. Cecilia (with brass) (Carl Fischer); A Jubilant Song (G. Schirmer-9580).

Diemer, E. L., Anthem of Faith (Standard Music-A25MX4); Spring Carol (Carl Fischer-CM7279); Three Madrigals (Boosey and Hawkes-5417).

Distler, H., How Lovely Shines the Morning Star (Arista-AE108); Praise to the Lord (J. Fischer-9695); Variations on "Lo How a Rose" (Concordia Pub. House).

Effinger, C., Four Pastorales (with oboe) (G. Schirmer); Set of Three (with brass) (Elkan-Vogel-1175).

Fauré, G., Cantique de Jean Racine (Broude Bros.).

Fetler, P., Praise Ye the Lord (Standard Music-A26MX1); Sing unto God (Augsburg Pub. House-1244); Snow toward Evening (Associated Music-A-245); Wild Swans (Associated Music-A-247).

Fink, M., Septum Angeli (E. C. Schirmer-2659); Te Deum (E. C. Schirmer-2673).

Finzi, G., My Spirit Sang All Day (Oxford Univ. Press-XVII-3).

Foss, L., Behold! I Build An House (Mercury Music).

Frackenpohl, A., Marches of Peace (with brass) (Shawnee Press-A-624).

Gabura, K., Ave Maria (World Library).

George, E., The Lamb (Summy-Birchard-2254).

Gustafson, D., Three Songs of Parting (Shawnee Press-A-897).

Hennagin, M., The Family of Man (Walton); Walking on the Green Grass (Boosey and Hawkes-5443).

Hindemith, P., Six Chansons (Schott and Co.-374).

Hooper, W., My Soul Waiteth in Silence (Carl Fischer-7705).

Hovhannes, A., O Lord of Hosts (with brass) (C. F. Peters).

Ives, C., Psalm 90 (Mercury Music); Serenity (Associated Music-A-377); Sixty-Seventh Psalm (Associated Music-A-274).

Jarrett, J., Three Christmas Songs (Standard Music-A37MX3).

Kirk, T., Alleluia, Praise the Lord (Standard Music-A36MX1); Blessed Art Thou, O Lord (Standard Music-A35MX1); Four Restoration Verses (MCA Music).

Kodaly, Z., All Men Draw Near (Oxford Univ. Press-X91).

Korte, K., O Give Thanks (Galaxy Music); I Will Make You Brooches (E. C. Schirmer-2728).

Kraehenbuehl, D., Ideo, Gloria in Excelsis (Associated Music-A-193).

Kubik, G., Household Magic (MCA Music Corp.); Scholastica: A Medieval Set (MCA Music Corp.).

Lamb, G., Aleatory Psalm (World Library); Hodie Christus Natus Est (Standard Music-A13-MX3); Three Choral Vignettes (E. B. Marks-4564).

Lekberg, S., A Villanelle (Galaxy Music-GMC 2286); Four Carols for a Holy Night (G. Schirmer-11646); Gladly for Aye We Adore Him (Standard Music-A28-MX1); Let All the World in Every Corner Sing (G. Schirmer-11616); Make a Joyful Noise unto the Lord (Galaxy Music-1837); Years Prophetical Standard Music-B400MX1).

Lenel, L., Christ Is Arisen (Concordia Pub. House-98-1572).

Lockwood, N., A Lullaby for Christmas (Neil Kjos-11); Hosanna (G. Schirmer-8391).

Lo Presti, R., Alleluia, Hodie (with brass) (Carl Fischer-CM7443).

Mechem, K., Sing unto the Lord a New Song (Mark Foster-403); Spring (Mercury Music-MC556).

Micheelsen, H., Der Morgenstern (Five variations on the Chorale) (Barenreiter-2149).

Moe, D., Hosanna to the Son of David (Mercury Music-MC252); The Lord Is My Strength (Sacred Music Press-S27); Psalm Concertato (with brass) (Augsburg Pub. House-11-633).

Nelson, R., Three Ancient Prayers (Boosey and Hawkes-5439-41).

Nystedt, All the Ways of a Man (Augsburg Pub. House); Praise to God (Augsburg Pub. House-A59715); The Path of the Just (Augsburg Pub. House-11-933).

Pepping, E., Laud Him (Neil Kjos-30).

Persichetti, V., Jimmies Got A Goil (G. Schirmer-9860); Sam Was a man (G. Schirmer-9791).

Pfautsch, L., Sing Praises (Lawson-Gould-793).

Pinkham, D., In the Beginning (tape and chorus) (E. C. Schirmer); Christmas Cantata (with brass) (Robert King Music Co.-602); The Reproaches (Associated Music-A-431).

Poulenc, F., Four Motets for the Season of Christmas (Salabert-12-15); Four Motets for the Season of Lent (Salabert); Exultate Deo (Salabert).

Rorem, N., From an Unknown Past (Southern Music-139).

Rowley, A., Jig for Voices (Boosey and Hawkes-1699).

Sanders, R., Out of the Cradle (Broude Bros.).

Schickele, P., Three Choruses from E. E. Cummings (Broude Bros.).

Schumann, W., Holiday Song (G. Schirmer-8927); Prelude for Voices (G. Schirmer-8929).

Seiber, M., Three Hungarian Folk Songs (G. Schirmer-10715).

Smith, G., Landscapes (G. Schirmer-10818).

Stevens, H., Blessed by Thy Glorious Name (Mark Foster Music-114); Go Lovely Rose (Mark Foster Music); Lady, as Thy Fair Swan (Mark Foster Music-320); Like as a Culver (Associated Music-A-218); Magnificat (with trumpet) (Mark Foster Music); Weep, O Mine Eyes (Mark Foster Music).

Stravinsky, I., Anthem (Boosey and Hawkes-5438); Ave Maria (Boosey and Hawkes-1832).

Thompson, R., Alleluia (E. C. Schirmer-1786); Choose Something Like a Star (E. C. Schirmer-2487); Glory to God (E. C. Schirmer-2470); The Last Words of David (E. C. Schirmer-2294); The Paper Reeds by the Brook (E. C. Schirmer).

Vaughan-Williams, R., For All the Saints (G. Schirmer); Let Us Now Praise Famous Men (G. Schirmer); O Clap Your Hands (with brass) (Galaxy Music-CCL222); Three Shakespeare Songs (Oxford Univ. Press).

Washburn, R., A Child This Day Is Born (with brass) (Shawnee Press).

Willan, H., Hodie Christus Natus Est (Carl Fischer-A-575); The Three Kings (Oxford Univ. Press-43.214); What Is This Lovely Fragrance? (Oxford Univ. Press).

Zimmerman, H. W., Psalmkonzert (C. F. Peters-EM 521); Psalm 23 (Concordia Pub. House-11-0640); Psalm 100 (Concordia Pub. House-11-0638).

Major Works

The following works contain one or more movements that are suitable to performance by many nonprofessional choirs.

Bach, J. S., For Us a Child Is Born (Cantata #142) (Galaxy Music Corp.); Motets (G. Schirmer).

Brahms, J., Requiem (C. F. Peters).

Britten, B., Rejoice in the Lamb (Boosey and Hawkes).

Bruckner, A., Mass in E minor (Broude Bros.).

Buxtehude, D., Magnificat (Barenreiter).

Charpentier, M., Song of the Birth of Our Lord Jesus Christ (Concordia Pub. House); Magnificat (Concordia Pub. House).

Faure, G., Requiem (G. Schirmer).

Hanson, H., Song of Democracy (Carl Fischer).

Haydn, F., Harmonie Mass (G. Schirmer); Lord Nelson Mass (C. F. Peters).

Mendelssohn, F., Elijah (G. Schirmer).

Mozart, W., Requiem (G. Schirmer); Vesper Psalms (G. Schirmer).

Pergolesi, G., Magnificat (Walton).

Poulenc, F., Gloria (Salabert); Mass (Salabert).

Schubert, F., Deutsche Messe (G. Schirmer); Mass in G. (G. Schirmer).

Schutz, H., The Christmas Story (G. Schirmer).

Stravinsky, I., Symphony of Psalms (G. Schirmer).

Vaughan Williams, R., A Prayer of Thanksgiving (Boosey and Hawkes); Hodie (Boosey and Hawkes).

Vivaldi, A., Gloria (Walton).

Music Publishers

Abingdon Press; 201 Eighth Ave., South; Nashville, Tenn. 37202.

Alfred Publishing Co., Inc.; 75 Channel Drive; Port Washington, N.Y. 11050.

AMSI (Art Masters Studios, Inc.); 2614 Nicollet Ave.; Minneapolis, Minn. 55408.

Arista Music Co.; Box 1596; Brooklyn, N.Y. 11201.

Associated Music Publishers, Inc.; 866 Third Ave.; New York, N.Y. 10022.

Augsburg Publishing House; 426 South Fifth St.; Minneapolis, Minn. 55415.

Bärenreiter; Heinrich Schutz Allee 29-37; 35 Kassel-Wilhelmeshöhe; Germany.

Belmont Music Publishers; P.O. Box 49961; Los Angeles, Calif. 90049.

Belwin-Mills Publishing Corp.; 25 Deshon Drive; Melville, N.Y. 11746.

Joseph Boonin, Inc.; Music Publications; P.O. Box 2124; So. Hackensack, N.J. 07606.

Boosey & Hawkes, Inc.; P.O. Box 130; Oceanside, N.Y. 11572.

Boston Music Co. *See* Frank Music Affiliates/Boston Music Co.

Bourne Co.; 136 West 52nd St.; New York, N.Y. 10019.

Breitkopf and Härtel. *See* Associated Music Publishers, Inc.

Broadman Press; 127 Ninth Ave. North; Nashville, Tenn. 37203.

Brodt Music Co.; P.O. Box 1207; Charlotte, N.C. 28201.

Alexander Broude, Inc.; 1619 Broadway; New York, N.Y. 10019.

Broude Brothers Limited; 56 West 45th St.; New York, N.Y. 10036.

Byron-Douglas Publications; P.O. Box 565; Phoenix, Arizona 85001.

Cambiata Press; P.O. Box 1151; Conway, Arkansas 72032.

Chappel & Co., Inc.; 866 Third Ave.; New York, N.Y. 10022.

Chor Publications; Box 4037; Wichita, Kansas 67204.

Choral Art Publications; 1540 Broadway; New York, N.Y. 10036.

Franco Colombo, Inc. *See* Belwin-Mills Publishing Corp.

Composers' Autograph Publications; P.O. Box 7103; Cleveland, Ohio 44128.

Composers Facsimile Edition; 170 West 74th St.; New York, N.Y. 10023.

Concordia (Publishing House); 3558 South Jefferson Ave.; St. Louis, Mo. 63118.

Crescendo Music Publishing; P.O. Box 11208; Dallas, Texas 75223.

Crescendo Publishing Co.; 48-50 Melrose St.; Boston, Mass. 02116.

Edition Musicus New York; 333 West 52nd St.; New York, N.Y. 10019.

Editions Salabert *See* Belwin-Mills Publishing Corp.

Elkan-Vogel, Inc.; Presser Place; Bryn Maur, Pa. 19010.

Fine Arts Press; P.O. Box 45144; Tulsa, Okla. 74145.

Carl Fischer, Inc.; 56-62 Cooper Square; New York, N.Y. 10003.

J. Fischer & Bro. *See* Belwin-Mills Publishing Corp.

H. T. FitzSimons Co., Inc. Publishers; 615 North La Salle St.; Chicago, Ill. 60610.

Harold Flammer, Inc. *See* Shawnee Press, Inc.

Mark Foster Music Co.; P.O. Box 4012; Champaign, Ill. 61820.

Sam Fox Publishing Co., Inc.; 1540 Broadway; New York, N.Y. 10036.

Frank Music Affiliates/Boston Music Co., Frank Distributing Corp.; 116 Boylston St.; Boston, Mass. 02116.

Frank Music Corp.; 119 West 57th St.; New York, N.Y. 10019.

Galaxy Music Corp.; 2121 Broadway; New York, N.Y. 10023.

General Music Publishing Co., Inc. *See* Frank Music Affiliates/Boston Music Co.

General Words and Music Co. *See* Neil A. Kjos Music Co.

Gentry Publications *See* Theodore Presser Co.

G.I.A. Publications, Inc., Gregorian Institute of America; 2115 West 63rd St.; Chicago, Ill. 60636.

H. W. Gray Co., Inc. *See* Belwin-Mills Publishing Corp.

Greenwood Press; 2145 Central Parkway; Cincinnati, Ohio 45214.

Hansen Publications, Inc.; 182 West Ave.; Miami Beach, Florida 33133.

Frederick Harris Music Co., Ltd.; Box 670; Oakville; Ontario, Canada.

Heritage Music Press; 501 E. 3rd St.; Dayton, Ohio 45401.

Hope Publishing Co.; 380 South Main Place; Carol Stream, Ill. 60187.

Edwin F. Kalmus; Miami-Dade Industrial Park; P.O. Box 1007; Opa-Locka, Florida 33054.

Kendor Music, Inc.; Delevan, N.Y. 14042.

Robert King Music Co.; North Easton, Mass.

Neil A. Kjos Music Co.; 525 Busse Highway; Park Ridge, Ill 60068.

Lawson-Gould Music Publishers, Inc.; 866 Third Ave.; New York, N.Y. 10022.

Hal Leonard Music, Inc.; P.O. Box 227; Winona, Minn. 55987.

Loop Music Co. *See* Neil A. Kjos Music Co.

Lorenz Publishing Co.; 501 East Third St.; Dayton, Ohio 45401.

Ludwig Music Publishing Co.; 557-67 East 140th St.; Cleveland, Ohio 44110.

Edward B. Marks Music Corp.; 1790 Broadway; New York, N.Y. 10019.

MCA Music; 445 Park Ave.; New York, N.Y. 10022.

Mercury Music Corp. *See* Theodore Presser Co.

Merion Music, Inc. *See* Theodore Presser Co.

Mills Music, Inc. *See* Belwin-Mills Publishing Corp.

Edwin H. Morris & Co., Inc.; 1370 Avenue of the Americas; New York, N.Y. 10019.

Novello & Co., Ltd. *See* Belwin-Mills Publishing Corp.

Oxford University Press; 200 Madison Ave.; New York, N.Y. 10016.

Pallma Music Co. *See* Neil A. Kjos Music Co.

Parks Music Corp. *See* Neil A. Kjos Music Co.

Peer-Southern Organization; 1740 Broadway; New York, N.Y. 10019.

C. F. Peters Corp.; 373 Park Ave. South; New York, N.Y. 10016.

Plymouth Music Co., Inc.; 17 West 60th St.; New York, N.Y. 10023.

Theodore Presser Co.; Presser Place; Bryn Mawr, Pa. 19010.

Pro Art Publications, Inc.; 469 Union Ave.; Westbury, N.Y. 11590.

Richmond Music Press, Inc.; P.O. Box 465, P.P. Station; Richmond, Indiana 47374.

G. Ricordi. *See* Belwin-Mills Publishing Corp.

Sacred Music Press; 501 East Third St.; Dayton, Ohio 45401.
E. C. Schirmer Music Co.; 112 South St.; Boston, Mass. 02111.
G. Schirmer, Inc.; 866 Third Avenue; New York, N.Y. 10022.
Schmitt, Hall & McCreary Co.; 110 North Fifth St.; Minneapolis, Minn. 55403.
Schott & Co., Ltd. *See* Belwin-Mills Publishing Corp.
Seesaw Music Corp.; 177 East 87th St.; New York, N.Y. 10028.
Shapiro, Bernstein & Co., Inc.; 666 Fifth Ave.; New York, N.Y. 10019.
Shawnee Press, Inc.; Delaware Water Gap, Pa. 18327.
John Sheppard Music Press. *See* Joseph Boonin, Inc.
Southern Music Co. (New York). *See* Peer-Southern Organization.
Southern Music Co. (San Antonio); P.O. Box 329; San Antonio, Texas 78292.
Spratt Music Publishers; 17 West 60th St.; New York, N.Y. 10023.
Standard Music Publishing, Inc.; P.O. Box 1043, Whitman Square; Turnersville, N.J. 08012.
Summy-Birchard Co.; 1834 Ridge Ave.; Evanston, Ill. 60204.
Tuskegee Music Press. *See* Neil A. Kjos Music Co.
Volkwein Brothers, Inc.; 117 Sandusky St.; Pittsburgh, Pa. 15212.
Walton Music Corp.; 17 West 60th St.; New York, N.Y. 10023.
Warner Bros, Publication Inc.; 1230 Avenue of the Americas; New York, N.Y. 10020.
Westwood Press, Inc. *See* Greenwood Press.
Willis Music Co.; 7380 Industrial Road; Florence, Kentucky 41042.
M. Witmark & Sons. *See* Warner Bros. Publication Inc.
Word, Inc.; 4800 West Waco Dr.; Waco, Texas 76703.
World Library Publications, Inc.; 2145 Central Parkway; Cincinnati, Ohio 45214.

Music Dealers

Byron Hoyt Sheet Music Service; 972 Mission Street; San Francisco, California 94103.
Dorn and Kirschner Band Instrument Co.; 1565 Union Avenue; Union, New Jersey.
Hallmark Music, Inc.; 147 Scranton; Lynbrook, New York 11563.
H & H Music Company; 1211 Caroline Street; Houston, Texas 77002.
J. W. Pepper and Son; 231 North Third Street; Philadelphia, Pennsylvania 19106.
Keynote Music Service, Inc.; 833 South Olive; Los Angeles, California 90014.
Magnamusic-Baton, Inc.; 6390 Delmar Blvd.; St. Louis, Missouri 63130.
Nationwide Sheet Music Service of Kansas City, Inc.; P.O. Box 2058; Kansas City, Missouri 64142.
Schmitt, Hall and McCreary; 110 North 5th; Minneapolis, Minnesota 55403.
Southern Music Company; Box 329; San Antonio, Texas 78292.
Universal Musical Instrument Company; 732 Broadway; New York, New York 10003.
Volkwein Bros., Inc.; 117 Sandusky; Pittsburgh, Pennsylvania 15212.
Werlein's for Music; 605 Canal Street; New Orleans, Louisiana 70130.

Concert Apparel

Collegiate Cap & Gown Co.; 1000 N. Market St.; Champaign, Illinois 61820.
DeMoulin Bros. & Co.; 1083 S. Fourth St.; Greenville, Illinois 62246.

E. R. Moore Company; 7230 North Caldwell; Niles, Illinois 60648.
Rollins Blazers; 242 Park Avenue South; New York, New York 10003.
C. E. Ward Co.; New London, Ohio 44851.

Choral Risers

Humes & Berg Mfg. Co., Inc.; 4801 Railroad Ave.; East Chicago, Indiana 46312.
Wenger Corporation; Owatonna, Minnesota 55060.

Recorders

Hargail Music, Inc.; 28 West 38th St.; New York, New York 10018.
The Empire Music Co., Inc.; 2707 California Ave. S. W.; Seattle, Washington 98116.
The Empire Music Co., Inc.; P.O. Box 413; Port Huron, Michigan 48060.

Professional Organizations

American Choral Directors Association; P.O. Box 17736; Tampa, Florida 33612.
American Choral Foundation; 130 West 56th Street; New York, N.Y. 10019.
Music Educators National Conference; 1201 Sixteenth Street N. W.; Washington, D.C. 20036.

Apel, Willi. *Harvard Dictionary of Music*. 2d. rev. ed. Cambridge, Mass.: Harvard University Press, 1969.

Boney, Joan, and Rhea, Lois. *A Guide to Student Teaching in Music*. Englewood Cliffs, N. J.: Prentice-Hall, 1970.

Boyd, Jack. *Rehearsal Guide for the Choral Director*. West Nyack, N. Y.: Parker Publishing Co., 1970.

Bragg, George. "The Adolescent Voice." *The Choral Journal* May 1971, pp. 10-11.

Brownell, Samuel M. "If I Were Starting to Teach." *The Bulletin* (NASP) 52: 2-5.

Bukofzer, Manfred F. *Music in the Baroque Era: From Monteverdi to Bach*. New York: W. W. Norton and Company, Inc., 1947.

———. *Studies in Medieval and Renaissance Music*. New York: W. W. Norton and Company, Inc., 1950.

Chapman, Rebecca. "Teaching Is Also Learning." *The Bulletin* (NASP) 52: 6-10.

Cope, David. *New Directions in Music*. Dubuque, Iowa: Wm. C. Brown Company, Publishers, 1971.

Crocker, Richard L. *A History of Musical Style*. New York: McGraw-Hill Book Company, 1966.

Dart, Thurston. *The Interpretation of Early Music*. Rev. ed. London: Hutchinson University Library, 1960.

Dolmetsch, Arnold. *The Interpretation of the Music of the Seventeenth and Eighteenth Centuries*. London: Oxford University Press, 1946.

Donington, Robert. *The Interpretation of Music*. London: Faber and Faber Limited, 1963.

Green, Elizabeth A. H. *The Modern Conductor*. 2d ed. Englewood Cliffs, N. J.: Prentice-Hall Inc., 1969.

Grout, Donald Jay. *A History of Western Music*. New York: W. W. Norton and Company, Inc., 1960.

Hansen, Peter S. *An Introduction to Twentieth Century Music*. 2d ed. Boston: Allyn and Bacon, Inc., 1967.

Hillis, Margaret. *At Rehearsals*. New York: American Choral Foundation, 1969.

Hoffer, Charles R. *Teaching Music in the Secondary Schools*. Belmont, California: Wadsworth Publishing Company, 1964.

Howerton, George. *Technique and Style in Choral Singing.* New York: Carl Fischer, Inc., 1957.

How to Promote Your Band (A Manual of Public Relations). Elkhart, Indiana: H. and A. Selmer, Inc., 1957.

Huls, Helen Steen. *The Adolescent Voice: A Study.* New York: Vantage Press, 1957.

Jones, Archie N., ed. *Music Education in Action.* Dubuque, Iowa: Wm. C. Brown Company, Publishers, 1964.

Kagen, Sergius. *On Studying Singing.* New York: Dover Publications, 1960.

Klotman, Robert H. *Scheduling Music Classes.* Washington D. C.: Music Educators National Conference, 1968.

————. *The School Music Administrator and Supervisor: Catalysts for Change in Music Education.* Englewood Cliffs, N. J.: Prentice-Hall, Inc., 1973.

Lamb, Gordon H., ed. *Guide for the Beginning Choral Director.* American Choral Directors Association, 1972.

————. *Choral Director's Guide to Repertoire for Mixed Choir: An Annotated Bibliography.* West Nyack, N. Y.: Parker Publishing Co., 1974.

————. "Indeterminate Music for Chorus." *The Choral Journal* May 1970.

————. "Selection of Music for the High School Choir." *The Choral Journal* November 1971.

Lang, Paul Henry. *Music in Western Civilization.* New York: W. W. Norton and Company, Inc., 1941.

Lehl, Allen. "Developing Choral Leadership through Solo Singing." *The Choral Journal* March-April 1969.

Machlis, Joseph. *The Enjoyment of Music.* 3d ed. New York: W. W. Norton and Company, Inc., 1970.

Marshall, Madeline. *The Singer's Manual of English Diction.* New York: G. Schirmer, 1953.

McElheran, Brock. *Conducting Techniques: For Beginners and Professionals.* New York: Oxford University Press, 1966.

Montani, Nicola A., ed. *Latin Pronunciation according to Roman Usage.* Philadelphia: St. Gregory Guild, Inc., 1937.

Morris, Jean. "Diary of a Beginning Teacher." *The Bulletin* (NASP) 52: 23-27.

Marple, Hugo D. *The Beginning Conductor.* New York: McGraw-Hill Book Company, 1972.

Myers, Bernard S. *Understanding the Arts.* Rev. ed. New York: Holt, Rinehart and Winston, 1966.

National Association of Teachers of Singing Committee. "The Solo Voice and Choral Singing." *The Choral Journal* December 1970, pp. 11-12.

Neidig, Kenneth, and Jennings, John, eds. *Choral Director's Guide.* West Nyack, N. Y.: Parker Publishing, Inc., 1967.

Pooler, Frank, and Pierce, Brent. *New Choral Notation (A Handbook).* New York: Walton Music Corporation, 1971.

Reece, Gustave. *Music in the Renaissance.* New York: W. W. Norton and Company, Inc., 1954.

Robbins, Jerry H. "Hot Spots in Student Activities-How to Deal with Them." *The Bulletin* (NASP) 55: 34.

Sachs, Curt. *The Commonwealth of Art.* W. W. Norton and Company, Inc., 1946.

Simons, Harriet. "Problems to Anticipate in Preparing Your Chorus for Another Conductor." *The Choral Journal* May 1970.

Snyder, Keith D. *School Music Administration and Supervision,* 2d ed. Boston: Allyn and Bacon, Inc., 1965.

Stevens, Denis, ed. *A History of Song.* New York: W. W. Norton and Company, Inc., 1960.

Shrunk, Oliver, ed. *Source Readings in Music History.* New York: W. W. Norton and Company, Inc., 1950.

Sunderman, Lloyd F. *Choral Organization and Administration.* Rockville Centre, L. I.: Belwin, Inc., 1954.

————. *School Music Teaching: Its Theory and Practice.* New York: The Scarecrow Press, Inc., 1965.

Swan, Howard. "Style, Performance Practice and Choral Tone." *The Choral Journal* July-August 1960, pp. 12-13.

Thomas, Kurt. *The Choral Conductor.* New York: Associated Music Publishers, 1971.

Ulrich, Homer, and Pisk, Paul A. *A History of Music and Musical Style.* New York: Harcourt, Brace and World, Inc., 1963.

Van Camp, Leonard. *Warm-ups for Minds, Ears, and Voices.* New York: Lawson-Gould Music Publishers, Inc., 1973.

Vennard, William. *Singing: The Mechanism and the Technic.* Rev. ed. New York: Carl Fischer, Inc., 1967.

Weyland, Rudolph H. *Guide to Effective Music Supervision.* Dubuque: Wm. C. Brown Company, Publishers, 1968.

Wienandt, Elwyn. *Choral Music of the Church.* New York: The Free Press, 1965.

Winning Public Support for the School Choral Group. Chicago: E. R. Moore Company.

Wilson, Harry, R. *Artistic Choral Singing.* New York: G. Schirmer, Inc., 1959.

————. *A Guide for Choral Conductors.* New York: Silver Burdette Co., 1950.

Young, Percy. *The Choral Tradition.* New York: W. W. Norton and Company, Inc., 1962.

Zipser, Burton A. "When Chorus and Orchestra Get Together, Harmony or Discord?" *The Choral Journal* July-August 1968.